Becoming Christian

Becoming Christian

The Demise of the Jesus Movement

NANCY L. KUEHL

Foreword by
Jeffrey J. Bütz

RESOURCE *Publications* · Eugene, Oregon

BECOMING CHRISTIAN
The Demise of the Jesus Movement

Copyright © 2014 Nancy L. Kuehl. All rights reserved. Except for brief quotations in critical publications or reviews, no part of this book may be reproduced in any manner without prior written permission from the publisher. Write: Permissions, Wipf and Stock Publishers, 199 W. 8th Ave., Suite 3, Eugene, OR 97401.

Resource Publications
An Imprint of Wipf and Stock Publishers
199 W. 8th Ave., Suite 3
Eugene, OR 97401

www.wipfandstock.com

ISBN 13: 978-1-62564-984-3

Manufactured in the U.S.A.

JPS TANAKH 1985 (English). The TANAKH, a new translation (into contemporary English) of The Holy Scriptures according to the traditional Hebrew text (Masoretic). The Jewish Bible: Torah, Nevi'im, Kethuvim. Copyright © 1985 by The Jewish Publication Society. All rights reserved. This fresh translation began work in 1955. Used by permission.

The Archeology of the New Testament: The Life of Jesus and the Beginning of the Early Church. © 1969, 1997 Princeton University Press. Reprinted by permission of Princeton University Press

Tomb of Philip the Apostle, Courtesy of Carl Rasmussen, www.HolyLandPhotos.org

To my children: Rob, Kris, and Kerry

This people draweth nigh unto me with their mouth, and honoureth me with their lips; but their heart is far from me. But in vain they do worship me, teaching for doctrines the commandments of men.

Contents

List of Illustrations | viii
Foreword by Jeffrey J. Bütz | ix
Preface | xv
Acknowledgments | xix
Abbreviations | xx

1. In the Beginning | 1
2. James, the Brother of Jesus | 23
3. Judaism in the First Century | 42
4. The Apostles | 69
5. Antioch and Transculturation | 107
6. Pella and the *Despoysni* | 116
7. From Nazaraean to Christian | 139
8. Becoming Christian | 152

Bibliography | 163

Illustrations

FIGURE 1   Seat of Moses | 40
FIGURE 2   Simeon bar Yonah Ossuary | 76
FIGURE 3   Tomb of Philip the Apostle | 82
FIGURE 4   Ossuary of Kyrthas | 97
FIGURE 5   Eleona Church | 133

Foreword

I AM MOST THANKFUL that Nancy Kuehl invited me to write the Foreword to her new book *Becoming Christian*. While I had heard of her previous book *A Book of Evidence: The Trials and Execution of Jesus*, I had not had the opportunity to read it and was not very familiar with her work. I did know that her work was generally along the same line as my own (examining the life of Jesus from a Jewish perspective), and I agreed to read her manuscript. And from the first few pages, *Becoming Christian* was a serendipitous revelation for me. I was immediately surprised at how many new insights Kuehl was able to provide into the life of Jesus and the development of earliest Christianity that I had not previously considered. While her work is rooted in the best current scholarship, she explores her own unique insights and develops new understandings of the beginnings of Christianity that make eminent sense of preceding scholarship. I learned a lot from this book both on an intellectual level, as well as a spiritual level (something rarely found in academically oriented books), and I knew I would be honored to write the Foreword to this groundbreaking work.

Becoming Christian builds upon a mass of research generated in the last half–century or so which has come to be called the "Third Quest for the Historical Jesus," a scholarly movement which takes as its basis the thorough Jewishness of Jesus' ministry and teachings. This line of thought is rooted in the groundbreaking work of Albert Schweitzer in the earliest years of the 20th century, especially his seminal *The Quest of the Historical Jesus*. The new trajectory engendered by Schweitzer—which took seriously Jesus as an eschatological Jewish prophet who believed he was the Messiah—began to fully flourish in the latter half of the 20th century, especially with works such as E. P. Sanders' *Jesus and Judaism,* and today the "Jewish

Jesus" is an unquestioned tenet of any work on recovering the "historical Jesus."

In the last couple of decades quite a number of popular level books have been produced examining various aspects of Jesus' life and teachings through a Jewish lens, many of the best being by Jewish scholars, perhaps best exemplified in the work of Amy-Jill Levine. All these works take as their starting point the basic tenet that Jesus was a Jewish rabbi whose teachings and religious practice were thoroughly rooted in the Torah and who never intended to create a new religion distinct from Judaism. For a majority of scholars today, of all religious persuasions, this is simply a given. Nancy Kuehl's work follows in this vein and is solidly grounded in the best of both Jewish and Christian scholarship.

The great value of *Becoming Christian* is that it builds upon this rock-solid foundation of work that has gone before and takes it in a fresh, new direction which has only recently developed (and which I have tried to develop in my own books). This new direction for understanding the historical Jesus takes seriously some rather startling new insights into the life of Jesus that break with long-held Christian tradition. Primary among these is the thesis, originally developed by Robert Eisenman, John Painter, and Richard Bauckham, and most recently championed by James D. Tabor (*The Jesus Dynasty*), that Jesus' family were not estranged from him (as Christian tradition has generally held), but were in fact intimate followers of Jesus, and that Jesus' own brothers and cousins were likely among the twelve apostles. Kuehl accepts this as a fundamental starting point (a stance I feel to be completely sound historically) and she also accepts the new insight that Jesus' eldest brother James took over the reins of leadership of the disciples after Jesus' crucifixion, not Peter as Christian tradition has held. In my own mind, these new understandings are as near to proven facts as one can get in historical Jesus studies. I am heartened to see Nancy Kuehl take all this as a given and builds upon it.

These insights provide many new avenues for exploration of the historical Jesus and they enable Kuehl to provide some illuminating, and at times astonishing new insights into the life and ministry of Jesus. Kuehl believes that Jesus was not the poor uneducated peasant of Christian tradition, but a highly educated rabbi who followed in the steps of his predecessor and mentor, John the Baptist. Through in-depth research into ancient Jewish genealogies and priestly lists, she shows that Jesus came from a long line of Zadokite priests of Davidic and Aaronic lineage and that not only

Foreword

Jesus, but his father Joseph and Uncle Cleophas as well as his brothers, were likely all priests, or *kohens* of the ancient order of Melchizedek. She convincingly shows that Jesus would have been seen by his followers as uniquely fulfilling the dual messianic roles of both priest and king.

Following upon this, Kuehl shows how Jesus' teaching and ministry was in no way unprecedented or at odds with traditional first-century Judaism. She provides an interesting new insight into one of Jesus' most beloved teachings—the Beatitudes—as being an exemplary example of Jewish Midrash. Going against S.G.F. Brandon and a school of thought (perhaps best exemplified in the work of Robert Eisenman) that understands the Jesus movement as militantly political, Kuehl puts forth compelling insights that the traditional pacifistic picture of Jesus is more historically accurate and that Jesus was not at all accepting of the approach of the Zealots. Kuehl's in-depth knowledge of first-century Judaism also helps throw light on some of Paul's more controversial and misunderstood statements. As a bonus, *Becoming Christian* also gives new insights into the development of the New Testament canon, especially the place of the Johannine literature. The book provides a number of unexpected new insights into New Testament passages that I thought I fully understood, but can now see in a whole different light.

And that is all in just the first half of the book! In the second half, all of the fresh analysis of the historical Jesus lays the groundwork for the real aim of this book—providing new insight into the development of the Christian religion out of its Jewish nexus. While the time period Kuehl primarily focuses on is between the death of Jesus' brother James in about 62 CE and the fall of Jerusalem in 70 CE, she also covers a wide range of material including the Antiochan bishops beginning with Ignatius, the apostolic fathers, and the Latin and Greek fathers on up through the edicts of the Roman church to about the year 500 or 600 CE. She also offers new and more accurate biographies of all the apostles, gives an overview of first-century Judaism and how it evolved into modern rabbinic Judaism, and provides a valuable history of the church at Antioch. She offers especially good insights into how Christianity as we know it germinated and blossomed at Antioch, and shows how Antiochan culture with its Hellenistic and Gnostic influences is the real source of Christianity. Another invaluable aspect of this book is her discussion of how original Jewish Christianity developed into a sect known as the Ebionites, who made their base in Pella at the time of the War with Rome and were denounced as heretics by both the early

Foreword

rabbis and Christian Fathers when ironically they were the *Desposyni*, the blood descendants of Jesus' family.

Becoming Christian sheds a lot of welcome light on a period some have called the "dark age" of Christianity, because so little has been previously known about it. Usually, Christian books begin with the apostolic fathers and very little has actually been written about the Jesus movement during the late first and early second centuries. Her sober analysis of this period is what makes this book especially valuable. *Becoming Christian* provides invaluable accounts of the debates between the Nazarenes and Pharisees as related in the Talmud during the first and second centuries and shows how the two groups, which originally shared so much in common, became rivals. Kuehl shows how in the end, due to the triumph of Pauline Christianity, the original Jewish Christianity of the Nazarenes and Ebionites slowly faded away, and she poignantly portrays the demise of the original Jewish Jesus movement as the tragic episode in history that it really was.

While this is a lot of territory to cover, Kuehl has a wonderful writing style that is both comprehensive and succinct, not an easy thing to do. While covering much ground, the book never becomes tedious because it is written in an engaging style that does not bog down in academic jargon. While thoroughly scholarly, it is a book that will engage laypeople and is a surprisingly easy read. What I also appreciated about Kuehl's narrative style is that she doesn't spend a lot of time quoting scholars for support of her positions (though the book is adequately footnoted), but simply accepts their findings and builds upon them to produce fascinating new insights into the implications of the Jewish Jesus for our knowledge of the development of earliest Christianity. Throughout, she refreshingly lets the scriptural texts speak for themselves without any theological manipulation to make them fit her thesis.

All in all, *Becoming Christian* is a major step forward in a growing body of knowledge of the historical Jesus and the true history of earliest Christianity. It is a thorough yet refreshingly succinct overview of Jesus' life and ministry, first-century Judaism and its many sects, and the cultural influence of both Hellenism and Gnosticism in producing two new religions: modern rabbinic Judaism and "catholic" Christianity. *Becoming Christian* is a first-rate analysis of what scholars now commonly call the "parting of the ways" between Judaism and Christianity.

The recently recovered message of the Jewish Jesus cannot be proclaimed enough, and this book is a most welcome addition to a growing body of literature from both Jewish and Christian scholars who share the common aim of restoring the teachings of Jesus to their Jewish context. Nancy Kuehl is the latest herald of this lost religious truth, and like Hugh Schonfield who paved the way she is a prophet of the original Nazarene gospel. Prepare to be enlightened.

The Rev. Jeffrey holds a Master of Divinity degree (*magna cum laude*) from Moravian Theological Seminary and a Master of Sacred Theology degree from the Lutheran Theological Seminary at Philadelphia, where he wrote his thesis on Jesus' brother James. He has been the pastor of Grace Lutheran Church in Nazareth, Pennsylvania since 1996 and an adjunct professor of Religious Studies and Philosophy at Pennsylvania State University since 2002. He has done archaeological work at Mt. Zion in Jerusalem and Tamar in southern Israel.

Bütz is the author of *The Brother of Jesus and the Lost Teachings of Christianity* (Inner Traditions International, 2005), which has received critical acclaim as the best book on Jesus' brother James written for a lay audience. His most recent book *The Secret Legacy of Jesus* (Inner Traditions, 2010), has been called "the new definitive work on Jewish Christianity." He has also written a screenplay, *James, Brother of Jesus,* with film producer Harvey Rochman and is a featured scholar in the groundbreaking new Robert Orlando film, *Apostle Paul: A Polite Bribe.*

The Rev. Jeffrey J. Bütz, S.T.M.

Preface

THIS BOOK IS NOT about Christianity per se but how traditional Christianity evolved. It is about the formation of the Jesus Movement and its history between the years when Jesus began his ministry in 29 CE through the year 66 CE when the movement ceased to be known as a Jewish phenomenon. Therefore, I shall not refer to the members of the movement – James and the apostles primarily – as "Christians" or "Jewish Christians" but as Jews who originally referred to themselves as Nazaraeans. The word "Nazaraean" does not refer to a location, nor does it refer to those individuals taking the oath of a Nazarite. The Hebrew word *natsar* (עָנַר) pronounced nawt-sar (or nazar) means to guard, protect, maintain, obey, or watch over. It was used in the sense of observing Torah and protecting it. By the time the Gospel of Matthew was written it was corrupted to conform to a location: Nazareth – Nazarene. It is referred to as a "sect" in Acts 24:5, where Paul is accused of being a "mover of sedition" and a "ringleader of the sect of Nazarenes" (as in the KJV; in YLT and other translations it is correctly rendered Nazaraeans). Considering the Jewish high priest (Ananias), the elders, and Tertullus were the accusers, they must have been referring to the Nazaraeans as a sect within Judaism. At that time then, the Nazaraeans as a community were still accepted within the normative religion of the day.

One of the most illusive periods in the history of Christianity is the period between the execution of Jesus in the 30s and the establishment of the first "Christian" church in Antioch about the year 66 CE when bishops became appointed. During this time we have only the writings of Paul of Tarsus to give some idea of the progression of the movement begun by the family and disciples of Jesus in Jerusalem after his death. These individuals believed Jesus was resurrected in bodily form, yet continued to practice the Torah of Moses, to keep the feast days, and to worship in the Temple.

Preface

This book is written in an attempt to shed light on what can only be referred to as the "Darkest Age" of Christianity, a time before our present gospels were written, before the teachings of Jesus and his disciples were changed, and a time before doctrines were fully established for the church. It is not difficult to pinpoint exactly when these changes began to occur. If we are to place any credence to the writings of Paul and the much later book of Acts, we must closely examine the controversy between James, his Jerusalem community, and Paul. The conflict between them occurred about 52 CE, long before the Antiochan community became established as what we now refer to as "Christian". If we follow the chronology given by Paul and by the author of Acts we can get a fair assessment of *how* the Jesus Movement eventually came to an end.

The first chapter of the book is an overview of Jesus, his life, and teachings, all focused on a single goal: the Kingdom of God. Emphasis is placed on the role of his education, the culture in which he lived, and the religion that he practiced, primarily his worship of Yahweh and the guidance of the Torah. Also provided is a review of his understanding of his own role in such a diversified religion.

No study of early Christianity would be complete without reviewing the position of Jesus' brother James and the influence he so obviously had in Jerusalem. His prominence extended well beyond the community of followers and disciples to some members of the elite priesthood, many of whom became involved in the Jesus Movement, themselves. His importance is evidenced by his illegal trial and execution by the Sanhedrin called by Annas II, son of the infamous high priest Annas of New Testament infamy.

The apostles were to carry the teachings of Jesus throughout Judea, Samaria, and Galilee at an early date, eventually extending beyond those borders into all areas of the Roman Empire and locations in the far East. A short review of their lives and missionary activities is included here.

Since Antioch, the new Babylon, became the location of the earliest church known as "Christian", its history and culture are examined as a background to what was to follow. The transculturation of Antioch became the driving force behind the Christian religion as it came to be known. It is in Antioch that bishops were first appointed and the foundation of church doctrine was laid.

At an early date a controversy arose within the various congregations about whether the succession of the true teachings of Jesus should lie with the apostles or with the heirs (known as the Despoysni) of Jesus. The church

Preface

in Antioch claimed apostolic succession, while the disciples claimed the succession belonged to the Despoysni.

The last two chapters explain how the original movement was pushed aside to accommodate the creation of doctrines favorable to the Roman Empire. Here is a study of the church fathers and their beliefs, along with an examination of the history of the gospel writings. Because these men were politically ambitious, connected with the Roman Empire, and knew little about Judaism, the edicts and councils that followed were set into motion, creating a system that to this day has remained unchallenged. The Jesus Movement, composed primarily of Jews, was soon forgotten and slowly died out while the new Christian religion gained a foothold in the Gentile world.

Acknowledgments

Although it is impossible to acknowledge all the pioneers in the field of early Christianity, there are those who have made significant contributions. Included among them are Hugh Schonfield, Raymond E. Brown, David Flusser, Richard Bauckham, and James D. G. Dunn.

More recently, scholars have focused on the writings of Paul, contrasting his teachings with those of Jesus and James. Robert Eisenman, James Tabor, Richard Bauckham, and Jeffrey Bütz are among those who have made considerable contributions to Christian origins in recent years and must receive mention.

I would also like to gratefully acknowledge Laura Poncy and Matthew Wimer of Wipf and Stock Publishers for their help in the publication of this book.

Finally, I would like to thank my family and my friends for the support they have given me in this endeavor.

Abbreviations

ABD	Anchor Bible Dictionary
Abod.	*Zar. Abod Zarah*
Abot.	Avot
Acts Phil	Acts of Philip
Ant.	*Antiquities of the Jews*
b.	Babylonian Talmud
BAR	Biblical Archaeology Review
BCE	Before the Common Era
Ber.	*Berakoth*
b. kam.	*Baba Kamma*
b.m.	*Baba Mezi'a*
CBN	Companion Bible
CE	Common Era
CJZC	Corpus jüdischer Zeugnisse aus der Cyrenaika
EBR	Rotherham's Emphasized Bible
Eccl.	*Hist. Ecclesiastical History*
ISR	The Scriptures
1 Clem	1 Clement
JE	Jerusalem Encyclopedia
JPS	The Hebrew Tanakh
Kel.	*Kelim*

Abbreviations

KJV	King James Bible
M.	Mishnah
Macc.	Maccabees
Meg.	*Megillah*
Men.	*Menahot*
Mid.	*Middot*
NIV	New International Version
NRM	Netzarim Reconstruction of Matthew
Nah. Pesh.	*Nahum Pesher*
Nid.	*Niddah*
Neg.	*Nega'im*
Par.	*Parah*
Pes.	*Pesahim*
R. H.	*Rosh Hashanah*
ROSN	Restoration of the Sacred Name Bible
Sanh.	*Sanhedrin*
Shab.	*Shabbat*
Shebu.	*Shebuot*
Sot.	*Sotah*
Suk.	*Sukkah*
Ta'an.	*Ta'anit*
Tam.	*Tamid*
Toh.	*Tohoroth*
Tosef.	Tosefta
y.	Jerusalem or Palestinian Talmud
Yeb.	*Yebamoth*
YLT	Young's Literal Translation
Yom.	*Yoma*

1

In the Beginning

After the people were baptized, Jesus also came and was baptized by John. And as he came up from the water, the heavens were opened, and he saw the Holy Spirit descend in the form of a dove and enter into him. And a voice from heaven said, "Thou art my beloved Son; with thee I am well pleased." And again, "Today I have begotten thee." And immediately a great light shone around the place; and John, seeing it, said to him, "Who are you, Lord?" And again a voice from heaven said to him, "This is my beloved Son, with whom I am well pleased." Then John, falling down before him, said, "I beseech you, Lord, baptize me!" But he forbade him, saying, "Let it be so; for thus it is fitting that all things be fulfilled."

To Matt 3:13–17 cf. Gospel of the Ebionites

The earliest followers (Nazaraeans) of Jesus re-titled themselves as Ebionites (the "humble") after the death of James when some Greek members of the congregation began to pervert the beliefs of James and the original apostles. This occurred prior to the election of Simeon, son of Cleophas as the second leader of the community. You will notice the similarities to the passage in the Gospel of Matthew within the wording above: "the heavens were opened", "like [the form of] a dove" "lighting" ["light shone"]. What we have here is the "consecration" and "acceptance" of Jesus by Yahweh into Sonship. The anointing of Elohim came down upon Jesus in the same manner as the priestly anointings in the Temple: in the shape of the letter *kaph* (a dove with wings backward), the symbol of which is a "dove". Furthermore, the number of the letter *kaph* is 100, the number of sheep in Jesus' parable, and is symbolic of the messianic ministry he is about to begin [i.e., implying the process of unifying of the congregation—99+1].

These earlier believers, like Jesus himself, were entrenched in the teachings and commandments of the Scriptures, or what Christians presently refer to as the "Old Covenant". The Babylonian Talmud reminds us that the canonization of the Tanach took place between the years 200 BCE to 200 CE; however, the discovery of the Dead Sea Scrolls gives evidence that at least the Torah and Nevi'im were canonized before 68 CE and describes some of the debate over the status of some books of Ketuvim, and in particular whether or not they render the hands "impure". In the Mishnah (200 CE) Yadaim 3:5 calls attention to the debate over Song of Songs and Ecclesiastes. Josephus also refers to sacred scriptures divided into three parts, the five books of the Torah, thirteen books of the Nevi'im, and four other books of hymns and wisdom.[1] The Nazaraeans had also read and studied the intertestamentary apocalyptic books written between the years 100 BCE and the first century along with the Book of Daniel, written sometime after 167 when Antiochus Epiphanes had desecrated the Jerusalem temple. It was upon that book that the apocalpytic fervor began. The Jewish people had viewed the Hasmonian dynasty as their saviors from foreign rule, but after the Romans defeated them Israel found itself once again ruled by a ruthless overlord. Since the days of Seleucid domination they had begun to expect their messiah to appear.

Christians generally believe the population of Israel looked for a militant messiah, primarily because Judas the Galilean had revolted against the Roman–Herodian rule. Nothing could be farther from the truth. They expected a messiah that fit the description given by the prophets, a messiah who would usher in the Reign of Yahweh on earth, bring peace to a downtrodden nation and institute a brotherhood of man, uniting all nations under the banner of the "Kingdom of God". The Pharisees, in particular, espoused the messianic hope in the synagogues and taught the people that these were the "Last Days" when messiah would suddenly appear. They expected a messiah who, as Isaiah wrote, would with righteousness "judge the poor, and reprove with equity for the meek of the earth: and he shall smite the earth with the rod of his mouth, and with the breath of his lips shall he slay the wicked" (Isa 11:4). The earth would be smitten by his instruction

---

1. Josephus, *Against Apion* 1:8.

and his words, not with a weapon of destruction. This two-edged sword is spoken of in the book of Revelation: "And I saw heaven opened, and behold a white horse; and he that sat upon him was called Faithful and True, and in righteousness he doth judge and make war . . . And out of his mouth goeth a sharp sword, that with it he should smite the nations" (Rev 19:11–15). This sword is symbolic for the words of his mouth, which are the righteous commandments of Yahweh.

Jesus' education and intelligence were the products of learning on several fronts. It was the responsibility of the father of the household as the religious leader to begin to teach Torah to his son as soon as the child could utter its first words. Joseph would have begun to teach the toddler Jesus during their stay in Egypt. By the time they returned, when Archelaus was ethnarch of Judea, Jesus would have been about six or seven years of age. Joseph would have been his constant companion, teaching him the Jewish prayers, taking him to synagogue, and teaching him a trade.

> One should view Jesus against his Jewish background, the world of the Sages, to recognize and appreciate his great influence on those around him. Only thus shall we be able to understand how Christianity was formed. Jesus was part and parcel of the world of the Jewish Sages. He was no ignorant peasant, and his acquaintance with the Written and Oral Law was considerable.[2]

The family was a deeply spiritual one, so it is no surprise that Jesus would have been indoctrinated from the time he was a child in the prophecies about the coming of messiah. He would have felt in his spirit that he was being groomed for something important. It was at his messianic appointment on the day of his immersion that he knew his purpose in full.

He was tested in the wilderness where he overcame his doubts and fears, knowing the road that laid ahead for him through the prophecies he had studied. The point is that Jesus knew he was the expected messiah and boldly took upon himself all that was expected of him. He purposely chose twelve students to study "at his feet", to teach them the secrets of Torah and the coming Reign of Yahweh in order that they might carry forth his teachings after his resurrection. He and his students traveled the entire span of Galilee for three and a half years healing the sick, encouraging the poor, spreading the good news of the coming Kingdom. He taught in riddles (or parables) just as the sages before him had done, adding personal glimpses of the nation's ills that had accumulated around him during his lifetime,

---

2. Flusser, *Jewish Sources*, p. 19.

things that mattered to a people who had faced economic hardships, political unrest, and the unrealistic religious rites of a corrupt priesthood.

Jesus focused on the love of Yahweh for his people, whether in his healing activities or in his sermons. He knew from the Scriptures that Israel was to be a shining light to all nations to bring them within a brotherhood, a single community, over which Yahweh would reign. This was his unwavering quest. At every opportunity he expounded his reverence for the God of Israel and gave him glory. As the agent messiah for Yahweh, he knew it was his duty to enlighten a population that had gone astray and no longer knew their God. Because of what the nation had endured the people had lost their hope and faith. When Jesus appeared on the scene that faith and hope was revived for those who heard him and believed his words. The Kingdom was the root of his message: "The Kingdom of Heaven is at hand" (Matt 10:7); "repent ye and believe the good news" (Mark 1:15).

> In Jesus' own sayings, we do not find the word "redemption" in its religious eschatological sense; but Jesus did use the expression "the Kingdom of Heaven." This expression, which was current in many circles, combined in Matthew 5:3 the Essene attitude of respect for poverty with the idea of the Kingdom of Heaven. Jesus said: "Blessed are the poor in spirit, for theirs is the kingdom of heaven." Rabban Yohanan ben Zakkai, a contemporary of Jesus, also used the expression "the Kingdom of Heaven." From him and from other sources it appears that this expression, "the Kingdom of Heaven," is a well-defined concept which was employed in the polemics against the Zealots, who advocated a war against Rome.[3]

Jesus said, "And from the days of John the Baptist until now the kingdom of heaven suffereth violence, and the violent take it by force" (Matt 11:12). It is clear that Jesus used the phrase in speaking of the Zealots who had wanted to make Jesus "king" and institute the Kingdom with force. Jesus, wanting to establish the Kingdom through peace, rejected their offer. "When Jesus therefore perceived that they [i.e., the Zealots] would come and take him by force, to make him a king, he departed again into a mountain himself alone" (John 6:15).

And it was to the "Lost Sheep of the House of Israel" to whom he was going and not to the Samaritans nor to the Gentiles (Matt 10:5). It was Israel, Yahweh's peculiar people, who would enlighten the Gentiles (Isa 42:6). That was the duty of Israel not messiah's.

---

3. Ibid., p. 50.

Jesus summed up his testimony of faith and obedience to Yahweh in one Scripture: "Hear, O Israel; The LORD our God is one Lord: And thou shalt love the LORD thy God with all thy heart, and with all thy soul, and with all thy mind, and with all thy strength: this is the first commandment" (Mark 12:29–30; Deut 6:4). This first commandment is the Jewish creed called the Shema Yisrael. That creed serves as a centerpiece for morning and evening prayers and expresses the monotheism of the nation of Israel. The name of Yahweh has always been pronounced as a euphemism, Adonai, which is used only of the God of the Old Covenant Scriptures. Jesus emphatically urged the people to keep the commandments of Yahweh: "Why callest thou me good? there is none good but one, that is, God: but if thou wilt enter into life, keep the commandments" (Matt 19:17).

Jesus began his ministry within his *mispahah* or clan community. These clan communities consisted of family groups inhabiting the same settlements, the forerunners of villages. These family groups were interdependent and relied on each other for economic and emotional support. This particular clan community would have consisted of the family of Jesus' father, Joseph. It was small but large enough for a synagogue, where Jesus stood up to read the *parashah* (portion) of the prophet Isaiah some time after his immersion (Luke 4:16). His relatives were astonished at his teaching, this quiet and intelligent boy who had grown up in their midst. "Is not this Joseph's son?" (Luke 4:22). Rejection by his clan relatives led him to conclude "a man's foes shall be they of his own household" (Matt 10:36). His mother and brothers, however, did not abandon him. He and his students were invited to a wedding in Cana where it is probable that one of his sisters married. Mary presided over the arrangements, and it was the duty of the parent(s) to oversee the necessary requirements for the ceremony. It was after the wedding that "he went down to Capernaum, he, and his mother, and his brethren, and his disciples: and they continued there not many days" (John 2:12). It is, therefore, probable that not only did his mother and brothers accept his messianic claim but that they traveled with him throughout his entire ministry.

It was in Capernaum at one of his student's homes (Simon Peter's: Mark 1:29–34) that Jesus first based his operations, although he had his own house in Capernaum as well (Mark 2:14–15) where he and his family lived together. His family would have included not only his mother and brothers but also their wives and mothers–in–law if they were widows, along with any children the brothers might have had. It was centered in the region of the Sea of Galilee where he and his disciples traveled the circuit of fishing villages. These villages were the hub of commerce where large contingencies of Jews gathered to conduct their business. There were synagogues in most of these villages, and on the Sabbath Jesus could be found in these synagogues healing the sick and expounding the Laws of Moses and the Kingdom of Yahweh (Mark 1:38–39; Matt 4:23). The Gospel of John tells us that Jesus was faithful to attend the major festivals in Jerusalem, especially Passover and Sukkot. His primary ministry, however, was in Galilee. He followed the Torah's requirements when healing, sending the healed to show the priest that he had been healed and to offer for the cleansing "those things which Moses commanded, for a testimony unto them" (Mark 1:44; Matt 8:4; Lev 13:13). It was in these synagogues, also, he encountered opposition from groups of Pharisees. The Pharisees, though lax in Galilee, were the religious leaders for the people. They had taught the people that the "last days" were upon them and advised them of all the prophecies concerning the messiah. It is not until the Judean Pharisees come to Galilee to listen to Jesus preach that the debates begin. They had also been sent to the Jordan to question John, thinking even he might be the messiah they had expected (John 1:19–24). Of these Pharisees there were priests and Levites. Most of the Jerusalem priests were Sadducean, but there were also priests who were Pharisees (such as Joazer had been and his brother Simon ben Cantheras, son of Boethus).[4] The Judean Pharisees, who were strict in their purity regulations and believed themselves superior to the Galileans, objected to Jesus' healings. They had considered themselves as the nations' only healers. There had been little opposition to Jesus until the Judeans began to control the people.

In Capernaum those Pharisees had decided Jesus was a nuisance. "And the Pharisees went forth, and straightway took counsel with the Herodians against him, how they might destroy him" (Mark 3:6). It was not their wish that he should be killed at that point but that, perhaps, he be arrested and placed in prison as John had been. He became their mortal enemy from the moment he had healed the palsied man Capernaum. The people who had been present at the healing were "amazed" and glorified Yahweh for giving Jesus the ability to heal this man (Mark 2:12). We know these were Judean Pharisees because "when he was *reclining* at meat in *his house*, many publicans and sinners sat also together with Jesus and his disciples"

---

4. Josephus, *Life* 39:197; See also: Josephus, *Ant.* 17.6.4; 18.1.1 where he is mentioned as "Joazar, son of Boethos.

(Mark 2:14–15; compare Luke 15:2 Matt 9:10; Luke 5:29; Luke 7:34; Matt 11:19, italics mine), and "when the scribes and Pharisees saw him eat with publicans and sinners, they said unto his disciples, How is it that he eateth and drinketh with publicans and sinners?" (Mark 2:16). They also asked him why his disciples did not fast like John's did (Mark 2:18), and finally, they had objected to the disciples not "washing" before eating. "Why walk not thy disciples according to the tradition of the elders, but eat bread with unwashen hands?" (Mark 7:5) Already, this particular branch of Judean Pharisees had placed impossible burdens on the people, burdens which would later become the laws of the Mishnah (200 CE), although they were not associated with the Sanhedrin at the time. Jesus entertained ordinary common people in his house in Capernaum. They were not just having a meal, they were having what is referred to as "table fellowship", a feast or a banquet. The Judean Pharisees did not have table fellowship with anyone except their own group. They would not have considered having table fellowship with anyone below their social strata nor with other Pharisees who did not keep their purity regulations. They, therefore, would have disapproved of Jesus and his disciples.

> In societies where there are barriers between classes, races or other status groups, the separation is maintained by means of a taboo on social mixing. You do not share a meal or a dinner party, you do not celebrate, or participate in entertainments, with people who belong to another social group. In the Middle East sharing a meal at table with someone is a particularly intimate form of association and friendship. They would never even out of politeness eat and drink with a person of a lower class or status or with any person of whom they disapproved.[5]

The primary focus of Jesus' teachings was of the coming Reign of Yahweh. "And it came to pass afterward, that he went throughout every city and village, preaching and shewing the glad tidings of the kingdom of God: and the twelve were with him" (Luke 8:1). Much of the content of his sermons was in riddles (parables). Those who were seeking the Kingdom of God in earnest would understand them, but those hangers-on who were only interested in his healings would not. He gained many followers in Galilee but only a few from Judea. Although Nicodemus (Nakdimon ben Gorion) was an Elder in the Sanhedrin in Jerusalem, he was a native of Galilee. In John 7:50–52 "Nicodemus (he who came to Jesus by night, being one of

---

5. Nolan, *Jesus Before Christianity*, p. 45.

them) said to them, "Does our law judge a man before it hears him and knows what he is doing?" They answered and said to him, "Are you also from Galilee? Search and look, for no prophet has arisen out of Galilee."

The irony is that Nicodemus ben Gorion *was* from Galilee, from a village called Rumah, Ruma, or Roma (Aroma in the Talmud), which is the site of Tell Rumeh, six miles north of present–day Nazareth and three miles north of Sepphoris. The Talmud tells us the wealthy family of Gorion had their estates there. "R. Judah related: It once happened that the Memel and Gorion families at Aroma distributed dried figs and dried grapes to the poor in a time of dearth."[6] Not only does a footnote by the editor explain that this village is "Ruma, identified with Chirbet Rume", but it is also identified in the history of Josephus: "Next to him, two brothers showed their courage; their names were Netir and Philip, both of them of the village Ruma, and both of them Galileans also . . ."[7]

As a *batlain* (or 'Bouleutai' or counselor), one of the three counselors of Jerusalem, Nicodemus was assigned to sing prayers at deaths and is available for making up the number required for religious services (ten men—a *minyan*) or for singing prayers in memory of the dead. This is what he probably did at the tomb of Jesus while preparing his body for burial and could be one factor in his helping to prepare his body. Josephus also mentions the place where the *bouleutai*, "the councilors," met at the *boule*, outside the Temple.[8] He would have been more inclined to show interest in the Kingdom of God than most citizens of Jerusalem since he derived from Galilee very near Jesus' own home. It is entirely possible that he had known Jesus and/or his family at a much earlier date.

The Kingdom of God was to be inaugurated on earth by peaceful means. This meant that Yahweh's righteous rule over all nations would be centered in Jerusalem under the kingship of his messiah. Jesus taught what the kingdom would resemble, stressing the commandments. "Full well ye reject the commandment of Yahweh, that ye may keep your own tradition" (Mark 7:9). The very first words Jesus spoke about the kingdom in his sermons can be found in Matthew 4:17: "Repent: for the kingdom of heaven is at hand" (compare Mark 1:15). Jesus mentions the "kingdom" one hundred seventeen times in the New Testament. The sermon on the mountain describes who will become citizens of the kingdom: the humble (Luke 6:20),

---

6. *b. Erub.* 51b.
7. J. W. 3.7.21.
8. BJ, 5.4.2.

those who mourn, the meek, those who hunger after righteousness, the merciful, the pure in heart, the peacemakers, the persecuted, and those falsely accused (Matt 5:3–12).

"Jesus himself had a profound Jewish education, and it is obvious that he was familiar with numerous Midrashim."[9] The "Beatitudes" were a form of Midrash, an ancient method of explaining Scripture.

> Even at the beginning of the Sermon on the Mount, we already have a hint to Midrashim: "Blessed are the poor in spirit, for theirs is the Kingdom of Heaven: Blessed are the meek, for they shall inherit the earth." It is obvious that the second of these verses is taken from Psalms 37:11: "But the meek shall inherit the earth." Jesus takes the word "meek" (Hebrew *anavim*) to mean the poor (Hebrew *ani'yim*) in spirit, on the authority of verses in Isaiah (57:15; 61:1) which speak of the meek and the humble in spirit; and he explains in a Midrashic manner the expression "they will inherit the earth" in the sense of "theirs is the Kingdom of Heaven."[10]

In other words, those who keep the commandments and seek righteousness, those who worship the Father (Matt 5:16) will be the heirs. It is here that Jesus boldly makes the claim: "Think not that I am come to destroy the law [Torah], or the prophets: I am not come to destroy, but to fulfil [instruct]. For verily I say unto you, Till heaven and earth pass, one jot or one tittle shall in no wise pass from the law, till all be fulfilled. Whosoever therefore shall break one of these least commandments, and shall teach men so, he shall be called the least in the kingdom of heaven, but *whosoever shall do and teach them* [the commandments], the same shall be called great in the kingdom of heaven" (Matt 5:17–19, italics mine).

When Jesus taught his students to pray, he emphatically stressed that the kingdom belonged to Yahweh. "Thy kingdom come, Thy will be done in earth as it is in heaven . . . For Thine is the kingdom, and the power, and the glory, for ever" (Matt 6:10–13). He clarifies here that the kingdom will be on earth and will reflect the holiness of Yahweh's Spirit. He submits to the belief that it is Yahweh who possesses the kingdom, that his is the great power, and that he is to be respected (glorified) perpetually.

Jesus speaks directly to the Jewish people about their yearning for material wealth ("For after all these things do the Gentiles seek" Matt 6:32).

---

9. Flusser, *Jewish Sources*, p. 62.
10. Ibid., p. 62.

He tells them to "seek ye first the kingdom of God, and *his righteousness*; and all these things shall be added unto you" (Matt 6:33, italics mine). He informs the people that they should seek the kingdom of God and *his* [Yahweh's] *righteousness* before they will ever truly prosper. He also warns them that even though they have used his name to prophesy and perfect all sorts of good works that they should not expect to enter the kingdom unless "he . . . doeth the will of [his] Father which is in heaven" (Matt 7:21).

We might ask, what is the kingdom of God? The expression kingdom of God (*basileia tou theou* in Greek, *malkuth Yahweh* in Hebrew) points to the ruling activity of Yahweh as the universal king over Yahweh's people and over the world Yahweh has created, a kingdom on earth ruled by his chosen king (that is, his messiah). The author of the Gospel of Matthew often prefers to use "kingdom of heaven" instead of "kingdom of God", perhaps because that author was sensitive to the fact that Jews were not allowed (by law) to pronounce the name of God. The kingdom of God can be said to be a vision of a radical transformation of human beings and institutions that expresses the character and nature of God, thus it was necessary that the messiah (Jesus) reflect the righteousness of God, ruling by his will. The kingdom or reign of God was, in fact, the "good news" ("gospel") Jesus preached throughout the land. The good news of the kingdom included both spiritual and socio–economic conditions for the land of Israel. The messiah was to be a servant, not only to Yahweh, but also to the people of the land. It was both present in his day and yet to come. The Jewish people believed in the "here and now", and Jesus, who advocated a peaceful establishment of the Kingdom, also believed that it was not only to come in the future but was, in fact, being established at the present time.

> The Sages believed that even when a man recites "Hear O Israel," he is taking upon himself the Kingdom of Heaven and is living under it. The Kingdom of Heaven existed there and then, and was in no way conditioned by a rebellion against Rome, but only by the purity of the people of Israel. Jesus employed this term, "the Kingdom of Heaven," exactly in this sense. For him too, the Kingdom of Heaven already existed, and one needed to work for its complete realization.
>
> In Jesus' view, John the Baptist had also fulfilled a task in the process of the realization of the Kingdom of Heaven. Jesus said that "All the prophets . . . prophesied until John" (Matthew 11:13). In other words, John the Baptist was the man who had begun the process of the realization of the Kingdom of Heaven, and Jesus

had then brought it to fulfillment through the dissemination of his ideas and the foundation of his movement.[11]

When the scribe came to him and asked him what the first commandment was he repeated the words of Jesus: "Well, Master, thou hast said the truth: for there is one God; and there is none other but he: And to love him with all the heart, and with all the understanding, and with all the soul, and with all the strength, and to love his neighbour as himself, is more than all whole burnt offerings and sacrifices. And when Jesus saw that he answered discreetly, he said unto him, *Thou art not far from the kingdom of God*" (Mark 12:32–34, italics mine). Jesus was indicating that the kingdom was not at that time a location but a state of the heart and mind. He also indicated that the reign of God was still *coming*, that it would not come in full as a natural event until a future time when he would return to "set up the kingdom". This is illustrated in Jesus' parable of the nobleman who went into a far country to receive for himself a kingdom and return (Luke 19:12–27). In it he refers to his receiving the kingdom and his return in the "last day". This is clearly the impression the apostles received once Jesus had been resurrected and ascended to the Father (Acts 1:9–12). "When the Son of man comes in His glory, and all the holy messengers with him, then shall he sit upon the throne of his glory; And before him shall be gathered all nations: and he shall separate them one from another as a shepherd divideth his sheep from the goats: And he shall set the sheep on his right hand, but the goats on the left. Then shall the King [Messiah] say unto them on his right hand, Come, ye blessed of my Father, inherit the kingdom prepared for you from the foundation of the world" (Matt 25:31–34). The Last Judgment, Final Judgment, Day of Judgment, Judgment Day, and The Day of the Lord are some of the Old Covenant terms for the "last day".

Jesus is to be King Messiah at some future date just as his ancestor David was King Messiah over the land and kingdom of Israel in the rank of "Melchizedek" (Psa 110). This title is in Hebrew *melek-zedek*, king-priest. Ancient kings were also the priests of their nations, and all Hebrew kings were "messiahs" (anointed). Jesus legally descended from David's sons, Solomon and Nathan, who were also king–priests. As Psalm 110 states, this was a designation that was to be "for ever", or perpetually, meaning that the descendants of his sons would also be of that rank, kings of "righteousness". At the time David organized his kingdom he made his sons *kohen* (priests):

11. Ibid., p. 51.

"... and David's sons were priests (כהן *kohen*; Sam. 8:18; JPS Tanach). The word *kohen* in Hebrew means "one officiating, a priest".

"And Azariah the son of Nathan was over the officers: and Zabud the son of Nathan was principal officer, and the king's friend" (1 Ki. 4:5). Barnes Notes on the Bible states: "Principal officer—Or, 'cohen.' The fact that the title (כהן) kohen was borne by sons of David (2 Samuel 8:18), who could not be 'priests' in the ordinary sense of the word, seems to identify Nathan of this verse with David's son (2 Samuel 5:14) rather than with the prophet."

The word *kohen* is very important in that it signifies that these were legitimate priests of a *special lineage* and "order", the order of *melek-zedek*, appointed by God, and *they* were destined to be the lineage of the Messiah. Much has been discussed about Jesus having been a priest in the rank of *melek-zedek*, a mediator between Yahweh and mankind, but when this reasoning is applied, it is evident that God is bringing back the "old order" of things when the kingdom is set up. Further, there is an early second century gospel (destroyed or lost) known as *The Legal Priesthood of Christ*. It is an obscure book and little is known of its contents,[12] but it likely contained information that established the *melek-zedek* priesthood of Jesus from the sons of David. The "old order" was changed when David's son exchanged the Tabernacle of David for the building of the Temple. This "old order" is prophesied: "In that day [meaning the "last day"] will I raise up the tabernacle of David that is fallen, and close up the breaches thereof; and I will raise up his ruins, and I will build it as in the days of old" (Amos 9:11). "Instead the new rule's origin goes back to the beginning of the davidic dynasty tradition—to Bethlehem Ephrathah and to 'days of old' have led some to see in this text a hope for the return of David himself, the so-called David *redivivus*."[13]

In a discussion of the "Branch", Pomykala states "that this future king will come from the source of the davidic tradition and not from the current royal line in Jerusalem."[14] He also discusses the role of the future leader in Ezekiel's prophecy. "Thirdly, this future leader is not explicitly called מלך ("king") [*melek*], but נשיא ("prince") [*nasi*]."[15] The "days of old" would seem to indicate a reversal from the dynastic formula to the *melek-zedek* tradition. The fact that the kingdom is merged with the priesthood can be found

---

12. Waite, *History*, p. 99.
13. Pomykala, *Davidic Dynasty Tradition*, p. 18.
14. Ibid., p. 20.
15. Ibid., p. 28.

In the Beginning

in that Zerubbabel is given *two crowns* to place on Joshua's head, but it is really only one crown of a priest who begins to rule as a king.

> Several problems must be addressed. The first has to do with the number of crowns involved. צטרות *is plural in form*, and thus, some commentators have spoken of two crowns. Yet, in Job 31:36 this identical plural form clearly refers *to only one crown*. Likewise, here in 6:11-14 [Zech], there is only *one crown* as the singular form of the verb in v. 14 (תהיה) confirms.[16]
>
> In 3:5, Joshua receives a clean turban (צניף), *a headdress indicative of royalty*. In 3:7 he is charged with executing judgment (תדין), *a duty formerly possessed by Judean kings*, and given access to the heavenly council, making him the mediator between God and Israel, *again a function formerly exercised by kings*. In 6:11, Joshua gets a crown (צטרות) in terminology *appropriate to royal, not priestly, power*.[17]

Thus this change in the priesthood indicates that the royal lineage would now pass down through the high priest, who in fact, is again the *melek-zedek* ruler as in the "days of old" when David and his sons were the *melek-zedek* of Israel until the messiah's advent. Although Jesus was both Davidic and Aaronic, he also now qualified as the *melek-zedek*, or king-priest, through the sons of David. This is why there was confusion as to whether the messiah would be of royal lineage or priestly lineage in the Dead Sea Scrolls and other intertestamentary books. This clarifies the statement attributed to Paul: "For there is one God [Yahweh], and one mediator [high priest] between God [Yahweh] and men, the *man*, Christ [Messiah] Jesus" (1 Tim 2:5). It explains how, although Jesus might have been Aaronic it was entirely unnecessary for him to be of that lineage in order to be "high priest". He was a high priest in the rank of *melek-zedek*.

As the king-priest, David was not only Yahweh's servant (2 Sam 3:19) but also a servant to his people: "And Yahweh thy Elohim said unto thee, Thou shalt feed my people Israel, and thou shalt be ruler over my people Israel" (1 Chr 11:2). Jesus, like David, was a servant of Yahweh and his people. In speaking of the future King Messiah Ezekiel prophesied about the messiah as God's servant: "And I will set up one shepherd over them, and he shall feed them, even my servant David [the future Son of David]; he shall feed them, and he shall be their shepherd. And I Yahweh will be

---

16. Ibid., p. 58, italics mine.
17. Ibid., pp. 55-56, italics mine.

their Elohim, and my servant David [Son of David] a prince among them; I Yahweh have spoken it"(Ezek 34:23–24). David was long dead at the time Ezekiel spoke this prophesy, but he referred to the future messiah as king, prince, and servant to the people. The appellation "Son of David" referred to David's messianic descendant who would rule as he did in the days of old. Blind Bartimaeus referred to Jesus as that messiah: "And when he heard that it was Jesus of Nazareth, he began to cry out, and say, Jesus thou son of David, have mercy on me" (Mark 10:47).

As a Jewish man and servant of God, Jesus was concerned with brotherly love and compassion for one's neighbor. The people of Israel had been taught that their "brothers" were not simply the people of their households but extended to everyone in the community. As such they were to have compassion on their fellow man. As we learn in the gospel narratives Jesus was "moved", "he felt sorry for" or "his heart went out to them", depending on which version is consulted, but these words do not accurately express his feelings. As Albert Nolan tells us, "The English word 'compassion' is far too weak to express the emotion that moved Jesus. The Greek verb *splagchnizomai* used in all these texts is derived from the noun *splagchnon*, which means intestines, bowels, entrails or heart, that is to say, the inward parts from which strong emotions seem to arise. The Greek verb therefore means a movement or impulse wells up from one's very entrails, a gut reaction."[18] Jesus did not simply *feel* compassion; he acted upon it. He healed the sick, raised the dead, encouraged the people, gave them hope, and gave them self-esteem in a frustrating and dangerous world. This is what Isaiah had prophesied the messiah would do, and this is what was still expected just before and during the first century. From prison John asks if Jesus is the one who was "to come or do we look for another?" Jesus echoed Isaiah's prophecy by telling the disciples to tell John that "the blind receive their sight, and the lame walk, the lepers are cleansed, and the deaf hear, the dead are raised up, and the poor have the gospel preached to them" (Matt. 11:5). These words are also echoed in the Dead Sea Scrolls. A manuscript found in Cave 4 entitled the Messianic Apocalypse and copied in the first century BCE, describes the anticipated ministry of the Messiah. "For He will honor the pious upon the throne of His eternal kingdom, *release the captives, open the eyes of the blind, lifting up those who are oppressed . . . For He shall heal*

---

18. Nolan, *Jesus Before Christianity*, p. 35.

the critically wounded, He shall raise the dead, He shall bring good news to the poor".[19]

The two sources sound almost identical. There can be little doubt that the words exchanged between John and Jesus refer to the Zadokite Essenes' expectation of Messiah as prophesied by Isaiah.

"I Yahweh have called thee in righteousness, and will hold thine hand, and will keep thee, and give thee for a covenant of the people, for a light of the Gentiles; To open the blind eyes, to bring out the prisoners from the prison, and them that sit in darkness out of the prison house" (Isa 42:6–7).

"The Spirit of Yahweh Elohim is upon me; because Yahweh hath anointed me [anointed as messiah] to preach good tidings unto the meek; he hath sent me to bind up the brokenhearted, to proclaim liberty to the captives, and the opening of the prison to them that are bound" (Isa 61:1).

The Essenes were known for their prophetic prowess, and from the Dead Sea Scrolls we have learned of their elaborate Jubilee calendar. Furthermore, it was a grand Jubilee year, a time for "releasing the prisoners". Jesus, shortly after his immersion, was to appear in the synagogue near Nazareth (as in Luke) or Capernaum (as in Mark) during the week of the Day of Atonement to announce the fifty-year release by reading Isaiah 61. Was the meeting between Jesus and John prearranged? We might never know, but John was certainly expecting the "messiah" to appear at that time. If John was truly an Essene then he would have recognized the Messianic Scroll's wording that Jesus used, and it would have confirmed to him that Jesus was the one sent as messiah. Since John came from the "wilderness" it is likely he was, indeed, an Essene.

Something now must be said about the hometown of Jesus. There is some confusion about his being from "Nazareth". His followers were known as Nazaraeans and he himself was known as "the Nazaraean". The Hebrew of that word is *Notzrim*, which is not connected with a location or the messianic *Nezer* (root) of Jesse. Christians believe that Jesus was supposed to be born in Bethlehem of Judea because of a prophecy in Micah 5:2: "But thou, Bethlehem Ephratah, though thou be little among the thousands of Judah, yet out of thee shall he come forth unto me that is to be ruler in Israel; whose goings forth have been from of old, from everlasting." However, that verse does not speak of the everlasting messiah; it is speaking of David. When one reads the verses directly afterward in the Old Covenant it is clarified. "And this man shall be the peace, *when the Assyrian shall come*

---

19. 4Q521, italics mine.

Becoming Christian

into our land: and when he shall tread in our palaces, then shall we raise against him seven shepherds, and eight principal men. And they shall waste the land of Assyria with the sword, and the land of Nimrod in the entrances thereof: thus shall he [David and his lineage] deliver us from the Assyrian, when he cometh into our land, and when he treadeth within our borders" (Micah 5:5–6, italics mine).

Assyria was not a threat to Israel during the lifetime of Jesus, but it *was* during the days of David and his kingdom. This is evidenced by constant threat of the Assyrians to the kings of Judah who followed him (2 Ki 15–23; 1 Chr 5; 2 Chr 28–33). Further, the Bethlehem mentioned as David's ancestor is not a location but a man. "Penuel was the father of Gedor, and Ezer the father of Hushah. These were the sons of Hur, the firstborn of Ephrathah, *the father of Bethlehem*" (1 Chr 4:4, italics mine). This means the father of Bethlehem was Hur, who was the firstborn of Ephrath. These were members of the clan of Caleb the Spy whose clan was "little among the thousands of Judah", the least of the clans of Judah. David descended from this man named Bethlehem. The prophecy is not dealing with a location but a person. Ephrahtha or Ephrath had married Caleb. To explain the close links between Moses and Hur, Josephus in *Antiquities* states that Hur was the husband of Moses' sister Miriam. However, in the Targum to I Chron. ii. 19, iv. 4, Miriam is said to be Hur's mother, asserting that Ephrath was another name for Miriam, the sister of Moses. "The name Ephrath is the basis of the Rabbinical connection of Miriam with the Davidic dynasty (i.e., the royal line that she merited), since David is called (I Sam. 17: 12): "the son of a certain Ephrathite."[20]

"These were the sons of Caleb, the son of Hur, the first-born of Ephrathah (or the rabbinical "Miriam", his wife): Shobal the father of Kiriath-jearim; And Shobal the father of Kiriath-jearim had sons: Haroeh, half of the Menuhoth" (1 Chr 2:50, 52). In Psalm 132:6 "the same is Bethlehem" or in the KJV "we found it in the fields of the wood" is a gloss and the word "Ephraim" is found in the margin to replace "Ephratah". This would indicate that Ephratah is in the northern region of Ephraim.

In fact, there is a Bethlehem of Galilee referred to in Joshua 19:14–16: "And the border turned about it on the north to Hannathon; and the goings out thereof were at the valley of Iphtahel; and Kattath, and Nahalal, and Shimron, and Idalah, and *Beth-lehem*; twelve cities with their villages. *This is the inheritance of the children of Zebulun* according to their families,

---

20. Sifrei on Numbers, 72; *b*. Sotah loc. Cit.

these cities with their villages" [italics mine]. This Bethlehem is referred to in the Talmud as *Beth Lechem Zoria* and *Beit Lehem HaGlilit*, Bethlehem of Galilee. Josephus (19:15) refers to it as one of the twelve cities of Zebulon. It is located a little less than seven miles southwest of Sepphoris (Zippori) and seven miles northwest of the present village of Nazareth. Some scholars place the nativity of Jesus in Bethlehem of Zebulon, and it is referred to in the Talmud[21] as Bethlehem *seriyyah*, which is the equivalent of *noseryyah* or Bethlehem of Nazareth (of Galilee), a combination of two names mentioned in the gospels. Beth Lechem of Galilee is touted as one of the birthplaces of Rabbinical Judaism.

"If the historical Jesus were truly born in Bethlehem, it was most likely the Bethlehem of Galilee, not that in Judaea. The archaeological evidence certainly seems to favor the former, a busy center [of Jewish life] a few miles from the home of Joseph and Mary, as opposed to an unpopulated spot almost a hundred miles from home."[22] In this Galilean Bethlehem, the Israeli archaeologist Oshri and his team uncovered the remains of a later monastery and the largest Byzantine church in Israel, which raises the question of why such a huge house of Christian worship was built in the heart of a Jewish area. He believes that it is because early Christians revered Bethlehem of Galilee as the birthplace of Jesus. "It was inhabited by Jews. I know it was Jews because we found here remnants of an industry of stone vessels, and it was used only by Jews and only in the period of Jesus," Oshri says.

Logic tells us that it would be more sensible if Joseph went from the village called Nazareth the seven miles to his hometown of Bethlehem of Galilee to pay taxes. Further, if Mary were fully nine months pregnant, a donkey ride to Bethlehem of Judea (ninety miles) would have been unbearable for her, but seven miles is not too far and would seem more reasonable. Since most of Jesus' ministry occurred in Galilee, it is entirely possible that he was born in the northern location. Since we know that the Gospel of Matthew and Luke were "reworked" it is entirely possible that the theological bent of individuals who did not understand the Micah prophecy assumed Bethlehem of Judea to be a location and not a dynasty.

The site was Jewish as early as the second century. In 1 Chronicles 24:5, 6, 9 there is a list of the twenty–four priestly families. The priests of Malchijah were known to have settled in Bethlehem of Galilee after the

---

21. *b. Meg.* 70a.
22. Oshri, "Where was Jesus Born?"

Bar Kochba revolt and served in the synagogue there until the village was destroyed in the seventh century CE by the Persian or Arab conquests.

Jesus had spent much of his ministry in this northern region, but near the end of that time period he began his journey to Jerusalem for the final time. It was at this crucial time that Antipas sought to "kill him" (Luke 13:31). For what reason, we cannot truly know. We might suspect that Antipas was in a precarious situation, having divorced his Nabataean wife and married the wife of his half–brother. He had, not long before, executed John the Baptist. Josephus claims:

> Herod, who feared lest the great influence John had over the people might put it into his power and inclination to raise a rebellion (for they seemed ready to do any thing he should advise), thought it best, by putting him to death, to prevent any mischief he might cause, and not bring himself into difficulties, by sparing a man who might make him repent of it when it should be too late. Accordingly he was sent a prisoner, out of Herod's suspicious temper, to Macherus, the castle I before mentioned, and was there put to death.[23]

Herod also feared an attack from Aretas of Arabia. "So Aretas made this the first occasion of his enmity between him and Herod, who had also some quarrel with him about their limits at the country of Gamalitis. So they raised armies on both sides, and prepared for war."[24] This war did not occur until sometime later, but he was preparing his army for an invasion. If Herod thought Jesus had fomented discontent among the natives of Galilee he might have believed it best to arrest him and execute him as he had John. The gospels tell us over and again that Jesus drew large crowds. The feeding of the five thousand might have been interpreted as the raising of a standing army. Jesus, therefore, left the territories over which Antipas ruled and traveled on the other side of Jordan and through the dangerous country of Samaria to avoid areas in which the army of Antipas might seize him.

Once Jesus arrived in Jerusalem he made instant enemies. He had not rebuked his disciples and those traveling with him when they exclaimed "Blessed be the King [Messiah] that cometh in the name of the LORD [Yahweh]: peace in heaven, and glory in the highest" (Luke 19:38). Further, upon entering the precincts at Beth Pagi he overturned the dovecotes and the moneychangers' tables at the Bazaars of Annas. From that

23. Josephus, *Ant.* 4:5.2.
24. Ibid., 4.5.1.

point forward, Annas, the infamous high priest who ruled from behind his son-in-law, sought to have him executed. The family of Annas ruled the priesthood until the destruction of Jerusalem. They had profited from their sale of sacrificial items required for temple sacrifice, and the fact that Jesus interfered with their trafficking could not have set well with them. The chief priests (family of Annas, primarily) and scribes "and the chief of the people" (high priest) sought to destroy him, even as he daily taught in the temple precincts (Luke 19:47). From the so-called "cleansing" of the temple until the Passover Jesus was harassed and questioned at every turn by the Sadducees (priests), the Pharisees and their scribes. It had been determined that he was disturbing the status quo. The priests, in particular, were terrified that Jesus might foment a rebellion among the people causing them to lose their auspicious positions, afraid that the Romans would not only rid themselves of the Jewish rule but also annihilate their nation. Ironically, this is exactly what happened some forty years later.

Eventually, members of the Sanhedrin were able to capture Jesus in the sleepy garden orchard of Gethsemane while the people were celebrating their peace offerings the night before Passover. He was taken first to Annas, who interrogated him as to his disciples and his doctrines, determining him to be a *mesith*, leading the nation astray by his doctrines, the worst blasphemy in all Judaism. He was then sent to Caiaphas who rubber-stamped the verdict of blasphemy and sent to the Roman Pilate for approval of his execution.

Jesus was executed the following morning, on a day appointed for celebration. His broken body was taken to a garden tomb belonging to one Joseph of Arimathea, an Elder in the Sanhedrin, who might well have also been a kinsman. Accompanying Joseph was Nicodemus (Nakdimon) ben Gorion to prepare the body for burial and sing prayers for the dead. While it was a necessity and was allowable by Jewish law to prepare the body for burial, no mourning for the deceased was allowed until after the Sabbath. The women who followed would have gone to their homes after locating the specific tomb where Jesus was laid where they might prepare the necessary spices and ointments for use after the Sabbath. There, the family would have gathered and mourned privately in the home. They would sit on the floor of the home, praying, singing hymns, and mourning their dead. Friends would come and supply them with food that they would, again, eat while remaining on the floor in lamentation. After the Sabbath on the first day of the week (Sunday), the women would take their prepared spices to properly anoint the body. The gospels indicate that several women, particularly Mary Magdalene, arrived at the tomb only to learn that the body of Jesus was no longer there. Mark isolates Mary Magdalene as the first to see the risen Jesus. This is where the gospel writers were confused. In Matthew the direction of the messenger is to tell the disciples that Jesus "goeth before you into Galilee" (Matt 28:7). The Gospel of Mark agrees in that Mary Magdalene was the first to see the risen Jesus. He, too, directs Mary to go to the disciples and Peter that he "goeth before you into Galilee: there shall ye see him, as he said unto you" (Mark 16:9). However, in Luke (24) Jesus first appeared to two disciples on the road to Emmaus and when they returned to Jerusalem, the disciples told them Jesus had appeared first to Simon *in Jerusalem*. In the Gospel of John, Jesus appears to the disciples *in Jerusalem*, but Thomas was not with them at the time. Eight days later Jesus again appears to them while Thomas was present, again *in Jerusalem*. In the book of Acts he stayed *in Jerusalem* for forty days with the disciples "speaking of the things pertaining to the Kingdom of God: And, being assembled together with them, commanded them that they should not depart from Jerusalem, but wait for the promise of the Father, which saith he, ye have heard of me" (Acts 1:3–4).

In all likelihood Jesus did not go to Galilee but met them in Jerusalem. We learn that the disciples witnessed his ascension from Bethany (Beth Hini, the Sabbath Limit) and immediately "went up into an upper room, where abode both Peter, and James, and John, and Andrew, Philip, and Thomas, Bartholomew, and Matthew, James the son of Alphaeus, and Simon Zelotes, and Judas the brother of James. These all continued with one accord in prayer and supplication, *with the women, and Mary the mother of Jesus, and with his brethren*" (Acts 1:13–14, italics mine).

Jesus ascended ten days before Pentecost (Shavuot, Feast of Weeks), and "in those days" Peter stood on the Mount of Olives and gave an oration to the Diaspora Jews (on Pentecost) while they awaited the opening of the gates of the temple at midnight (when Pentecost had *fully come*) (Acts 2). During the three festival days the time had "fully come" at midnight. At that time the gates to the temple were opened so that the festival pilgrims might view inside the temple. It is in that manner that we know Peter's oration occurred in the night hours before midnight (*kachatzot halailah*—at the dividing of the night) on the fiftieth day of Matzoh. Midnight was an auspicious time for the Jewish people. At Passover it commemorated the Exodus which began at midnight. In Matthew 25:6–13

In the Beginning

the call of the bridegroom comes at midnight. It was also the time when the rabbis claimed David would enter the garden to speak with Yahweh. That day was the day designated as the giving of the Torah to the people of Israel, thus it is associated with Yahweh's close presence, and this is reflected in the giving of the Holy Spirit.

The disciples had no doubt that they had seen, touched, and ate with Jesus during the forty days after his resurrection. Paul, writing to the Corinthians (1 Cor 15:5–7) sometime between 50 and 60 CE (usually dated about 53 CE), states: "And that he was seen of Cephas, *then of the twelve*: After that, he was seen of above five hundred brethren at once; of whom the greater part remain unto this present, but some are fallen asleep. After that, *he was seen of James; then of all the apostles*" [italics mine]. Once again, it is Peter who first sees Jesus after his resurrection, then *all* the apostles, and finally James, the brother of Jesus. We are instantly reminded that all these disciples and the family of Jesus were lodged in Jerusalem just before Pentecost and shortly after his ascension. This fact indicates that his family, including his brothers, believed Jesus was messiah. It also indicates they had taken up residence in Jerusalem before the execution of Jesus, apparently for some time. It appears that James, the brother of Jesus and leader of the Jerusalem community of Nazaraeans had lived there some time with his own family. There can be little doubt that the earliest Nazaraeans believed in the resurrection and soon return of Jesus to set up the Kingdom of God. They continued to worship Yahweh in the temple at the time of the morning and evening prayers (Acts 3:1) and kept the Sabbath as they always had. Peter expressly stated before the court of the Sanhedrin that they had "killed the Prince [messiah] of life, whom God [Yahweh] hath raised form the dead; whereof we are witnesses" (Acts 3:15) He, again, emphasizes this point: "Unto you first God [Yahweh], having raised up his son Jesus, sent him to bless you, in turning away every one of you from his iniquities" (Acts 3:26). Although the disciples were brought before the court they continued teaching the resurrection of Messiah Jesus. The book of Acts states that "many thousands of Jews there are which believe; and they are all zealous of the law [Torah]" (Acts 21:20). There were among these Jews "a great company" of the priesthood (Acts 6:7) along with Pharisees (Acts 15:5) who had come to believe Jesus was the messiah. All these were faithful to Judaism as it existed at the time, yet they also believed with all their understanding that Jesus was the risen messiah of Yahweh.

Becoming Christian

James, the brother of Jesus, makes it clear that Paul, who had been telling the Diaspora Jews they no longer had to circumcise their children and to "forsake Moses", nor "to walk after their customs" (Acts 21:21) that he could now preach only to the Gentiles. He then took over the ministry of Peter, who had first had been sent to the Gentiles in order to invite them into the community as Proselytes (full Jews). James, the leader of the Nazaraean community in Jerusalem, the central authority over all the messianic communities issued a letter to the Gentile communities outlining the commandments they must keep (Noachide commandments). The disciples, the elders, and the whole assembly approved it. James' authority was not challenged. In fact, Paul makes mention of the fact that James, along with Peter and John, "seemed to be pillars" of the Jerusalem community (Gal 2:9). While in Jerusalem the first time he saw none of the apostles, "save James the Lord's brother" (Gal. 1:19) and Peter.

The members of the earliest Jerusalem community under the leadership of Jesus' brother James remained fully within Judaism. They still followed Torah, kept the Sabbath, worshiped in the temple, attended daily prayers, and still maintained that Yahweh was their God. They lived in expectation of the return of Jesus to set up the Kingdom of God, beginning in Jerusalem.

> It should be remembered that Jewish believers remained largely undisturbed in Jerusalem for most of the period 30–62 CE. The spasms of persecution are not recalled as particularly motivated by hostility to Christ-devotion . . . the bulk of Jewish believers in Jerusalem could subsequently be described as 'all zealous for the law' (Acts 21.20) suggests that their reverence of Jesus did not incite open opposition from the Jewish authorities in Jerusalem.[25]

The fact that James as the highest authority of the Jerusalem community continued in public view of the ruling priests and the Sanhedrin for the next thirty-one years until his death is an indication that he was a faithful believer in the God of the Jews and was fully accepted within the general religious community. It is with this backdrop that we might further investigate the beliefs and practices of the earliest Nazareans.

---

25. Dunn, *Did the First Christians Worship Jesus?*, p. 115.

2

James the Brother of Jesus

THE PERIOD BETWEEN JESUS' execution and 66 CE at the beginning of the Jewish Revolt the Nazaraeans (*Notzrim*) were a driving force in Jerusalem. Within a short time after the resurrection of Jesus numerous individuals joined the sect, at least three thousand at the time of the Feast of Weeks (Pentecost) (Acts 2:41), no small number considering the population of first century Jerusalem. At the time of the revolt (in 66 CE) Tacitus had estimated the population of Jerusalem at 600,000, but during the time of its greatest prosperity it is believed the population was more in the range of 40,000 to 60,000. It can be estimated more accurately that the population of Jerusalem reached 120,000–200,000 under Herod's rule.[1] A clear number of Passover pilgrims from the Diaspora and Israel itself can be found during the reign of Agrippa II when he wanted to number the male participants. Recorded in the Talmud is the method by which the high priests counted the census that year:

> Agrippa the king once wanted to know how many male Israelites there were. So he told the high-priest to keep account of the paschal lambs. The high-priest then ordered, that one kidney of each paschal lamb be preserved, and it was found that six hundred thousand pairs of kidneys were preserved; and this was twice the number of the Israelites who went out of Egypt. Naturally, this was exclusive of all Israelites who were unclean and could not offer the sacrifice, and all those who lived at a great distance from Jerusalem

1. History of Jerusalem, http://www.shalomjerusalem.com/jerusalem/jerusalem3.htm.

and were not in duty bound to be present. *There was not a single paschal lamb that did not represent at least more than ten persons.*[2]

This would mean that there were about 3,000,000 celebrants for Passover that year! It later became referred to as the "large Passover". This certainly must be where Josephus derives his figure for the numbers of Passover pilgrims in the city of Jerusalem. He mentions more than once the large numbers that came up to the feast.[3] He calculates that there were 2,700,200 capable of celebrating the Passover at the time of the destruction of Jerusalem.[4] Whatever exaggeration there may be in these numbers, it is clear that the number of people at the feast must have been great. The numbers seem a little extraordinary but is entirely within possibility. The James community, however, would have had ample opportunity to expound the resurrection of Jesus at each of these required feasts.

Each day brought new converts (Acts 2:47) and each year many more Jewish converts to the sect, including "a great company of the priests" (Acts 6:7), both from Jerusalem itself and from other major Jewish centers from Judea and Samaria to Egypt and from the Diaspora. The sect of the Nazaraeans grew in numbers so great that their synagogues spread throughout the city of Jerusalem.

The sect, under the leadership of James, the brother of Jesus, was well respected and fully accepted within the larger Jewish community as it existed during the first century. The Nazaraeans were known to have observed the Torah, worshiped in the Temple, continued to keep the festivals (including the Day of Atonement), and engaged in the rites of circumcision.

> And all who believed were together and *had all things in common.* And they sold their possessions and property and shared the proceeds with any who had need. *And day by day, devoting much time to being in the temple together and breaking bread in their homes,* they received their food with glad and generous hearts, praising God and *finding favor with all the people.* And day by day the Lord added to their number those who were being saved (Acts 44–47, italics mine).

The only difference between the Nazaraeans and the Pharisaic and Essene sects was that they held a belief that Jesus was the resurrected Messiah.

---

2. *t. Pesah.* 4:15, italics mine.
3. Josephus, *Ant.* 17.9.3; 20.5.3.
4. Josephus, BJ 6.9.3.; BJ 2.14.3.

They, like the other two sects, held religious doctrines from ancient traditions and believed in a bodily resurrection of the dead. The Nazaraeans found "favor with all the people". Although the followers of Jesus remained in the Jewish faith as it was known at that time, there can be little doubt that the family and followers of Jesus believed he had been resurrected from the dead and would return in the "last days" which they believed was imminent, and this did not affect their orthodox dealings with other Jews.

> Among the original disciples were some drawn from these groups [i.e., Essenes, Pharisees, Zealots, and Therapeutae]. It is most significant that from its foundation the Nazorean Party exhibits a strong resemblance to Essenism, in both form and manners, and to a considerable extent in ideas and practices. So much so, that fourth-century investigators of Christian Beginnings could hold that the Essenes of Judea and the Therapeutai of Egypt were the early Christians. Also, like the Baptists, the Nazoreans emphasized baptism for the remission of sins, which was made a requisite of membership.[5]

In no manner did James and the Nazaraeans intend to found a new religion. During this time period, they were known as the Nazaraeans, not "Christians". They held no Pauline view of what would become dominant in Christianity. Had they not been accepted within the mainstream Jewish religion, they would have been excommunicated from Temple worship. It had, likewise, never occurred to them that circumcision ought to be abolished for the Jewish race. Yet these Nazaraeans were allowed to have their own synagogues and were allowed to co-exist with the priests, the Pharisees, and the Essenes in harmony. In general, they were not viewed as a threat to the populace. The only aggression toward the Nazaraeans was by the instigation of the Saducean family of Hanan (Annas) and their alliances. The *nasi* (president) of the Great Sanhedrin (the religious Sanhedrin) at the time was Gamaliel, the grandson of the famous teacher Hillel (Caiaphas was the *nasi* of the criminal Sanhedrin consisting of twenty-three members). At the time Peter and John were brought before Annas and Caiaphas and John (Jonathan) and Alexander (Eleazar), "and as many as were of the kindred of the high priest", who held the majority in the priesthood and all members of the criminal Sanhedrin. Gamaliel, the well known Pharisee and leader of the religious Sanhedrin, defended them (Acts 5:34–40). There can

---

5. Schonfield, *The Jesus Party*, p. 106.

be little doubt that the aristocratic family of Annas had wanted to execute them, just as they had executed Jesus. The logic and power of Gamaliel and his influence over the populace is the only thing that prevented them. It was also Caiaphas, the son-in-law of Annas, who had written letters to the synagogues along the way to Damascus, asking them to aid Paul in arrest of the Nazaraeans.

There appears to have been a deep conflict between James and his Jerusalem community and Paul.

> Paul lived in a state of tension with the Christian community of Jerusalem, all the members of which were observant Jews. He developed his own particular doctrine, or gospel, which took no account of Jesus' own preaching, but considered the core of Christianity to consist of the act of salvation by Jesus the Messiah, who redeemed the whole of mankind and opened the gate, as it were, to the Gentiles. Paul's attitude to the Torah and the commandments was in no way positive, and this attitude was an indirect cause of the Christians' rejection of the Torah and commandments.[6]

It is noticeable that neither Gamaliel (if he were still alive), who had defended Peter and John, nor any of the community headed by James were Paul's advocates when he was arrested. Their silence is deafening.

> [W]hen Paul was arrested and put on trial we hear nothing of any Jewish Christians [Nazaraeans] standing by him, speaking in his defence—and this despite James's apparent high standing among orthodox Jews ... Where were the Jerusalem Christians [Nazaraeans]? It looks very much as though they had washed their hands of Paul, left him to stew in his own juice. If so it implies a fundamental antipathy on the part of the Jewish Christians to Paul himself and what he stood for.[7]

It had been Paul who had presided over the stoning of Stephen and "*cast his vote* against the Nazarenes" (Acts 26:10, italics mine), clearly indicating he had been associated with the Jerusalem Sanhedrin and fastidiously aligned with the Sadducees, connected in some manner with the family of Annas, even though he claimed to be a Pharisee. Had he not been a member of the Chamber of Pharisees he would not have been able to "vote" in proceedings against Stephen and others. Only a member of the 23-member criminal Sanhedrin could "vote" to put a man to death. It was

---

6. Flusser, *Jewish Sources*, pp. 67–68.
7. Dunn, *Unity and Diversity*, p. 256, as quoted in Bütz, *The Brother of Jesus*, p. 89.

the Sadducees, and the family of Annas in particular, who Josephus informs us were strict in their criminal proceedings. In general, the Pharisees were known to have been much more liberal and certainly more compassionate in their interpretation of the law.[8] It was also the Sadducean Ananus II (son of Annas I) who called an illegal Sanhedrin and convicted and executed James and some other members of the Nazaraeans.

> But *this younger Ananus (Annas)*, who, as we have told you already, took the high-priesthood, was a bold man in his temper, and very insolent; *he was also of the sect of the Sadducees, who are very rigid in judging offenders, above all the rest of the Jews, as we have already observed*, when, therefore, Ananus was of this disposition, he thought he had now a proper opportunity [to exercise his authority]. Festus was now dead, and Albinus was but upon the road; so he assembled the sanhedrim of judges, and brought before them *the brother of Jesus, who was called Christ, whose name was James, and some others, [or, some of his companions]; and when he had formed an accusation against them as breakers of the law, he delivered them to be stoned.*[9]

So it wasn't the general population of the "Jews", nor even the Romans, who wanted to stamp out the family of Jesus and the Nazaraeans. His teachings were in line with the religious beliefs of the general population, the Pharisees, and the Essenes. It was the powerful family of Annas who held a long-standing feud with the family of Joseph and Jesus. The houses of Boethus and Annas were rivals throughout the first century. It is possible that Joseph, who might have been a member by marriage of the Boethus family, had incurred the ire of the most powerful priests (Ananelaus and Theophilus, father of Matthias the high Priest) in the land of Judea and it was probably the reason for the feud.

John Crossan realizes that James was an influential individual within the sphere of Jerusalem orthodoxy, so important that his execution caused Annas II to be deposed from the priesthood.

> Josephus tells us that Ananus was a Sadducee, but he was much more than that. His father, Ananus the Elder, was high priest from 6 to 15 C.E., and is known to us from the gospels as Annas. The elder Ananus was father-in-law of Joseph Caiaphas, High Priest from 18 to 36 C.E., a figure also known to us from the gospels.

---

8. Josephus, *Ant.* 13.10.6.
9. Ibid., 20.9.1, italics mine.

> He was furthermore the father of five other High Priests... The immediate family of Ananus the Elder had dominated the high priesthood for most of the preceding decades, with eight high priests in sixty years, yet the execution of James resulted in the deposition of Ananus the Younger after only three months in office. An abstract illegality could hardly have obtained such a reaction, so James must have had powerful, important, and even politically organized friends in Jerusalem.[10]

There can be little doubt that the Nazaraeans under the leadership of James, another son of Joseph, conducted their *administrative affairs* on the Mount of Olives or the new "Mt. Zion", as Eusebius informs us. While James headed the Nazaraean Sanhedrin (the "Seventy") in its administration, it was the apostles who became its teaching emissaries. James and Peter would have completed the Seventy-two (as president and vice president), making it a full Sanhedrin. It was from the Mount Olives then that the Sanhedrin of James met.

> Believers in Christ congregate from all parts of the world, not as of old time because of the glory of Jerusalem, nor that they may worship in the ancient Temple at Jerusalem, but... that they may worship at the Mount of Olives opposite to the city, whither the glory of the Lord migrated when it left the former city.[11]

In fact, Eusebius tells us exactly where the "throne of James" existed.

> And this Mount of Olives is said to be over against Jerusalem, instead of the old earthly Jerusalem and its worship... believers in Christ congregate from all parts of the world... that they may worship at the Mount of Olives opposite the city... *to the cave that is shown there.*[12]

Ernest Martin also connects Eusebius' description of the Mount of Olives with the New Mount Zion: "The Mount Sion of Eusebius was the Mount of Olives. He said: Mount Sion adjacent thereto [to Jerusalem] (where our Lord and Saviour for the most part lived and taught)"...[13]

---

10. Crossan, *Jesus, A Revolutionary Biography*, pp. 134–136.
11. Eusebius, *Proof* VI:18.
12. Ibid., VI:18, italics mine.
13. Martin, *Secrets*, p. 182.

James the Brother of Jesus

The "cave" can be found beneath the foundations of the ancient Eleona Church (now the Pater Noster Church). Dr. J. Wilkinson discusses this cave as the ascension site:

> Where did the Apostles experience this final parting? Though Luke says at the end of his Gospel that it was at *Bethany* no later pilgrims or Jerusalem Christians ever seemed to remember it there. Nor indeed was it in the place where the Jerusalemites first commemorated it, *for this was none other than the Eleona Cave*, and Acts 1:10 demands that the place of the Ascension should be in some open place from which it was possible to look up into the sky.[14]

There is really no contradiction here since "Bethany" is none other than "Beth Hini" (and not the "village" of Bethany) in the region of "Beth Pagi"[15] on the Mount of Olives and which is mentioned often in the Talmud as an ecclesiastical district attached to the Temple as a wing and surrounded by its own wall yet considered a part of the city. "Bethania" in Talmud Bqavliy show this place named spelled... (*Beyt Hiyniy'... Pesakhim* 53a [twice] and *Bava M'tziya* 88a)."[16]

> But [even] on R. Judah's view, *does it not require the [chomah or joining] wall [of Jerusalem]?*—He threshed it *within the walls of Beth Pagi*... I.e., since he tithed the crops in ear, nothing thereof is to be consumed—not even by beasts—*outside the walls of Jerusalem... the outer wall of Jerusalem, added to the original limits of the town*; v. Sanh. (Sonc. ed.) p. 67, no. 9.[17]

This region of Beth Pagi–Beth Hini was also where the twenty-three-member Jerusalem Sanhedrin met for criminal adjudication (a third of the religious Great Sanhedrin and conducted by the family of Annas).

> R. Joseph said, Come and hear: If they found a rebellious elder in *Beth Pagi*, and he rebelled against them, it is possible to think that his act of rebellion is punishable; therefore there is a text to state, *Then shalt thou arise and get thee up unto the place [the Plaza of Gulgoleth, called the topos in the New Testament Greek]. This teaches that the 'place' [the "town square"; Plaza] determines [whether the act of rebellion is punishable]*. Now how many of them had gone forth [from the Great Sanhedrin to *Beth Pagi*]?... *if they*

---

14. Wilkinson, *The Jerusalem Jesus Knew*, p. 173, italics mine.
15. See Kuehl, *A Book of Evidence*, "The Place of the Crux".
16. Ben-David, NRM, Vol. II: Miydrash, II:21, 17.1.
17. *b. B. Mes.* 90a, n. 5 and 6, italics mine.

> met in Beth Pagi, and [an elder] rebelled against them ... [This verse is applied to the Sanhedrin, called *'navel'*, because *it sat in a place [plaza] which was considered to be the centre of the world [the naval; daughter of Zion, the branch of Zion; part of Beth Pagi].* 'Mingled wine' is defined (Shab. 77a) as diluted with two-thirds of water. Hence *one third of the Sanhedrin must at least be present* at a session] ... e.g., they went forth to carry out a measurement in connection with the heifer, or to add to the boundaries of the city [of Jerusalem] or the Temple-courts, it is possible to think that his act of rebellion is punishable; therefore there is a text to state, *Then shalt thou arise and get thee up [etc.]. This teaches that the 'place'* [plaza at Beth Pagi] *determines [whether the act of rebellion is punishable].*[18]

It was at this site that Jesus "cursed" the fig tree with unripe figs. That tree had never fully matured: "And when he saw a fig tree in the way, he came to it, and found nothing thereon but leaves only, and said unto it Let no fruit grow on thee henceforward for ever. And presently the fig tree withered away" (Matt 21:19–20).

There is a discussion in the Talmud concerning the figs of Beth Pagi.[19] The unripe figs found in Beth Hini are referred to as *pagge* and are a species of figs referred to as *ahina* or *ahini* (plural) *that never reach full maturity*, but nevertheless are fit to eat. These are the type of figs in Jeremiah's basket of unripe figs that are considered evil and represent Zedekiah's destruction (Jer 24:1). Jesus is certain to have had Jeremiah in mind when he cursed the fig tree. It represented the government of the corrupt Sadducean priesthood and the Sanhedrin. The Sanhedrin is also represented by the fig tree. These figs are considered inferior. The sages refer to this place as Beth Hini and Bethania, by which it is called because the surrounding wall encompassed both Beth Hini as well as Beth Pagi, where the residents of the priests (or Tanaaim) were located.

Not only did this region encompass the two small villages of Bethphage and Bethany (not the present villages; Origen mentioned Beth Pagi as a "village of priests"), it was also the eastern plaza of the city where various ecclesiastical offices were situated and included also the execution site, the Miphkad Altar at which the Red Heifer rites were performed and the goat of atonement was burned. The *beth hadeshen* or place of ashes was also located there.

18. *b. Sotah* 45a, 1987 ed., italics mine.
19. *b. Pesah.* 53a.

James the Brother of Jesus

The surrounding wall of Beth Pagi is the Sabbath Limit. There is another discussion of the rabbis concerning the location of the prison regarding passover. There was a prison in Beth Pagi and is probably the prison where the apostles were held.

> And likewise one who has received a promise to be released from prison, and an invalid, and an aged person who can eat as much as an olive, one slaughters on their behalf. [Yet in the case of] all these, one may not slaughter for them alone, lest they bring the passover–offering to disqualification therefore if a disqualification occurs to them, they are exempt from keeping the second passover, except one who was removing debris, because he was unclean from the beginning.
>
> GEMARA. Rabbah son of R. Huna said in R. Johanan's name: They learned this only of a heathen prison; but [if he is incarcerated in] an Israelite prison, one slaughters for him separately; since he was promised, he will [definitely] be released, as it is written, The remnant of Israel shall not do iniquity, nor speak lies. R. Hisda observed: As to what you say, [If he is in] a heathen prison [one may] not [kill on his behalf alone]; *that was said only [when the prison is] without the walls of Beth Pagi; but [if it is] within the walls of Beth Pagi, one slaughters on his behalf alone.* What is the reason? It is possible to convey it [the flesh] to him and he will eat it.[20]

> Bethany is interpreted, the house of obedience, but Bethphage the house of cheek bones, being *a place belonging to the priests*, for cheek bones in the sacrifices were the right of the priests, as it is commanded in the law. To that place then where obedience is, and where the priests have the possession, our Savior sends His disciples to loose the ass' colt.[21]

The two are often confused in the literature. For instance, in the Syriac version Bethany is rendered "place of business". That is because in that general area were the bazaars and merchants, as well as the moneychangers. Also located there were the genealogical registers, which would have included those of the family of Jesus.

---

20. *b. Pesah.* 81a, italics mine.

21. Origen and Jerome; Comment. in Matt. vol. xvi. cap. xvii, italics mine. (Lommatzscli, iv. 52) In loc. & ad Eustoch, fol. 59. 3. Tom. 1.((r) Misn. Menachot, c. 11. sect. 2. B. Menachot fol. 63. 1. & 78. 2. Maimon. Hilch. Pesul. Hamukdash, c. 12. sect. 16. Gloss. in Pesach. fol. 63. 2.((s) T. Bab. Pesach. fol. 53. 1. & Erubin, fol. 28. 2.((t) Zechariah 14 4. Targum in Ezek. xi. 23. & Bartenora in Misn. Mid. dot. c. 1. sect. 3, italics mine.

Becoming Christian

> In a word, all matters involving genealogical or census records of the people of Israel were kept at the library at Bethphage (which was a village exclusively for priests and where the second court of the great Sanhedrin was located). Though Bethphage was reckoned to be an official part of the city of Jerusalem, it was actually situated outside the camp or just east of the summit of the Mount of Olives and a little further east of the Miphkad Altar. This eastern entrance to the camp was considered to be the eastern "gate" into the proper city limits of Jerusalem.[22]

However, both the royal bank and the genealogical registers (the archives) had been moved to Sepphoris *prior* to the destruction of Jerusalem and the temple in 61 CE under Agrippa II:

> But as for Justus, the son of Pistus, who was the head of the third faction, although he pretended to be doubtful about going to war, yet was he really desirous of innovation, as supposing that he should gain power to himself by the change of affairs. He therefore came into the midst of them, and endeavored to inform the multitude that the city Tiberius had ever been a city of Galilee, and that in the days of Herod the tetrarch, who had built it, it had obtained the principal place, and that he had ordered that the city Sepphoris should be subordinate to the city Tiberias; that they had not lost this preeminence even under Agrippa the father, but had retained it until Felix was procurator of Judea. *But he told them, that now they had been so unfortunate as to be made a present by Nero to Agrippa, junior; and that, upon Sepphoris's submission of itself to the Romans, that was become the capital city of Galilee, and that the royal library and the archives were now removed from them.*[23]

So the archives were removed from Beth Pagi to Sepphoris in Galilee long before the war (also verified by Rabbi Jose, whose father was the leader of the government at Sepphoris at the time), and the *despoysni* were able to obtain and hold on to their genealogy. At a later date the Romans also destroyed the genealogical records at Sepphoris but not before the families had obtained a copy. Most families kept not only an oral record but a scrolled record of their genealogies as well.

The Eleona Church was a building constructed at the instance of Queen Helena, the mother of Constantine, over the cave where Jesus and the disciples often met and is sometimes referred to as the "Church of the

---

22. Martin, *Restoring*, Chap. 11.
23. Josephus, *Life* 9, italics mine.

Disciples". Although there is a fourth century crypt located in the cave, the first leaders of the Nazaraeans were also said to have been buried somewhere in that vicinity as well, perhaps in the cave itself. Nearby in the Dominus Flevit tombs can be found the ossuaries of Simon bar Jonah (Peter), Mary, Martha, and Eleazar (Lazarus) and other Nazaraeans.

The Nazaraean headquarters then appears to have been situated on the Mount of Olives, the "New Mount Zion" near the location where Jesus ascended, but synagogues might have been dispersed throughout the City of David and Mount Zion. We do know of synagogues in Jerusalem that were the meeting places for Jews of the Diaspora while they visited Jerusalem (Acts 21:27). They are referred to as "Grecians" in the New Testament, but they were really Hellenistic Jews, as we know from Acts 6:1 where the "Grecians" (Hellenists) murmured against the "Hebrews", the Hebrews representing the administrative leaders of the Nazaraeans, because their widows were neglected.

> The Hellenized Jews visited the Temple. They also founded in Palestine their own synagogues, as we are told in the New Testament. It is true that their knowledge of Judaism could not be compared with that of the Palestinian Jews, and their children did not receive as good a Jewish education as did the children of Palestinian Jews, but they did remain loyal to Judaism, and one can take it that most of them kept the commandments—at least to the extent to which they were familiar with them. Perhaps it was the fulfilling of the commandments on a soil which was not part of their motherland which aroused in them a sense of insecurity and suspicion. They were, for example, suspicious of Paul. It was these Hellenized Jews who persecuted Paul and brought about his arrest by the Romans when he visited Jerusalem. The tension between Paul and the Hellenistic Jews was great, since they were terrified of a new faith which could have shaken their Jewish faith to its foundations.[24]

The Mount of Olives would, logically, be a place the community would set up the royal "kingdom" on earth to await Jesus' return since the two men in white apparel declared to them that "this same Jesus, which is taken up from you into heaven, shall so come in like manner as ye have seen him go into heaven" (Acts 1:11). After this, they had returned "unto Jerusalem from the mount called Olivet, *which is from Jerusalem a sabbath day's journey*" (Acts 1:12, italics mine). Beth Pagi–Beth Hini was, in fact, considered to be the sabbath limit. The sabbath limit was measured from the Holy

---

24. Flusser, *Jewish Sources*, pp. 75, 78.

Becoming Christian

of Holies. As we know, Jesus was executed "outside the camp" in a plaza (*topos*) as is described in the book of Revelation as the place "where also the Lord was slain" (Rev 11:8). The *spot* in Beth Pagi near Jerusalem is there referred to as spiritually Sodom and Egypt.[25]

Since Jesus was executed on the Mount of Olives just a sabbath's journey from Jerusalem in Beth Pagi and buried in a garden tomb in Bethphage, it is also reasonable that James and the apostles chose to set up their administration headquarters at the cave near where Jesus ascended to await his return.[26]

Although James is mentioned only some seventeen times in the New Testament, there is much to know about him.

1. James was a Hasidic Jew who sought to study and follow the precepts of Torah in the strictest manner. He had grown up in Galilee, a region known as a haven for its meticulous study of Torah.

2. He (along with his surviving brothers) was married and probably had children (1 Cor. 9:5).

3. He was a natural leader and head administrator and made final decisions for the sect. His word was "law" as we learn in Acts 21 where James clarifies to Paul that the Gentiles must keep the Noachide commandments only, and that Paul could no longer teach the Diaspora Jews that they did not need to become circumcised.

4. He wore linen clothing and mitre (a priest's turban) and was allowed to enter the Holy of Holies, indicating he was of the lineage of the legitimate high priesthood, the Zadokites (the Essenes were also Zadokites). Eusebius, quoting Hegessipus:

> *He alone was permitted to enter the sanctum, for he wore not wool but linen.* He used to enter the temple alone and was often found kneeling and imploring forgiveness for the people, so that his knees became hard like a camel's from his continual kneeling in worship of God and in prayer for the people. Because of his superior righteousness he was called the Just and Oblias—meaning, in Greek, "Bulwark of the People" and "Righteousness"—as the prophets declare regarding him.[27]

---

25. See Kuehl, Nancy, *A Book of Evidence*.
26. See Kuehl, *A Book of Evidence* on the subject of the execution and tomb site.
27. Eusebius, HE 2:23, italics mine.

Oblias, which Eusebius renders, "Protection of the People" (*perioche to lao*) would indicate he was brought to trial by Ananus II for "protecting the people"; i.e., the poor priests from whom the high priests were stealing tithes, thus leaving them to starve.

I would suggest, however, that the term "Just" or *zedek* referred more correctly to the fact that he was of the priestly lineage of legitimate Zadokites.

5. James had associated with other sects, including the sects of the Essenes and the Pharisees, as well as other righteous Jews before his execution in 62 CE, as Josephus informs us:

> But as *for those who seemed the most equitable of the citizens*, and such as were the most uneasy at the breach of laws, they disliked what was done; they also sent to the king [Agrippa II, actually a tetrarch], desiring him to send to Ananaus that he should act so no more.[28]

6. We know he had four brothers: Jesus (Yehoshua), Joses (Joseph), Juda (Jude/Judah/Judas), and Simon (Shimon) and at least three sisters (Mark 6:3), all of whom, along with his mother Mary were involved in the ministry of Jesus and found praying earnestly with the apostles (Acts 1:14).

7. It is probable that his father was a priest, and that it would have been from him that he would have inherited the Zadokite priesthood, and that his mother was named Mary (Miriam).

8. We also know that his cousins were priests; for instance, Simeon, who was said to have been allowed to enter the Holy of Holies, indicating that his uncle Cleophas (Joseph's brother) was *also* a priest.

> In a late Jewish source the composition of all three works is ascribed to Simeon ben Calpus, an honorable old man, stated to have been an uncle of Jesus. *The uncle, of course, was Calpus (Cleophas)* . . . The man they select is "a certain aged man from among the Elders . . . *who frequented the Holy of Holies*." He is called in one text Simeon Cepha, but correctly in another Simeon ben Calpus.[29]

Cleophas was, indeed, the brother of Joseph (not Mary) as Hegessipus relates:

---

28. Josephus, *Ant.* 20.9.1, italics mine.
29. Schonfield, *The Jesus Party*, p. 231, italics mine.

> [T]hey all with one consent approved Symeon the son of Clopas, of whom also the book of the Gospels makes mention, as worthy of *the throne of the community* in that place. *He was a cousin—so it is said—of the Saviour; for indeed Hegesippus relates that Clopas was Joseph's brother.*[30]

9. Simon Peter recognized his authority, reporting to him after his escape from prison: "Go shew these things unto James, and to the brethren" (Acts 12:17), indicating that it was James, not Peter who became head of the Nazaraean community. Peter, at first, was a missionary to the Gentiles but became the missionary to the Jews ("the circumcised" as in Galatians).

10. While Peter was a traveling missionary (as the New Testament verifies), James was the administrative (and most powerful) leader of the community in Jerusalem and the authority for the Nazaraean communities in the Diaspora (as is clear by his edict setting down the "law" or rules for converts to the sect).

"Peter, like Paul, is portrayed as a "missionary" rather than as the leader of a settled community."[31]

11. He was entombed by the "Sanctuary" as Hegessipus informs. Had he not been well respected by other orthodox Jews he would not have been accorded such an honor. Not just anyone could be buried near the Temple. The James ossuary is believed to have come from a location near the Temple."[32]

James and the Nazaraeans taught what Jesus taught, that not one "jot" (*yod*) nor "tittle" (*keren* used in making the *tagin* or "crowns" that ornamented the letters), diacritics in the Hebrew *aleph–beth* would disappear from the Torah *until heaven and earth passed away* (Matt 5:18, Luke 16:17, italics mine). These marks were so important that one small error could change the meaning of an important sentence. Thus the Nazaraeans were accepted as "Jews" within the sphere of the first century Jewish community. They were in no way persecuted because of their belief in Jesus as the resurrected Messiah. In fact, the Pharisees (rabbis) during Hadrian's reign were still meeting with them for discussion of Torah. Furthermore, during the

---

30. Eusebius, HE 3.9, italics mine.
31. Painter, *Just James*, pp. 43–44.
32. Bütz, *The Brother of Jesus*, p. 112. (See also Shanks and Witherington, *The Brother of Jesus*).

reign of Domitian (81–96 CE) a group of rabbis journeyed to the Christian Diaspora in Rome.

> Under Domitian, Gamaliel II made a journey thither in company with Eleazar ben Azariah, Joshua ben Hananiah, and Akiba, and it is related that they discoursed in synagogues and school-houses, and discussed religious subjects with heathen and Christians.[33]

We can well imagine the government of the community rested on the normal Jewish hierarchy; i.e., a seventy-two member religious Sanhedrin. James, as "high priest" and "prince regent" was the ultimate authority of this group, and they would judge religious matters, similar to the *Great Sanhedrin* or the *Great Beth Din*. There were also three "pillars" or "secretaries" (Peter, James, who would have headed all the Sanhedrins, and John) who represented a three-member Sanhedrin (or *Beth Din*), "judges" who sat to determine civil matters such as monetary disputes and donations (such as that made by "Barnabas"), to administer charities and to record the proceedings of the Great Sanhedrin headed by James. There were also seven overseers, called *sheliach tzibburim* or "emissaries of the congregation", appointed as leaders and teachers for the community in Antioch, but who reported to James in Jerusalem. They were primarily "prayer leaders" of the community synagogues. There were twelve original disciples to represent the twelve tribes, although each man did not derive from those tribes since we know there were at least three sets of brothers. More likely, they were each to sit as judges, each appointed to serve as an arbitrator for a specific tribe. It is entirely probable that each of the twelve disciples was related to Jesus. We know that several were his cousins (for example, *at least* the sons of Jesus' uncle Cleophas: Matthew Levi, Simon, James the Less, and Judas, as well as their brother John Mark). Their form of government, therefore, required that a man replace Judas Iscariot as the twelfth disciple. The man chosen for that position (the thirteenth in number) was Matthias who we believe died in about 53 CE, about the time Paul's messianic teachings began to take hold among the Gentiles.

> To be an apostle one must first have been with Jesus during the whole time from his baptism (Luke 3:21) to his ascension: It is noteworthy that Luke omits the flight of the disciples reported in Mark 14:50, and in Luke 23:49 tells us that all Jesus' acquaintances are witnesses to the crucifixion. An apostle also must have been— by divine determination—a witness of his resurrection (verse 22).

33. Moore, *Judaism*, p. 106.

Becoming Christian

> Since the number of apostles is evidently restricted to twelve, both this limitation and the stated criteria implicitly exclude Paul (but see Acts 14:4, 14). The subsequent election of Matthias restores the apostolate to its full complement of twelve before the outpouring of the Spirit.[34]

At the time of the replacement two men were put forth as candidates, Matthias (who, again, was probably a cousin) and a man named Justus (Joses). It is probable that Justus became the third leader of the Jerusalem community (after Simon, son of Cleophas). He might be the "Joseph" who is a brother to Simon and another son of Cleophas.

From the 60s until 135 CE the Nazaraeans tried to keep the essence of the original movement of Jesus alive, but Paul's opposing teachings became the death knell for the orthodox community and formed the basis for the Catholic Church.

> The emerging Catholic Church quickly abandoned the dogmas associated with adherence to the Law, but it soon developed dogmas of its own to replace them, one of which was the doctrine of the virgin birth. With the rise of this doctrine, and especially with the growth of the belief in the perpetual virginity of Mary, James and the rest of Jesus' siblings became an embarrassment that needed to be hidden in the closet. Soon the memory of their importance, and even of their existence, was tragically lost.[35]

Sadly, the splinter groups from the early Nazaraeans, the real followers of Jesus, including his family and his disciples, were labeled heretics by the Pauline church.

> Scholars today realize that early Christianity was by no means homogeneous; there were many competing factions within the early church, each holding different interpretations of Jesus. Tensions and disagreements, especially over the nature of Jesus (i.e., whether he was human or divine) built up over the years and were eventually resolved (certainly not to everyone's satisfaction) at the Council of Nicaea in 325 C.E. *Those who disagreed with the majority vote at Nicaea were forever afterward declared to be heretics.*[36]

Those who accepted Jesus as a human who had been called by God to be his Messiah, executed, and resurrected from the dead (by Yahweh's

---

34. Ludemann, *The Acts of the Apostles*, p. 42.
35. Bütz, *The Brother of Jesus*, p. 111.
36. Ibid., p. 41, italics mine.

Spirit) were among those who began to be called "heretics". The sects that had derived from the Nazaraeans became those heretics, including the Nazaraeans, who might well have been the Nazaraeans themselves. Certainly, these sects held James in high esteem.

Had Jesus truly been executed by the Romans by his having claimed to be king, his family would also have been hunted down and wiped out at the time to prevent a royal line from inheriting the throne of Israel.

> James, as the next of kin, would have had even more to fear. If Jesus was, as the gospels attest and as most historical Jesus scholars agree, crucified for the crime of treason against the Roman Empire (as Pilate's placard on the cross, reading "the King of the Jews," plainly delcared), the Romans would indeed have cast a wary eye on James, whom as Jesus' eldest brother, they would have expected to be next in line to succeed him.[37]

Yet if it were the family of Annas who desired to rid themselves of the family of Joseph and Jesus, it would make perfect sense that they would continue to pursue the family and followers of Jesus under trumped-up charges, and that is exactly what they did. Of course, Annas, who was in league with the Romans, would have been required to seek approval from them to execute a Jew. It is certain the criminal Sanhedrin (headed by Annas) still had the right to do so, especially when it concerned the Temple or religious matters. Of course, the Hanan family was both wealthy and powerful, and they were known to use trumped charges when it was to their advantage to do so (as an example, the execution of James by Annas II). It was this family who stood the most to lose during the first century, and any threat to their power structure would have been dealt with speedily. As long as the Nazaraeans did not "make waves", they would have been safe. This family would have been under constant vigil with the presence of a legitimate royal family seeking the "kingdom". The Nazaraeans, however, did not cause trouble. They were simply awaiting the return of their "king", continuing their religious duties as would any other Jewish sect.

James had served as the "regent" of the "king", administering Jesus' kingdom for him in his absence. There is evidence that the "throne" of James was passed on through the family of Joseph and Jesus. Eusebius, in his day, claims that an actual "throne" or seat did exist on which James sat.

---

37. Ibid., p. 55.

Now *the throne of James*, who was the first to receive from the savior and the apostles the episcopate of the Jerusalem church and who was called a brother of Christ, as the divine books show, *has been preserved to this day*; and by the honor that *the brethren in succession pay there to it*, they show clearly to all the reverence in which the holy men were and still are held by the men of old time and those in our day, because of the love shown them by God.[38]

Today this (unlikely) "throne" is preserved in the Armenian cathedral of St. James in Jerusalem. While this symbolic throne is a "relic" shown there, it is probable that there was a "seat", much like Moses' seat that might have been shown there upon which James sat.

A basalt seat, known as "Moses' Seat" was found in excavations at the Synagogue of Chorazin in Galilee. The Aramaic inscription of the front of the stone reads: "Remembered be for good Judah ben Ishmael who made this stoa and its staircase. As his reward may he have a share with the righteous".

This find illuminates a passage in Matthew 23.2,3, where Jesus said: "The scribes and the Pharisees sit in Moses' seat: all therefore

---

38. Eusebius, HE, 7.19.1, italics mine.

whatsoever they bid you observe, that observe and do; but do not ye after their works: for they say, and do not."

The meaning of the words in the Gospel of Matthew are that people should obey the commandments of Moses and not copy the deeds of the Pharisees.

The Law of Moses was read every sabbath in the synagogue: "Moses of old time hath in every city them that preach him, being read in the synagogues every sabbath day" (Acts 15.21). The public teaching in the synagogue was usually done from a chair called the 'Moses's Seat', as illustrated in Luke 4.20: When Jesus spoke in the synagogue of Nazareth, after having read from the prophet Isaiah, 'he closed the book, and he gave it again to the minister, and sat down.' The place where he sat down was called 'Moses' Seat'.[39]

Eusebius' claim and his listing of the first overseers of the Jerusalem community "of the circumcision" is an indication that the leadership of the religion was not through apostolic succession (as the Christian church indicates) but through the royal dynastic family of Jesus. That family became known as the *despoysni*. These "heirs" remained in the religion of Israel as it existed in the first century.

---

39. Ritmeyer Archaeology Design, http://store.ritmeyer.com/node/555.

3

Judaism in the First Century

THE FORM OF RELIGION in Israel during the first century can hardly be referred to as "Judaism". That term developed over the centuries and did not exist to a great extent at that time. Rather, the religion of the Jews was mostly referred to as the "Law of Moses", which was Torah but also included the Prophets. It included both the written and the oral Torah. The Pharisees understood that God had not only given a written Torah to Moses but that Moses was instructed to teach or instruct (the general meaning of *torah*) from the commandments and precepts given to him. "Judaism" derives from the Greek *Ioudaismos*, a term first used in the intertestamentary period by Greek–speaking Jews to distinguish their religion from Hellenism (2 Macc. 2:21; 8:1; 14:38). In the New Testament the word appears only twice (Gal. 1:13—14) in reference to Paul's prior consuming devotion to Jewish faith and life. Rabbinic Judaism developed slowly over a period of several centuries and today includes Orthodox, Conservative, and Reform divisions that are based on Rabbinic Judaism. All sectors of the religion depend on the Scriptures (Torah, Prophets, and Writings), or Tanach, and the Mishnah, Talmud, and Midrash. The modern divisions were formed from the Orthodox about two hundred years ago in Germany.

This trend toward rabbinical organization had begun with the Pharisees two centuries before 1 CE. Because the Sadducees were the ruling class the two sects vied for domination over the people. During the first century, there were numerous Pharisees of differing viewpoints. The Pharisees with whom Jesus debated were a small group whose purity regulations kept them from intermingling with other Pharisees. They were not influential in the Sanhedrin and were not involved in the Chamber of the Pharisees and Scribes. Other Pharisees were more relaxed in their devotions, such as those with whom Jesus had table fellowship. The Galilean Pharisees generally did not object to Jesus as is clear in that they sought to warn him that Herod Antipas sought to "kill him".

The Sadducees, on the other hand, were not a very lenient group, tending to strictly enforce the Torah's precepts in a court of law. They consisted primarily of aristocratic and wealthy men who were interested in upward political advancement. They were also involved in Temple administration as "bankers" hiring moneychangers to exchange foreign coins for shekels for money to maintain the temple. They were also the merchants of sacrificial items that must be purchased for the temple sacrifices and involved in the incense trade as well, which made them extremely wealthy.

The Sadducees, unlike the Pharisees, did not believe in the resurrection of the dead, claiming nowhere in the Torah could there be found a reference to it. This was only one of the many conflicts between them. Beginning with Alexander Jannaeus, the Hasmonian king of the earlier century, the Sadducees gained power over the Pharisees. That king was known to have *hanged hundreds of Pharisees alive* in his war against them. When his wife, Shalom-Zion, became queen, he advised her to side with the Pharisees, a political maneuver she was wise to heed, thus they had begun to rise in status in the political structure during her reign.

By the first century the Pharisees were the "teachers" of the people of Israel. They believed it was their responsibility to advise the people in the Torah concerning everyday life. It was during this period that the laws of the Mishnah (200 CE) began to take shape. The "law" was not yet settled and debates between sages were conducted on a daily basis. We find these Pharisees debating with Jesus on numerous occasions. They might not have liked the *torah* of Jesus (his oral *torah* or instruction), but they were powerless to prevent it. The Sabbath regulations were not yet firmly set, but the Pharisees believed theirs were the most relevant and rebuked Jesus for his relaxation of their rules.

The various sects of Judaism, as it developed, vied for dominance. Debate was a common occurrence since all these sects believed their rule was the one that should be followed. By the destruction of the Jewish Temple the Talmud states that there were twenty-four varieties of "heretics" (sectarians).[1] The "heretics" are all referred to as the *minim* (heretics); however, this description is a general one and included all other sects of Pharisees and Jewish gnostics. While it does include the Nazaraean and Ebionite sects, it also includes the numerous other sects (Essene, Zealot, *et cetera*) that rose during the early first century in Jerusalem. Later, after the Bar Kochba Revolt, it also included "Pauline Christians" and the Roman church, what had been then become known as "Christianity". The winners write history, and it was the development of the laws of the rabbinic Pharisees that won the day. Josephus only names three of the five sects he claims existed during the early part of the war, the Sadducees, the Essenes, and the Pharisees. Although he also describes the Zealots (who were also Pharisees), we can conclude that he considered them a fourth. Since there were so many different religious ideas of what form Judaism should take in a period of internal and external strife, it is hardly fair to debase the Pharisees of the gospels, since they believed theirs to be the correct path. "The impurity from which these sectarians wished to separate themselves was that of other Jews, whom these sectarians treated as outsiders, and contact with whom they believed imperiled the soul."[2]

There were numerous other Pharisees who had completely different agendas. Jesus' teachings, for example, were just as "correct" as any others. There were also the sects of John the Baptist and Bannus under whom Josephus studied for three years.[3] Some sects were stricter than others. Bannus lived off the land and dressed only in clothing made from trees. He rejected outsiders who might make him impure. The Essenes, too, separated themselves from the priests and Pharisees of Jerusalem, living aesthetic lives in devotion to God. Various small groups gathered together to protest some aspect of their religious life. For some it was the mode of dress, for some it was for food and purity rules, for some it was Scriptural disagreements, and for the Jesus movement it was messianic apocalypticism. So there was a wide range of subjects on which these sects might disagree.

Jewish gnosticism, for instance, had existed for some five hundred years prior to the first century CE, but it reached its height during the intertestamentary period (200 BCE–200 CE). Much gnostic thought was derived from Babylonian and Syrian religions. Johanan ben Zakkai, born at the turn of the first century and surviving the destruction of Jerusalem,

1. *y. Sanh.* 10.6 29c.
2. Baumgarten, "Ancient Jewish Sectarianism".
3. Josephus, *Life* 10–12.

Judaism in the First Century

was thought to be a Jewish gnostic.[4] Gnosticism was considered legitimate within Judaism; there were both good and bad gnostics. Christian gnosticism developed from Jewish gnosticism as it existed within the Jewish religion. The most common gnostic pairing in the Christian gnostic writings was between Jesus and the Sophia (wisdom). Wisdom in Hebrew is the word *hokmah*. By the time the Gospel of John was redacted with its gnostic tendencies Jesus was associated with the *logos* ("word"), but that word within the Hellenic world had already been defined as being associated with wisdom. Philo, an Alexandrian Jew, compared the *logos* with the wisdom of Yahweh in a Greek philosophical sense. Since Philo knew only the Septuagint, the Greek version of the Old Covenant, he used the word *logos* in its Greek context of combining "thought" and "word", rather than the Hebrew word *dabar*, meaning strictly the "word" as uttered.

> The Greek, metaphysical concept of the Logos is in sharp contrast to the concept of a personal God described in anthropomorphic terms typical of Hebrew thought. Thus when Hebrew mythical thought met the Greek philosophical thought it was only natural that some would try to develop speculative and philosophical justification for Judaism in terms of Greek philosophy. Philo of Alexandria (20 BCE–50 CE), a Hellenized Jew, produced a synthesis of both traditions developing concepts for the future Hellenistic interpretation of messianic Hebrew thought. In the process, he laid the foundations for the development of Christianity as we know it today.[5]

It was Philo, an Egyptian Jew, who introduced the Stoic concept of *logos* into Judaism. The author of the late Gospel of John found it useful in his redaction of the gospel for his community. Paul, a Hellenized Jew himself, followed Philo's philosophy in his own teachings. Josephus presented the three known sects of Judaism as the Jewish equivalent of Greek philosophies. For instance, he identified the Pharisees with the Stoics[6] and the Essenes with the Pythagoreans.[7]

Gnosticism was a curious synthesis of Jewish apocalypticism, Platonism, ideas from pagan religions, and finally affected second century Christianity, through sects like the Ophites. Montanism, though classified

---

4. *b. Suk.* 28a.
5. Hillar, "The Logos", pp. 36–53.
6. Josephus, *Life* 12.
7. Josephus, *Ant.* 15.371.

Becoming Christian

by the church fathers as gnosticism, would be accepted within some denominations of Christianity today. In the region of Turkey Montanus, along with two women, Maximilla and Priscilla, claimed to have been visited by the Holy Spirit, believing he had the ability to deliver messages from God. The church fathers believed he was fanatical. Even Tertullian, considered one of the "fathers", joined the sect!

We find all these different sects, including Jewish gnostic sects, referred to as the *minim*, criticized as "heretics" by the Rabbis. It is a mistake to assume that those the Rabbis referred to as the *minim* were entirely "Christian". It is a fact that after the destruction of Jerusalem the Pharisaical Rabbis often visited and debated with the Ebionites. In order to understand the period shortly after the destruction of Jerusalem and the temple, it becomes necessary to also understand the Pharisees who inherited a place in world religion known as Judaism.

THE PHARISEES AND THE BEGINNINGS OF MODERN JUDAISM: CONFLICT WITH CHRISTIANITY

Many of both the upper and lower classes of the Pharisees fled before or during the Jewish war. Most of the Sadducees did not and, therefore, no longer exist. It is through the Pharisees that the religion called Judaism developed. The Jewish religion during the first century was not referred to as "Judaism". That term developed over the centuries through the efforts of the Pharisees in keeping the Torah and the Jewish religion alive. At first, the word "Judaism" only applied to the people of Judah, but over time it became a religion for all Jews. The term "Pharisee" or "Perisha" is from the Aramaic root *prš*, meaning both "separate" and "to interpret". The fact that they became the "interpreters" of Torah also implied that they separated themselves from the general population. Although they were sectarian, they were a collection of teachers who interpreted Torah and instructed the people in "The Land". They were most likely the teachers in the synagogues. Josephus give us a definition of the Pharisees:

> They give credit for wisdom to those alone who have an *exact knowledge of the laws* and who *are capable of interpreting the meaning of the Holy Scriptures*. Consequently, though many have laboriously undertaken this training, scarcely two or three have succeeded, and have forthwith reaped the fruit of their labors.[8]

8. Josephus *Ant.* 20.12.1 (264), italics mine.

Yohanan ben Zakkai, a disciple of Hillel and native of Galilee, was one of the first Pharisees to escape Jerusalem during its fall (68 CE). He faked his death and had his disciples carry his coffin to Vespasian's tent where he emerged and prophesied that Vespasian would become the emperor of Rome. In exchange, he requested a place in Yavne in order to *set up a school to teach Torah*. Vespasian agreed if he became emperor Zakkai would have his school. Within a year Vespasian was Emperor of Rome and did not forget his promise to Zakkai. Yavneh then became the headquarters of the Sanhedrin. This would be the birth of Judaism as a recognized religion.

After the war, numerous Pharisees gathered in Yavne. Johanan's last words were messianic. He died in 90 CE. His final request was to prepare a throne for Hezekiah, the king of Judah, who is coming.[9] Hezekiah was a euphemism for the messiah. The messianic fervor and apocalyptic atmosphere of the previous two centuries had been quelled but was not completely dead. The Jews who survived believed God would deliver them to rebuild the temple and Jerusalem, though it had been destroyed in the war, just as he had brought them back from the captivity of Babylon. Before his death, however, Zakkai had begun to lose faith that the messiah would soon come. He told his students if someone were to say "'Come quickly, the messiah is here!', first finish planting the tree and then go to greet the messiah."[10]

These were the beginnings of change. Zakkai was responsible for replacing the rituals performed in the temple with new edicts. Synagogues became the places of worship and took on many of the functions of the temple. They had existed for at least two centuries and probably longer. There were numerous synagogues during the time of Jesus all over the land and in Jerusalem, including the "Great Synagogue" within the temple, itself. These synagogues were for meeting on the Sabbath, for worship and study of Torah for the people. The temple, while it stood, remained the primary focus and pride of the Jewish people; however, once it was destroyed, the synagogue became the place of worship.

Within two centuries the Mishnah, an organized system of both religious and political laws, became the norm. The collection of laws that passed down from Torah and Tradition (*halakah*) were compiled by Rabbi Judah, *nasi*. It became a system of human conduct, the law of righteousness by which man might live outside Jerusalem. By the fifth century the Babylonian Talmud, consisting of Gemara (discussion or *haggadah* on the

9. *b. Ber.* 28b.
10. Rabbi Nathan, *Abot* 31b.

Mishnah) was compiled. There had been an earlier Jerusalem Talmud a couple of centuries before, and the Tosefta had come before that.

With the destruction of the temple, numerous precepts in the written Torah had become obsolete, but what is termed the Oral Torah, or the Traditions, had always existed and had been handed down from teacher to student throughout the centuries. They based their tradition on Scripture: "And thou shalt come unto the priests the Levites, and unto the judge that shall be in those days, and enquire; and they shall shew thee the sentence of judgment: And thou shalt do according to the sentence, which they of that place which the LORD shall choose shall shew thee; and thou shalt observe to do according to all that *they instruct thee*: According to the sentence of the law *which they shall teach thee*, and according to the judgment which *they shall tell thee*, thou shalt do: thou shalt not decline from the sentence which they shall shew thee, to the right hand, nor to the left" (Deut 17:9-11; italics mine).

God had given Moses his Word (Torah), of which he, in turn, instructed the people and introduced the priesthood. That word of instruction was handed down to the next generation, instructing them of the precepts of God. As times and circumstances changed, the instruction also changed, but that instruction was always based on the Torah. The instruction was given by way of explanation, which was the scribe's "instruction" based on a particular set of circumstances. It became the body of the law for both religious and political courts. By the first century the Tradition had existed for centuries. Each scribe or sage had his *own* torah to explain and add to the written Torah. Jesus also used Traditions in his teaching. For example, the author of Matthew has him say: "Ye have heard that it was said by them of old time, Thou shalt not commit adultery: But I say unto you, That whosoever looketh on a woman to lust after her hath committed adultery with her already in his heart" (Matt 5:27-28). We must assume that Jesus quoted the Scripture. This was Jesus' *oral torah* (instruction), based on the Old Covenant laws already in place. What he did was to *clarify* the edict of adultery, stating that one should prevent lust in his heart in the first place. He did the same thing with "do not kill"; he carried it even farther by implying that one should not even have the kind of anger in his heart that would cause him to kill in the first place.

So this individual *torah* instruction was based on the Old Covenant laws with an explanation. Jacob Neusner explains the three torahs that Jesus elaborates in the Sermon on the Mount:

> These formulations represent an elaboration of three of the Ten Commandments ... In the language of a text of Judaism attributed to authorities long before Jesus' own time, 'Make a fence around the Torah.' That is to say, conduct yourself in such a way that you will avoid even the things that cause you to sin, not only sin itself."[11]

He compares the form Jesus uses with the teaching of Rabbi Yohanan ben Zakkai:

> "Not only so, but the teaching of the Torah by a paraphrase of the Torah would form a staple of rabbis' teaching later on. For we have access to a great master, Yohanan ben Zakkai ... In sayings associated with him and his disciples, we have exactly the same program: restate in concrete terms, and in a more profound setting, the requirements of the Torah of Sinai.[12]

He also explains the difference between Torah and torah:

> It bears two meanings, one with a capital *T*, the other with a small *t*. Torah with a capital T stands for God's revelation to Moses at Mount Sinai. When we write 'torah' with a small t, we mean, 'the instruction of a master—in the context of the teaching of the Torah.' It is a somewhat odd shift; what Jesus does is teach the Torah, and what he teaches also is torah. For his engagement with the Torah of Moses—and Matthew makes clear Jesus is profoundly engaged in Torah-learning—means that things that he will say also form a continuation, expansion, elaboration, and clarification, for instance of the Torah. He is a teacher of the Torah, so in the framework of the Torah, he teaches the Torah and he himself adds to the Torah: so his is a labor of torah, too.[13]

This is how the Pharisees, who were teachers, taught Torah as well. Although the Pharisees numbered only at 6,000 in all the land (per Josephus), these were split into factions. The fact that there were two well known factions, that of Hillel and that of Shammai who are mentioned in the Talmud, give us an indication that there were many others that had developed certain interests in particular social situations. Jesus bridged the two groups. The group with which Jesus contends was one of those factions that was rigid in its purity laws, therefore, placing a burden on an already burdened population.

11. Neusner, *A Rabbi*, p. 40.
12. Ibid., p. 41.
13. Ibid., p. 21.

Becoming Christian

Generally, however, the Pharisees were instructors (scribes) who visited synagogues throughout the land. A select few were associated with the temple. While they might condemn Jesus and his disciples for their lack of performing the ritual regulations, there was really nothing they might do about it. These particular Pharisees also condemned other Pharisees who did not follow their guidance. It will be remembered that there were both Pharisees and a "great company of" priests who joined the earliest messianic community led by James, the brother of Jesus (Acts 15:4–5; 15:6–7). Some Pharisees warned Jesus of Herod Antipas' desire to kill him, and Jesus was known to have had congenial relationships with other Pharisees, even so far as dining with them in what is termed "table fellowship". The authors of the gospels were writing *outside Judea* long after the destruction of the temple at a time when there was conflict between the Christian (mostly Gentile) communities, whose doctrines had changed immensely from the Jewish religion of the first century, and the Pharisees, who had remained within it. Jesus was no longer the resurrected Jewish messiah that James, Peter, John, and the Jerusalem community had known; he had become divine, the "risen Christ" preached in Paul's cosmic theology.

While the Jews who followed the teachings of Jesus remained within what is now referred to as "Judaism", worshiping in the temple, making sacrifices, keeping the feasts, keeping the Torah and awaiting the return of Jesus at the "last day", the Hellenistic Gentiles had basically abandoned Torah and promoted Jesus to the ethereal "risen Christ" of Paul's teachings.

The Pharisaic response to the gospels (not written until at least 70–120 CE) was open hostility. In those gospels Jesus did not "fit" their conception of messiah. The basic premise of the Jewish religion is that of monotheism, God is one. Jesus himself believed this, as evidenced in his quotation of the creed, the Shema. We can rest assured that Jesus prayed during the three daily services: morning (*Shacharit*), afternoon (*Minchah*), and evening (*Ma'ariv* or *Arvit*); not only does the Shema consist of Deut 6:4–9, but also Deut 11:13–21 and Num 14:37–41 and its Blessings. The creed that Jesus pronounced follows.

> Hear, O Israel: The LORD our God is one LORD: And thou shalt love the LORD thy God with all thine heart, and with all thy soul, and with all thy might. And these words, which I command thee this day, shall be in thine heart: And thou shalt teach them diligently to thy children, and shalt talk of them when thou sittest in thine house, and when thou walkest by the way, and when thou liest down, and when thou risest up (Deut 6:4–9).

Judaism in the First Century

After 70 CE the hostility that arose between the Gentile Christian and the Pharisee became the basis for future anti-Semitism. The reason is given by Herford in his excellent book *The Pharisees*:

> The point is that his obedience to the Halachah [the body of laws] was the only side which the Gentile could in general observe of the religious life of the Jew; it was that side where his religion found its most characteristic expression in action. Not indeed, its only expression in action, because the Jew, as a humane and philanthropic man, did not wait for the directions of the Halachah to prescribe all his acts of kindness or to define the limits of his sympathy. It was certainly a mitzvah to help the poor and relieve the oppressed. But the kind heart and the generous hand could find their own way of fulfilling that mitzvah. But, apart from these, the fact remains that on the whole that side of the life of the Jew which chiefly came under the notice of Gentile neighbours and marked him off as different from them was the side which was concerned with Halachah. And, as the Halachah was the Torah on its perceptive side, made definite and explicit, I believe that here is to be found the reason why Torah was always rendered in Greek by νόμος (nomos), and why in all languages it is rendered by the equivalent of Law. Few Gentiles were or are in a position to know that Halachah was *only one element in Torah, not the whole of it* . . .[14]

The "law" or Halachah was one thing, but Haggadah was something entirely different. The Haggadah is found in the discussion of various laws and precepts of the Mishnah. The Mishnah originally contained the laws that were set out as *an agenda of holiness* for the people in response to a powerless people dominated by Romans. They pertained to "parts of domestic life which can be controlled by people out of power in their own society: food, sex and marriage. Food and reproduction within the household rather than the public cult at the Temple and the governance of society are within the grasp of a subject people."[15] The Haggadah is the portion of the Talmud known as Gemara, collected and developed much later and over the centuries. It allows for a greater amount of leverage in the deeper meanings of God and Torah. Yet it is *not* the law. Gentiles reading the Talmud misunderstand that these discussions are made by individuals who have differing opinions and understandings of what the law might be. They are sometimes used in determining what the law should *become* based

---

14. Herford, *The Pharisees*, p. 77, italics mine.
15. Saldarini, *Pharisees, Scribes and Sadducees*, p. 213.

on circumstances that might not have been prevalent in previous ages. The Haggadah took the forms of "stories founded on the lives of persons mentioned in Scripture, parables to illustrate types of character in which some virtue or vice was conspicuous, plays of fancy based on some slight hint hidden in a Scripture or phrase, arbitrary changes in the wording of a text for the sake of pointing a moral or deducing a religious lesson, even sometimes mere freaks of wit and grotesque fancy, intended, we may suppose, to arrest the attention of a drowsy audience. Almost everything that imagination could do is represented in the Haggadah."[16]

Jesus, too, used parables to illustrate points of Torah, as well as to describe the society in which he lived. The parable, or "riddle" as the actual term, was used to portray certain moral or immoral points in to teach a lesson, i.e., to give one's torah or explanation and instruction to a group of students. Those who condemn the Pharisees today find themselves doing the same thing, expounding doctrines by their imaginations.

The term *minim* (heretic) was not used by the Pharisees of the Jewish Ebionites but only of the *new* Nazaraeans and the Gentile Christians, and this at a much later date, a date long after the gospels were written. As stated previously not all Pharisees were in opposition to Jesus as the messiah (Acts 15:5), nor were all the priests (Acts 6:7). In fact, it was probably these "poor priests" who were the stimuli for James at his trial. They had been poorly abused by the ruling priests during those couple of decades before and after James' execution.

The Gospel of Mark (ca 70 CE is the norm), probably written in Alexandria, was the first of the gospels to mention antagonism toward the Pharisees. Since Mark was written *after* the destruction of Jerusalem from "outside" the Judean territory and his community was still awaiting the return of Jesus, his biography reflected the times in which he lived and *not those in which Jesus lived*. As time went by the author of Matthew (80–90 CE) displayed even more condemnation of them. By the time the gospel of Luke was written (ca 90 CE), Christians were warned to have nothing to do with the Pharisees at all. Finally, the author of the redaction of John (dated between 90–150 CE) couples them with the Saducean priests who were responsible for bringing Jesus to trial. So as time elapsed after the destruction of Jerusalem and more and more Gentiles were brought into Christianity, the Pharisees became the object of Christian anti–Semitism and hatred, a condition that has persisted even to the present day. True,

---

16. Herford, p. 81.

Judaism in the First Century

there is a current trend in scholastic circles to investigate the history and a desire to get back to Judaic roots through study of the historic Pharisees in order to learn more about the "historical Jesus", but in classic Christian circles the term "Pharisees" is sometimes still held in contempt. Much of that contempt is based on the writings of Paul, who despite claiming to be a Pharisee of the lower class (an artisan, a tentmaker), "was consciously creating a new community with a new understanding of purity, just as the Pharisees had for Judaism."[17]

It appears that Paul repeals his own Pharisee affiliation in Philippians 3:5–7, where he counts these things as "loss for Christ". It is fairly clear, however, that Paul was *not* a lower class citizen. It is likely he had been involved with Jewish leadership since he is known to have been influential in the execution of Stephen and the persecution of the original Nazaraeans. In the book of Acts he claims he "gave [his] voice [voted] against them" (Acts 26:10). The word used here is Ψῆφος (*psephos*), which means a pebble; i.e., a verdict, a vote (a white pebble was used as a vote to determine the verdict of the court). This appears to mean that Paul was, at the time, a member of the Chamber of Scribes in the Sanhedrin, and not just the religious Great Sanhedrin but the 23-member *beth din*, the criminal court. That is, he had been selected to sit on the judiciary. He certainly had access to the high priest at that time, either Joseph called Caiaphas or Jonathan ben Hanan, who would not only have been the president (*nasi*) of the Great Sanhedrin but also the head of the 23-member criminal sanhedrin (Acts 9:1–2; 22:4–5; 26:12). Annas, the most powerful member of the court, served as the *ab bet din*, or "father of the court", the Vice President. Certainly, Paul had abandoned his Judaism in favor of the easier path of his spiritual message, one that did not require the human aspect of Jesus. No longer does he feel he has to follow the purity rules of table fellowship.

The Pharisees of the gospels are what is termed those keeping "table fellowship" together and not political nor religious in any particular sense. They disagree with Jesus as to what the *rules for the community should be*, but they have no legal power or influence. While they might observe these rules in table fellowship with other Pharisees of their own faction, they would be disinclined to have table fellowship with Jesus. One Pharisee belonging to this faction invited Jesus for table fellowship at his home but was shocked when Jesus did not "wash" before eating (Luke 11:37–38). Table fellowship is distinguished from the simple fact of having a "meal". Ordinarily, when

---

17. Saldarini, p. 138.

having a meal or dinner on a daily basis a family would merely sit at a table to eat. Table fellowship was something more than that. It involved a group of people lying on couches, similar to holding a banquet or a "party" where guests were invited. Jesus did have table fellowship with Simon ben Cantheras, son of Boethus (the "Leper"), a Pharisee, and his family on another occasion (Mark 14:3; Matt 26:6; Luke 7:36–50; John 12:2–9). This common understanding of "table fellowship" is related by Albert Nolan:

> The fact that guests were invited and the fact that they reclined at a table show that the meals referred to in the gospels were feasts or dinner parties. At ordinary family meals to which guests had not been invited people sat upright at table in much the same way as we do. One reclined only at a feast or dinner party. Feasts or dinner parties need not be thought of as very elaborate or expensive meals (Lk 10:38–42). The company and conversation mattered more than the food.[18]

Jesus was also known to recline at these feasts with "sinners" and "tax-collectors", which to this particular rigid faction of Pharisees was akin to breaking the law.

It is interesting to note that Simon, a Pharisee, did not offer to wash the feet of Jesus (as was the custom of the head of the house in the case of a visiting guest): "And he turned to the woman, and said unto Simon, Seest thou this woman? I entered into thine house, thou gavest me no water for my feet: but she hath washed my feet with tears, and wiped them with the hairs of her head. Thou gavest me no kiss; but this woman since the time I came in hath not ceased to kiss my feet. My head with oil thou didst not anoint: but this woman hath anointed my feet with ointment" (Luke 7:44–47). It appears that Simon was not a "fastidious" Pharisee belonging to the rigid faction of Pharisees that Jesus condemned but a member of the group associated with the temple. Furthermore, priests were not all Saducean. Josephus relates to us that there were several priests who belonged to the "school" of the Pharisees (including Joazar and Simon Cantheras, both sons of Simon Boethus).

Most Pharisees did not accept Jesus' messianic claim, but some did. The ones who did split from that group fleeing to Yavne (Jabne, Jamnia). They, instead, followed the original Nazaraeans (now referred to as Ebionites) to Pella and other locations outside Judea. After leaving Jerusalem,

---

18. Nolan, *Jesus Before Christianity*, p. 46; Jeremias, *New Testament Theology*, p. 115 and *The Eucharistic Words of Jesus*, pp. 20f.

Judaism in the First Century

the original Nazaraeans had also split into diverse groups, each headed by a leader having different ideas about what it was to follow the teachings of Jesus. Those who invited Gentiles into "full fellowship" were the "Nazaraeans", and eventually were overtaken by them. Although the faction now known as "Ebionites" were the original followers of Jesus and James, Epiphanius refers to them as heretical:

> For they use not only the New Testament but also the Old . . . For they also accept the resurrection of the dead and that everything has origin in God . . . Only in this respect they differ from the Jews and Christians: with the Jews they do not agree because of their belief in Christ, with the Christians because they are trained in the Law, in circumcision, the Sabbath and the other things . . .

He confuses the two groups in his writings.

> This heresy of the Nazarenes exists in Beroea in the neighborhood of Coele Syria and the Decapolis in the region of Pella and in Basanitis in the so–called Kokabe, Chochabe in Hebrew. For from there it took its beginning after the exodus from Jerusalem and to go away since it would undergo a siege. Because of this advice they lived in Perea after having moved to that place as I said. There the Nazarene heresy had its beginning.[19]

The refutation of the "heretic" sect of the "Nazaraeans", however, began quite a bit earlier:

> We must consider this period of time within a larger context: the development of Christianity in the first century and its origins in the proclamation of Jesus of Nazareth. Jesus had announced that the Kingdom was at hand. After his resurrection, the apostles took that message, now altered slightly to accommodate the eschatological miracle they had just witnessed, to the synagogues of Judea and, shortly thereafter, the Diaspora. Those receiving their message—Jews, together with some Gentile God–fearers—formed or joined an ekklesia within the synagogue. *But within 50 years*, the movement was predominantly Gentile, and *within 150, the church regarded Jewish Christians as heretics.*[20]

By the fourth century the Christian "church" no longer wanted to be associated with the Ebionites, including James, the brother of Jesus and the *despoysni*. The teachings of Jesus had become unimportant, for now

19. Epiphanius. *Panarion* 29.
20. Fredericksen, *From Jesus to Christ*, p. 167, italics mine.

they had an ethereal Christ on whom they might depend. No longer was the testimony of Jesus, his teachings, the focal point of the religion. Now, the focus was *about* Jesus, or more specifically about the "Christ". As mentioned earlier, James, Peter, John, and the "elders", the community in Jerusalem, though believing in the resurrection of Jesus as messiah, continued to worship in the temple, continued to perform circumcision, and continued to study Torah while awaiting the "Last Day" and the return of Jesus. The "New Testament" had not yet been compiled by the church fathers, and *the only Scripture that existed was, in fact, the Old Covenant*. Further, they had never lost sight of the fact that there was only one God, Yahweh (this also formed Jesus' belief), and continued in the Jewish religion, even though they believed in Jesus as the messiah.

It follows that in 1 John these *new* Nazaraeans had gone out from the very core teachings of Jesus and James:

> Little children, it is the last time: and as ye have heard that antichrist shall come, even now are there many antichrists; whereby we know that it is the last time. *They went out from us, but they were not of us*; for if they had been of us, they would not doubt have continued with us: *but they went out*, that they might be made manifest that they were not *of* us (1 John 2:18–19, italics mine).

". . . many false prophets are gone out into the world" (1 John 4:1).

This became such a problem that it sullied the name "Nazaraean", thus the original movement took on the appellation "Ebionite" from the word *ebion* meaning "humble, poor". When the Gentiles overtook the Jesus movement they established their form of "Christianity" in opposition to the teachings of Jesus, James, and the disciples.

Among those anti–Semitics who denigrated the members of the original movement was Eusebius, who called them "poor in spirit", certainly a slur on their status:

"The Ebionites were a messianic sect. They denied the virgin birth and believed that Jesus's Sonship rested not on his birth but on the anointing of the Holy Spirit on him at his immersion." Eusebius calls them heretics and refers to them as "poor" in Spirit (the word *ebion* actually means "humble", "meek", or "poor"). He seems to have a particular dislike for them; among the reasons, his dislike for Symmachus, a translator. He states:

> Of these translators it should be observed that Symmachus was an Ebionite; but the heresy of the Ebionites as it is called, asserts

Judaism in the First Century

> that Christ was born of Joseph and Mary, and supposes him to be a mere man [i.e., not a "divine savior god–man"], and *insists upon an observance of the law too much after the manner of the Jews* [i.e., they kept the "feasts" and the "sabbaths", and studied Torah, even as Jesus did], as we have already seen in a previous part of our history. There are also commentaries of Symmachus still extant, in which he appears to direct his remarks against the gospel of Matthew [probably against the Latin vulgate and Greek translations, the "church" translations], in order to establish this heresy. But Origen remarks that he received these with interpretations of others, from one Juliana, who he also said, derived them by inheritance from Symmachus himself.[21]

When listing the disputed books, Eusebius states: "But there are also some who number among these [i.e., genuine], the gospel according to the Hebrews, with which those of the Hebrews that have received Christ [the Hebrews would call him Mashiach] are particularly delighted."[22]

Now, here is what Eusebius says against the practices of the Ebionites:

> The spirit of wickedness, however, being unable to shake some in their love of Christ, and yet finding them susceptible of his impressions in other respects, brought them over to his purposes. These are properly called Ebionites *by the ancients*, as those who cherished low and mean opinions of Christ [this is Eusebius' own opinion]. For they considered him a plain and common man [a "Son of Man", not the "divine god–man" of pagan motif], and justified only by his advances in virtue, and that he was born of the Virgin Mary, by natural generation [it was established as canon by the time of this writing that Mary would remain a perpetual virgin forever, even though it was well known that Jesus had sisters and brothers, two of whom wrote letters that were incorporated into the New Testament canon]. With them the observance of the law was altogether necessary [i.e., they kept the Torah], as if they could not be saved, only by faith in Christ and a corresponding life [note that not only Jesus, but also Paul who contradicts himself, and the other apostles, as well as Clement of Alexandria, explicitly states that the movement should obey the commandment to keep the feasts, "observed the law" or Torah]. Others, however, besides these [i.e., the *new* "Nazaraeans"], but of the same name, indeed avoided the absurdity of the opinions maintained by the former,

---

21. Eusebius, HE, 6.17, italics mine.
22. Eusebius, HE, 3.25.

not denying that the Lord was born of the Virgin by the Holy Ghost, and yet in like manner, not acknowledging his pre-existence, though he was God, the word and wisdom [Eusebius is fully entrenched in the pagan motif of the "god-man"], they turned aside into the same irreligion, as with the former they evinced great zeal to observe the ritual service of the law [and the "church" instituted its own "ritual services" to replace them]. These [the second group that he is speaking of], indeed, thought on the one hand that all the epistles of the apostles ought to be rejected, calling him an apostate from the law [Jesus, indeed, was legally an apostate from the Pharisaic law, and they were just stating a well known fact],[23] but on the other, only using the gospel according to the Hebrews [the Original Hebrew gospel], they esteem the others as of but little value [Matthew was the most Hebraic of all the New Testament books, but even it had been tampered with by the time of Eusebius]. They also observe the Sabbath [i.e., the seventh day being our present Friday-Saturday; the "church" under Constantine changed the day of worship to "Sun-Day" in honor of the "sun-god"] and other discipline of the Jews [as Clement stated in his Epistle to the Corinthians, "the feasts"], just like them, but on the other hand, they also celebrate the Lord's days very much like us, in commemoration of his resurrection [the early followers of Jesus celebrated the Resurrection Day by sharing a "meal" of fish, bread, and wine, the true commemoration of the "Last Supper" so-called, because it was symbolic of the messianic banquet, feasting on Leviathan's flesh]. Whence, in consequence of such a course, they have also received their epithet, the name of Ebionites, exhibiting the poverty of their intellect [now, this is just a boldly slanderous statement of prejudice and anti-Semitism by Eusebius, as is evidenced by his next statement]. For it is thus that the Hebrews call a poor man."[24]

The so-called "Lord's Day" was commemorated on the first day of the week (Sunday) in remembrance of the resurrection of Jesus. The eating of a meal of fish was symbolic of the messianic banquet. The messianic banquet is one in which the people will feast on the flesh of Leviathan. There are several different legends about the slaying of Leviathan. Leviathan is the "Beast of the Sea". In the book of Revelation it is that "dragon", that old "serpent" who is called the "devil" and "Satan" who sits atop the seven-hilled

23. Read *A Book of Evidence* "The Crime" and "The Jewish Trial" for an in-depth evaluation of this statement.
24. Eusebius, HE, 3.27, italics mine.

Mystery Babylon (Jerusalem, which is "situated on seven hills"—Pirke de-Rabbi Eliezer, 10) that shall be overcome and slain by the messiah, Jesus (Rev 19:20) at Har Megiddo (Mountain of Meeting; i.e., at Beth Pagi, the Place of Meeting; Zech. 14:2–5) where the merchants sell their wares (Rev. 18:11–13) near the Valley of Jehoshaphat (Joel 3:2, 12). Peter's soliloquy in the book of Acts (2:16–21) refers to this very day in relation to the return of Jesus as messiah. It is known as the Seudat HaMashiach or "Meal of Messiah". It later became a custom traced to the Baal Shem Tov, the founder of Hasidic Judaism, 1698–1760 and the author of *Eben Shettiyah*, *who also translates the Gospel of Matthew* in that treatise. On the seventh day of Passover, a meal celebrating the world to come and aspects of Messiah's coming and his healing the world. The *eighth* day of Passover is Firstfruits and was on the first day of the week (Sunday), the very day of Jesus' resurrection. Christianity has turned that meal into the so-called Eucharist, but this meal had nothing to do with the table fellowship of the "Last Supper", other than to be a meal in remembrance of the messiah.

It is referred to as *Seudat HaMashiach*, the meal of Messiah. A custom now not only for Hasidic Jews, but many Messianic Jews and Judeo-Christians as well. What is even more interesting is the fact that the Last Supper and the Messianic Banquet consisted of bread and wine as well. As a *melek-zedek* through the lineage of David's son Nathan Jesus offered the same offering that both Melquisedek offered to Abraham (Gen 14:18) and David gave to each person in Israel a cake of bread, and a flagon of wine (2 Sam. 26:39). When Jesus offered bread and wine to his disciples at the "Last Supper", he was alluding to his position as a *melek-zedek*, a perpetual position that could never be taken away from him. The metaphors of eating the bread as his body and drinking the wine as his blood was to inform them that if they followed him that God would make them a *kingdom of priests*, too. The fact is that Zerubbabel was told that a branch of righteousness would descend from him (Zech 3:8; 6:12). This means that a branch as extending outward (i.e., as descending from him) would be that "branch". Furthermore, that "branch" would be a priest who sits on a throne: "And he shall grow up out of his place [i.e., branch out], and he shall build the temple of the LORD: Even he shall build the temple of the LORD; and he shall bear the glory, and *shall sit and rule upon his throne, and he shall be a priest upon his throne*: and the counsel of peace shall be between them both [i.e., *both thrones, priestly and royal*] (Zech 6:12–13, italics mine).

Of the Ebionites Epiphanius says:

> And these too (like the Nazaraeans) receive the Gospel according to Matthew; for this they too, as also the Cerinthians and Merinthians, use to the exclusion of the rest. *And they call it 'according to the Hebrews,'* to tell the truth because Matthew alone in the New Testament set forth both the exposition and preaching of the Gospel *in Hebrew speech and Hebrew characters.*[25]

Thus, there was a two-fold sect of the movement; one was called Ebionites proper, while the other was called the "Nazaraeans." The Ebionites believed the Gentiles were entitled to their messiah, but realized the concept of "messiah" was alien to the non-Jewish. Therefore, James insisted on only two things: that they keep the Noachide commandments and to keep Torah. It is obvious from references in the book of Acts that James and the Jews of Jerusalem did not want Paul to include the "uncircumcised" in the messianic assembly, this Jerusalem group not accepting the doctrines of the Gentiles. We are reminded that the Jerusalem sect did keep the "law" and were, in fact, circumcised. It is clear from the altered text that the "Ebionites" or the "poor" (for whom Paul collects money from his own jurisdiction to send to Jerusalem) were quite strict in their dietary habits as well.

Hugh Schonfield writes:

> Just before the outbreak of the war with the Romans, in AD 67, a number of members of the *Jewish Christian Community*—informed it is said by a revelation—under the leadership of Simeon, a first cousin of Jesus, went to Syria where there were numerous Essenes. The exiles were ruled for half a century by relations of Jesus, known as "the Heirs"; but they failed to regain authority over the Christians at large, *who now [67–70], being predominantly Gentiles, were inclined to antisemitism*, especially after the disastrous ending of the Jewish Revolt, and still more the second revolt in the reign of Hadrian (in AD 132–135), when Simon Bar-Cochba had claimed the Messiahship.[26]

Between the years 70 and 500 CE Christian leaders became vehemently anti-Semitic, blaming the "Jews" (especially the Pharisees, which were the most visible group) as being "Christ-killers". During those early years there was little difference between the Jews of the Nazaraeans who followed Jesus' teachings and those of the Pharisees. The difference was

---

25. Epiphanius, *Panarion* 30.13, italics mine.
26. Schonfield, *The Original*, p. xix, italics mine.

Judaism in the First Century

that the Nazaraeans held an apocalpytic messianic belief in Jesus, while the Pharisees did not. With the Gentile Christians, however, it was another story entirely. Christian teaching of Gentiles under Paul's guidance had alienated the Jews for once and all from Jesus. He was now, not only messiah; he was God Incarnate, and this was unacceptable in every way since both the Pharisees and the Nazaraeans knew Yahweh was the only God. The daily prayer echoing the first commandment, the Shema (taken from the first word, "Hear"), given by Jesus "Hear, O Israel; The LORD [Yahweh] our God [Elohim] is one LORD [Yahweh]: And thou shalt love the LORD [Yahweh] thy God with all thy heart, and with all thy soul, and with all thy mind, and with all thy strength" places Jesus solidly within the sphere of the Jewish religion. The concept of monotheism is the primary belief of the Jewish people. Gentiles had long been adapted to the pagan mystery religions involving trinitarian figures, thus it was introduced quite early into the Christian religion. This, the Pharisees, could not accept. Those Jews called the new Nazaraeans were soon ostracized as well (by both Gentile Christians and Pharisees), the reason being that they had been associated with the Gentile Christians. Now, they were no longer viewed as original Nazaraean Jews but referred to by the name the pagan Antiochians had given them, which consolidated them into a single group: Christians. For decades the original Nazaraeans had tried to remain separate, but the war and destruction of the temple had split them into different factions and they then had only a shadow of a central "government", now under the leadership of the "heirs" of Jesus, the *despoysni*. With no real central community the various factions soon developed their own interpretations and beliefs about Jesus' teachings, adding to or taking away from the core teachings once held in Jerusalem under James' leadership in order to reflect conditions in their own communities. These became the groups from which the gospels derived. Each gospel represented a different community, and each community had a distinct set of concerns and problems. The later church would refer to some of them as "heretics". Since there was no central government (i.e., in a specific locale) to create laws by which to govern their members, and the government under James had disintegrated at the time of of his death just before the destruction, they were unable to form a separate organization like that of the Pharisees, who were successful in doing just that.

It is clear that most of the rabbis (Pharisees) during the reign of Hadrian (117–138 CE), after the destruction of Jerusalem, would not enter the *Be*

Nizerte (House of the Nazaraeans); however, they would enter into the *Be Abedan* (House of the Ebionites) for both discussion and disputation. The former they called *minim* (heretics). While Rabbi Samuel would enter the *Be Abedan*, one Rabbi Joseph even claimed to be one of the Ebionites[27] and would not enter the *Be Nizerte* (or "House of the Nazareans"), but would go to the *Be Adibian* ("House of the Ebionites"). One entry in the Babylonian Talmud, in discussing the trial of Rabbi Eleazar b. Penata reveals that this was one of the charges against him. His purpose in visiting the *Be Nizerte* was for discussion and debate of Torah. This "house" was a place where disputations were held. Hadrian had forbidden the study of Torah on pain of death, and this included all Jews, including the Ebionites and Nazaraeans. That Pharisees still associated with them at that time shows they had not yet completely separated from them. This means the Jewish Ebionites and its opposing sect, the Nazaraeans, were still in close contact with the Pharisees at the time and that they also still studied Torah. One Rabbi was arrested for just such a crime. "They asked him [Penata] 'Why did you go to the Meeting-House [*Be Nizerte*, House of the Nazareans, as is clarified in another tractate]?"[28]

They met to discuss local matters as well as for religious debates. Since this occurred during the reign of Hadrian, we can also surmise that James and Zocher, the grandsons of Jude, the brother of Jesus, were executed during Hadrian's reign not for being of the House of David but for studying Torah. They were Jews, albeit Ebionite Jews, who studied Torah. The fact that these Jews in the *Be Nizerte* were referred to as Nazaraeans tells us they were the divided sect.

Another instance in which we find that the Pharisees got along with the Nazaraeans at this point is that the "Men of Ma'amad" (compared with the "Men of the Mishmar"; i.e., priests of the temple) would not fast in the synagogue on Sunday in respect of the Nazaraeans. "Why did they not fast on Sunday?—R. Johanan said: Because of the Nazareans."[29]

The editor explains that it was "because they [the Nazaraeans] might take umbrage at the Jews turning their Sabbath into a fast-day."[30] Such respect for their fellow Jews, even though their beliefs were different, shows they were still not considered as being outside the Jewish religion.

27. *b. Shab.* 116a
28. *b. Abod. Zar.* 17b; *b. Shab.* 115a, b; 116a.
29. *b. Ta'an.* 27b.
30. *b. Ta'an.*, note.

Judaism in the First Century

It is clear that the Rabbis and the Ebionites continued to meet together and discuss local affairs, laws, and religious matters. "Under Domitian, Gamaliel II made a journey thither in company with Eleazar ben Azariah, Joshua ben Hananiah, and Akiba, and it is related that they discoursed in synagogues and school–houses, and discussed religious subjects with heathen and Christians."[31]

Because the Nazaraeans became divided and accepted Gentile Christians (of whom there were many more) a new set of rules and doctrines became necessary. By the middle of the second century there were numerous groups *calling themselves Christians*, many of them Jewish gnostics. Also by that time, there were numerous "sects" of Christianity.

It was at this time that the Pharisees began to concern themselves with the writings of the "Christians". By this time there were numerous gnostic texts. Their discussion in the Talmud related to which texts should be hidden (of their own) and which should be burned. For instance, there was an early Testament of Job that was known in the Hebrew that they decided should be done away with. Because of Hadrian's ban they hid their scrolls of the Torah, Prophets, and Writings at that time in storage places called genizas. The question as to whether to hide or burn the Christian writings was also discussed. One rabbi suggested cutting out the divine names [meaning Yahweh and his euphemisms were in those gospels] and hiding the rest. The debate was left undecided, but Rabbi Mier later (third generation from the destruction, ca 130–163) referred to the gospels as *Aven Gilyon* ["Blank Spaces of Falsehood], a play on the word *evangelion*, derived from the Greek εύαγγύλιον [*euangelion*] meaning "good message."

At this time, a conflict broke out between the Pharisees and the Nazaraeans. Samuel [Mar Samuel, the Exilarch of Babylonian Davidic lineage in Nehardea; *mar* means "my Lord"] had once visited with the Ebionites, apparently, those who were still practicing Judaism. The group now known as the "Nazaraeans" that included mostly Gentiles by this time had split from the original Nazaraeans and had become "Christians" of the Pauline theology. The Ebionites were assuredly the sect receiving their instruction from the *despoysni* and the original Nazaraeans who followed their teachings. *Rabbi Joseph claimed to be "one of them."*

> Come and hear: The blank spaces above and below, between the sections, between the columns, at the beginning and at the end of the Scroll, defile one's hands. 13—It may be that [when they are]

---

31 Moore, *Judaism*, p. 106.

Becoming Christian

together with the Scroll of the Law they are different. 14 Come and hear: The blank spaces 15 and the Books of the Minim 16 may not be saved from a fire, but they must be burnt in their place, they and the Divine Names occurring in them. Now surely it means the blank portions of a Scroll of the Law? No: the blank spaces in the Books of Minim. Seeing that we may not save the Books of Minim themselves, need their blank spaces [DIVINE SACRED NAMES] be stated?—This is its meaning: And the Books of Minim are like blank spaces.

The blank spaces and the Books of the Minim, we may not save them from a fire. R. Jose said: On *weekdays one must cut out the Divine Names which they contain, hide them*, and burn the rest. R. Tarfon said: May I bury my son if I would not burn them together with their Divine Names if they came to my hand. For even if one pursued me to slay me, or a snake pursued me to bite me, I would enter a heathen Temple [for refuge], but not the houses of these [people], for the latter know [of God] yet deny [Him], whereas the former are ignorant and deny [Him], and of them the Writ saith, and behind the doors and the posts hast thou set up thy memorial. R. Ishmael said: [One can reason] a minori: If in order to make peace between man and wife the Torah decreed, Let my Name, written in sanctity, be blotted out in water, these, who stir up jealousy, enmity, and wrath between Israel and their Father in Heaven, how much more so; and of them David said, Do not I hate them, O Lord, that hate thee? And am I not grieved with those that rise up against thee? I hate them with perfect hatred: I count them mine enemies. And just as we may not rescue them from a fire, so may we not rescue them from a collapse [of debris] or from water or from anything that may destroy them?

R. Joseph b. Hanin asked R. Abbahu: As for the Books of Be Abedan [Ebionites], may we save them from a fire or not?—Yes and No, and he was uncertain about the matter. Rab would not enter a Be Abedan, *and certainly not a Be Nizrefe* [House of the Nazaraenes]; Samuel would not enter a Be Nizrefe [House of the Nazaraenes], *yet he would enter a Be Abedan [House of the Ebionites]*. Raba was asked: Why did you not attend at the Be Abedan [House of the Ebionites]? A certain palm-tree stands in the way, replied he, and it is difficult for me [to pass it]. Then we will remove it?—Its spot will present difficulties to me. *Mar b. Joseph said: I am one of them and do not fear them. On one occasion he went there, [and] they wanted to harm him.*[32]

---

32. *b.* Shab. 116a, italics mine.

We know that Rabbis of undoubted Jewish orthodoxy, like R. Abahu, had close contact with the Ebionites. Rabbi Saphra was even appointed by the community of Ebionites in Ceasarea as their teacher on the recommendation of the same R. Abahu. Yet Abahu, like Rabbi Eliezer ben Hyrcanus (70–100 CE; the husband of Imma Shalom, sister of Gamaliel II) who was martyred and had enjoyed the *halakah* of Ebionites in Sepphoris, had contact with Jewish Christians, while also being rigorous opponents of their teachings, and had many debates with them. Even though the Jewish community at large held the Ebionites in contempt, there were among the Pharisees those who did visit and debate with them and not a few who were interested in their teachings. Rabbi Eliezer was charged with heresy and excommunicated. It was he who gave the explanation of execution by stoning and hanging:

> The place of stoning was the height of two men. One of the witnesses knocked (the convict) down on his back [lit.: "loins"]. If he turned over on his chest [lit: "heart"], the witness turned him on his back. If he died right away, that was enough; but if not, the second (witness) took a stone and dropped it on his chest. If he died right away, that was enough; but if not he was stoned by all Israelites (present) . . . 4b "All who were stoned were (then) hanged." These are the words of Rabbi Eliezer (ben Hyrcanus). But the sages said: "No one is hanged except the blasphemer and idol worshippers." "They hanged a man facing the people and a woman facing the tree." These are the words of Rabbi Eliezer (ben Hyrcanus). But the sages said:—"The man was hanged but the woman was not."[33]

He spent his last days in retirement at his home in Caesarea. His debates with the Ebionites are evident in his lament:

> Rabbi Eliezer (ben Hyrcanus) the great says: "From the day the Temple was burned the sages started to be like scribes, and the scribes like superintendents and the superintendents like peasants [*am de aretz*]. And the peasantry grew weak and died. And there is none who seeks. On whom can we rely? On our Father in heaven!
> "*With the footsteps of the Messiah* arrogance will spread and prices will rise; the vine will give its fruit, but the wine will cost more [Rev. 6:6: "hurt not the oil and the wine"]. Those who serve idols will turn to heresy [*minuth*] and there will be no reproof. The council house will be for prostitution. Galilee will be laid waste and Golan ruined. The men of the frontier will wander from city

---

33. *m. Sanh.* 6.4.

to city and there will be no favors [Matt 24:23–26 implying people will be searching for messiah]. The wisdom of the scribes will decay. Those who fear sin will be loathed and truth will be rejected [Rev. 11:3–9; truth and faith "lie dead in the street"]. The young shall shame the elders and the elders will stand up before inferiors: *'The sons dishonor the father, the daughter rise against her mother the daughter-in-law against her mother-in-law; a man's enemies (will be) men of his own house'* (Micah 7:6). This generation's face is like a dog's face: the son is not ashamed before his father. And on whom can we rely? On our Father in heaven!"[34]

It is evident that Eliezer had discussed the traditions of the messiah with the Ebionites in Galilee. He uses a Scripture from Micah 7:6 which Jesus also used: "For I am come to set a man at variance *against his father, and the daughter against her mother*, and the daughter in law against her mother in law. *And a man's foes shall be they of his own household*" (Matt 10:35; Luke 12:53, italics mine). He is purported to have been the author of the Seder Olam Habah, a second-century chronicle dating from the creation until the time of Hadrian, also known as Bariata di Jose ben Halafta.[35] His love of genealogy was apparent.

Mar Samuel bar Abba (200 CE), who had visited with the Ebionites sometime during the second century, had children who were captured by the Romans during the Jewish war, and was of the first generation of Pharisees in Babylonia. Samuel believed the Messianic Era would arrive through natural means. Whether he visited them in Galilee or in Persia cannot be determined. He is known to have gone to Galilee to be confirmed as Rabbi. "It is probable that it was at this time that the Nazarenes assumed the designation of Ebionites, signifying the contrast between themselves and the avaricious apostates and claiming that they were the true heirs of the Messianic kingdom."[36]

Schonfield claims this happened immediately after the death of James, the brother of Jesus in order to separate themselves from the "apostates" (Zealots); however, there is also some indication that they might have taken on this name even before Paul wrote in Galatians that he was making collection for the "poor" in Jerusalem (Gal 2:10; Rom 15, 26). Further, Jesus had decreed that the "poor in spirit" (the humble *ebion*) would inherit the Kingdom of God in his beatitudes (Matt 5:3). The name might have been

---

34. *m. Sotah* 9.15, italics mine.
35. *b. Yeb.* 82b; *b. Nid.* 46b.
36. Schonfield, *The History of Jewish Christianity*, pp. 16–17.

Judaism in the First Century

taken quite early since the Ebionites in Jerusalem were both poor in wealth and humble in spirit. Ebion (אביון) is a cryptic reading of אבידן (Be Abedan) in the passage above and translates as a settlement of Ebionites. R. Huna bar R. Judah met Raba there and consulted with him about a point of law.[37]

The church fathers believed it was their specific duty to weed out those who did not follow *their* doctrines and dogma, and that included the many sects of Jewish believers. By the time of Constantine Jesus had replaced Yahweh as God and Mary had become a perpetual virgin. Easter replaced Passover; the day of Sol Invictus became "Christ's Mass" or "Christmas". No longer was Jerusalem the capitol of the Christian world; Rome had superceded it. No longer was James the leader of the "church"; Peter had usurped his throne. No longer were the Christians of the Diaspora "outsiders"; now, the "outsiders" were the Jewish people who founded the true religion of Jesus. Over the centuries, the Roman church became a political organization, its pope the authority over kings. No longer was Jesus the intermediary between mankind and God; now, the pope usurped his throne. Not only had Paul reformed Judaism for the Gentiles; he had founded a new religion: Christianity! That religion was at odds with the sage Jesus and his followers that walked the land of Israel during the first century, and with the Pharisees. The word Nazaraean (or Nazarene) is derived from the Hebrew root *nsr* (*nazar*) and means "to observe" or "to keep", "to watch"; i.e., to observe Torah, keep its commandments, and guard it by "placing a fence around it". Abandonment of the Old Covenant has, in effect, displaced Jesus in his historical context.

Jacob Neusner sums it up well:

> I realize it is difficult for Christians today, as it was long ago to make sense of the continued vitality of the Torah, that is, of Judaism. To explain Israel's "unbelief," Christians have called Jews "perfidious," meaning "unbelieving"; have regarded them as stubborn or stiff-necked; have imputed to them invincible ignorance. The Gospels divide Israel behind believers and connivers, and for twenty centuries, Jews, faithful to the Torah of Moses were called Christ-killers. So there has been a certain impatience with us, eternal Israel, perhaps understandably so.[38]

Both the heirs of David, including some who were not of the *despoysni* and the Pharisees, were tortured and/or put to death by the Romans. Edicts

---

37. *b. B. Qam.* 117a.
38. Neusner, p. 23.

defined by Rome persecuted *all* Jews, including those belonging to the Ebionites and Nazaraeans. The Roman emperors used the church as the vehicle to persecute the Jews. They were regarded as second class citizens. There was a prohibition against circumcising slaves and many of the Jews had been enslaved. Constantine also issued a decree forbidding marriage between Jews and Christians. The violation of this edict was punishable by death. These edicts referred to the Jews as a "shameful" or "bestial" sect, "contemptible and perverse". The irony of all this is that Jesus was a Jew! Ironically, while worshiping a Jew as the "risen Christ", they were killing his brothers.

As time passed, the Pharisees developed a hatred for the Gentile Christian *minim*, and the conflict between the two religions continued unchecked for centuries. What had happened? "Too many Gentiles, too few Jews, and no End [i.e., the "last day"] in sight!"[39] So the Christian *minim* of the Talmud do not reflect those Jewish messianics, the Ebionites, at all but the Gentile Christians who had made it their task to convert the Jewish people to Paul's view of the cosmic Christ.

Pharisees still exist, but they are not known as Pharisees. Judaism has now split into three factions: conservative, reform, and orthodox. They still use Torah as their guide, and though the times and social settings have changed, they have adapted through their reliance on Torah.

---

39. Fredericksen, p. 169.

4

The Apostles

THE GREEK WORD "APOSTLE" is *apostolos*, meaning "one sent" with a message. In Hebrew the equivalent is *shalach*, "to send forth" (as in Thayer's). There are numerous traditions about the apostles and their lives after the resurrection of Jesus. Most are legendary, but a few historical facts can be attained. The Acts of the Apostles was written to magnify Paul's mission rather than trace the fates of the apostles. Few details are given in that book about the "twelve" and the community of Jerusalem. The traditions of the church are hardly historical. Many of the traditions contradict each other and it is difficult to ascertain the historical value of them. There is much confusion between the various church fathers who hand down these traditions as to what actually happened to the apostles. We have reliable witnesses only about the deaths of James, the brother of Jesus, James, the brother of John, and Judas Iscariot: Josephus and the New Testament. As for the rest of the apostles it is only conjecture as to their fates. Although there were only twelve original "disciples", there were actually fourteen "apostles", those "sent". Included among them here is a woman, Mary Magdalene (The Great).

MARY MAGDALENE, APOSTLE OF APOSTLES

The first apostle was actually Mary Magdalene. She was "sent" by Jesus himself to relay a message to the disciples from Jesus (John 20:16). Christians assume that she was Mary "of Magdala", but there appears to be something

Becoming Christian

more to the title "Magdalene" than the fact that she derived from that place. The primary meaning of the word Magdala is "elegant" or "great", "magnificent". It is derived from the word *migdal* meaning "tower". The meaning of "elegant" is one exhibiting refined, tasteful beauty of manner, form, or style, and this would "fit" our Mary. She might have been a tower, magnificent, or great, but elegant is the quality she most exhibits in the gospels, and her role in the ministry was perhaps "great". The first mention of her name in the gospels is in Matthew 27:56 where she is one of the women (the other is Mary, the mother of James and Joses, and the mother of Zebedee's children) are viewing the execution from the Women's Court balcony ("from afar"). She is apparently given the status of leader of the women who visited the tomb, and we are told by the author of Mark that "when he [Jesus] was in Galilee, followed him and ministered to him" (Mark 15:41). This would indicate that she might have been quite important since wealthy Jewish women were known to have subsidized sages in their ministries. We know that Joanna, the wife of Chuza, Herod Antipas' personal administrator, was also a wealthy woman and ministered to Jesus of her "substance", along with Susannah and "many others" (Luke 8:3). The word substance is rendered in the Greek as *huparchonts* meaning "possessions" or "property".

Later Christian attitudes regarding the place of women in worship had not yet come into vogue. Women were considered "equal partners" with their husbands based on the marriage of Adam and Eve, who were considered "one flesh". It is true that the woman was an integral and equal partner in marriages long before the first century. The family worked and lived as a unit. Each member of the household did his or her share to enjoy the fruits of their labors. Women were not subservient as reflected in later centuries.

> In the time of Jesus there was no separation of the sexes in the synagogue and women could be counted as part of the ten individuals needed for a religious quorum. This allowed women to be much more active in the religious life of the community than they are today.[1]

For seven centuries into the Common Era men and women sat together in the synagogue, while the Romans and the church separated the genders (evidencing the nature of male–dominated religion in the early Roman church).

Safrai further comments concerning women's education:

---

1. Safrai, "The Place of Women."

> In the Second Temple period women were religiously the equals of men: ancient Jewish sources from the land of Israel and from the Diaspora show that women frequented the synagogue and studied in the beit midrash (study hall). Women could be members of the quorum of ten needed to say the "Eighteen Benedictions" . . . and like men, women were permitted to say "Amen" in response to the priestly blessing.[2]

In the synagogue women also carried the title and held the responsibilities of *archisynagogissa*, head or leader of a synagogue.[3] They also had the right to be included as one of the seven people called to read from Torah on the Sabbath.[4] A woman treasurer (*gizbarit*) is mentioned in the Babylonian Talmud.[5] Synagogue inscriptions have also given titles like *presbytera* (elder), *mater* or *pateressa* (mother), and priestess to women in the Greco–Roman world. One late fourth or fifth century example is a funerary inscription from Crete, 'Sophia of Gortyn, *presbytera* and *archisynagogissa* of Kissamus (lies) here. The memory of the righteous woman (be) forever. Amen."[6] As heads of synagogues these women would have been, in the words of rabbi and scholar Shaye Cohen, "responsible for supervising the services, specifically for deciding who should read the Bible, lead the prayers, and give the sermon. The *archisynagogue* was something between a president and a rabbi."[7]

This carried over into the rabbinical years after the destruction of the Temple. "Scripture places men and women on an equality with regard to all the laws of the Torah."[8] Beruryah (wife of R. Meir) and Imma Shalom (wife of R. Eliezer) were scholars in their own right whose interpretations are quoted in the Talmud, while the wife of Jonah the prophet went up to Jerusalem for the three festivals, and Michal, the daughter of King Saul, donned *tefillin*. In several instances, Beruryah's opinions on *halakhah* (Jewish Law) were accepted over those of her male contemporaries. While it is the general consensus within Christian circles that the women received

---

2. Safrai, "Were Women Segregated?"

3. Cohick, *Women in the World of the Earliest Christians*, p. 223; b. Abod. Zar. 38a–b.

4. *t. Meg* 3, 11–12.

5. *b. Shab.* 62a.

6. English translation in Noy, Panayotov & Bloedhorn 2004, 252; Noy, D., A. Panayotov and H. Bloedhorn (eds.), *Inscriptiones Judaicae Orientis*, vol. 1: Eastern Europe, Tübingen 2004..

7. Cohen, "Women in the Synagogues", pp. 23–29.

8. *b B.K.* 15a.

no education, young girls were taught Torah either by their mothers or by women tutors.

Women had the right to buy, sell, and own property, and to make their own contracts. Proverbs 31:10–31, which is traditionally read at Jewish weddings, speaks repeatedly of business acumen as a trait to be prized in women (v. 11, 13, 16, and 18 especially). They might also have the right to be consulted about marriage and marital sex was the woman's right, not the man's. Widows had the right to their husband's property and could use it in any manner without the permission of her deceased husband's family. In Elephantine at the colony of the Jews, women might even initiate divorce.[9] They were also required to make the pilgrimage to Jerusalem for festival celebrations.

Seven of the prophets were women, and women are highly acclaimed in the Talmud as well as in the Old Covenant. We know of Hulda and the "prophetess", wife of Isaiah (8:3) from the Scriptures, who were important in political affairs, even advising Hilkiah the priest. Deborah, also a prophetess, served as a judge of Israel and women served in the army (Judges 4:9–10). Others became "philosophers" or Therapeutrides. These are mentioned by Philo and are investigated in Joan Taylor's *Jewish Women Philosophers of First Century Alexandria*. These female members were, in fact, not virgins; many had children of their own. They were referred to as Therapeutrides (Θεραπευτρίδες) and ministered to the sick as female physicians. These women were very similar to the women followers of Jesus; i.e., Joanna, Mary the Magdalene, and others, and later one of Philip's daughters, Hermione, who was said to have been a "doctor". Their healings were not only for the body but for the soul, thus they were also known as "curers" or "worshipers" (θεραπεύω).

This is not to say that Mary Magdalene was, indeed, a Therapeutride; however, she seems to fit the role of one who might accompany the great physician and aid him in his healing activities. Could Jesus have been a Therapeut? It is interesting that we have verses that indicate his healing prowess and he claims the title of "physician" for himself (Matt 9:12; Mark 2:17; Luke 4:23; Luke 5:31). Although the word "physician" is rendered in Greek in the New Testament as *iatros*, literally meaning "healer", the word *therapeut* indicates both physical and spiritual healing. We have no accounting of his youth, so it is possible. The sect known as the Therapeutae, one community existing in Alexandria at Lake Mareotis, were believed to

---

9. Collins, *Families*, p. 119.

have been similar in beliefs and practices to the Nazaraeans of Jerusalem. Eusebius even believed them to be early "Christians".[10] Philo gives the only complete description of their community. Their designation as Therapeutae (Θεραπευταί), or "Physicians" connects them as having branched off from the Essenes (Asaiai, or "Healers"). They spent their time in deep study of Torah and in reciting and composing hymns.

> Like the Essenes, they offered every morning at sunrise a prayer of thanksgiving to God for the light of day as well as for the light of the Torah, and again at sunset for the withdrawal of the sunlight and for the truth hidden within the soul. In studying the Scriptures they followed the allegorical system of interpretation, for which they used also works of their own sect. They took their meals only after sunset and attended to all their bodily necessities at night, holding that the light of day was given for study solely. Some ate only twice a week; others fasted from Sabbath to Sabbath.
>
> On the Sabbath they left their cells and assembled in a large hall for the common study of the Law as well as for their holy communion meal. The oldest member of the community began with a benediction over the Torah and then expounded the Law while all listened in silence; the others followed in turn. After this they sat down to a common meal, which was very simple, consisting of bread and salt and herbs (hyssop); and water from a spring was their drink in place of wine. The Therapeutæ, differing in this respect from the Essenes, *included women members. These, though advanced in years, were regarded as pure virgins on account of their lives of abstinence and chastity*; and they seem to have been helpful in nursing and educating waifs and non–Jewish children that took refuge in such Essene communities (Philo, l.c. § 8). Young men, but no slaves, waited at table . . . They all wore white raiments like the Essenes. After the repast, passages of Scripture were explained by the presiding officer and other speakers, with special reference to the mysteries of the Law; and each of these interpretations was followed by the singing of hymns in chorus, *in which both men and women invariably joined.*[11]

This woman was an exceptional follower of Jesus. We can conclude that she was an educated wealthy woman and, perhaps, served as a leader of

---

10. Eusebius, HE 2:16–17.

11. "Therapeutae", JE, http://www.jewishencyclopedia.com/articles/14366-therapeutae, italics mine.

Becoming Christian

the Jesus movement. She was faithful to him throughout his ministry, at his execution, at his tomb, and again at his resurrection. She certainly would merit the title of Magdalene in all its meanings. Her title in no manner indicates the notion that she was Jesus' wife. Instead, it reflects her status as a female *archisynagogissa*, a female leader of the movement.

SIMON (SIMEON, "PETER", "CEPHAS")

Simon bar Jonah is considered the foremost and greatest of all the apostles. He was the first, along with his brother Andrew whom we know little about, to be chosen as one of Jesus' students (Matt 4:18). The Roman church designated him as its founder based on a verse in Matthew, "And I say also unto thee, that thou art Peter, and upon this rock I will build my church" (Matt 18:17). However, the "rock" on which Jesus claimed to found his church was the statement Peter had made. "Thou art the Christ [Messiah], the Son of the living God [Yahweh]" (Matt 18:16). Needless to say, Jesus was pointing to the fact that he, as Messiah, was the foundation of the Kingdom of God, as exclaimed by Peter. The word play between "Cephas" and "Rock" (or the nickname "Rocky") is evident since the name Cephas means "rock". It is upon the basis of the revelation that Jesus is Messiah that his "church" would be built, not upon Peter. The nickname Rocky appears to have been given to Peter because of his impetuousness and his wavering faith. Time and again in the New Testament we find Peter's wavering personality. Peter reported to James how he had been instrumental in the conversion of a Gentile proselyte, Cornelius, a Roman soldier, yet when dining with the Gentiles and Paul, succumbed to the men sent from James.

In fact, it was Jesus' brother, James, who inherited the status of head of the Jesus movement in Jerusalem after the resurrection. Peter is clearly an apostle to the Gentiles. "And when there had been much disputing, Peter rose up, and said unto them, Men and brethren, ye know how that a good while ago God made choice among us, that the Gentiles by my mouth should hear the word of the gospel, and believe" (Acts 15:7). Peter is here referring to the vision he had on the roof of the house in Joppa (Acts 10:10–16) before Paul's encounter with the Gentiles. Paul reflects upon Peter's mission and his own, indicating the language of the edict that he was no longer allowed to preach to the Jews. "But contrariwise, when they saw that the gospel of the uncircumcision was committed unto me, as the gospel of the circumcision was unto Peter; (For he that wrought effectually in Peter to the apostleship of the circumcision, the same was mighty in me toward the Gentiles: And when James, Cephas, and John, who seemed to be pillars, perceived the grace that was given unto me, they gave to me and Barnabas the right hands of fellowship; that we should go unto the heathen, and they unto the circumcision" (Gal 2:7–9). Although Peter's speech concerning the Gentiles was heard by the council, it was James who made the final decision and issued the edict to the Gentile God-fearers in the Diaspora. "Wherefore my sentence is, that we trouble not them, which from among the Gentiles are turned to God: But that we write unto them, that they abstain from pollutions of idols, and from fornication, and from things strangled, and from blood" (Acts 15:19). The entire council "the whole church" (22), the apostles and the elders agreed with his judgment. They did not look to Peter for judgment; they looked to James. Peter, however, was one of the three "pillars" (James, Peter, and John) and an important administrator in the movement.

In 43–44 CE King Agrippa executed James, the brother of John, and arrested Peter and put him in prison. This occurred during the intermediate days between Passover and Pentecost, Agrippa fully intending to have him executed shortly after the festive days were completed. The "angel" who released him was probably Barnabas, who appears to have been related to Agrippa and knew the workings of the prison and the guards. Peter was told to go to the house of Mary, the mother of John "whose surname was Mark", Barnabas' nephew. Mary was Barnabas' sister (Acts 12:6–16) and the wife of Cleophas, the brother of Joseph. Peter recognizes the authority of James since his instructions were to "Go shew these things unto James, and to the brethren. And he departed, and went into another place" (Acts 12:17). It is at this time that tradition holds Peter went to Rome; however, if we can accept the Epistle of First Peter as the work of Peter, he went to Babylon to the Nazaraean assembly there. It is unknown which of the apostles had established the movement in Babylon, but it was apparently established quite early on, perhaps by Peter himself. There had been a large population of Jews who had lived there since the captivity, and before the destruction of Jerusalem numerous members of the Jerusalem community fled to that location as well as to Parthia and other eastern locations. There were three Syrian Jews there who had founded an early community of Nazaraeans (so-called) in central Mesopotamia in Ctesiphon–Seleucia on the Tigris during the second century by the names of Abris (Eber?—121–137 CE), Abraham (159–171 CE) and Ya'qub (James; ca 190 CE). Bauckham

Becoming Christian

relates that "Abris is said to have been 'of the family and race of Joseph' the husband of Mary, while Abraham was 'of the kin of James called a brother of the Lord' and Ya'qub was Abraham's son."[12] These men had ancestors who had been residents in that area since the first century.

We are told in the end of that letter "The church that is at Babylon, elected together with you, saluteth you; and so doth Marcus [Mark] my son" (1 Pet 5:13). Tradition holds that Peter had married a daughter (The Hebrew Adah, referred to as Concordia or Perpetua in the traditions) of Aristobulus III, one of the "Seventy", a brother of Mary and Barnabas (also of the Seventy). This would make Mark the nephew of Peter as well, and he might well have referred to him as "son" in the sense of family relationship if he were watching over him for his parents in a foreign land. It is entirely probable that several of the disciples were the children of Mary and Cleophas-Alphaeus.

It is highly unlikely that Simon bar Jonah (Yonah) ever went to Rome and certainly not during his latter career. An ossuary discovered on the Mount of Olives at the Dominus Flevit cemetery is believed to have been Peter's and contradicts the idea that Peter's bones are in Rome. It is very near other ossuaries with the names Mary and Martha and Eleazar (Lazarus). This cemetery is clearly one that is associated with the early Nazaraeans.

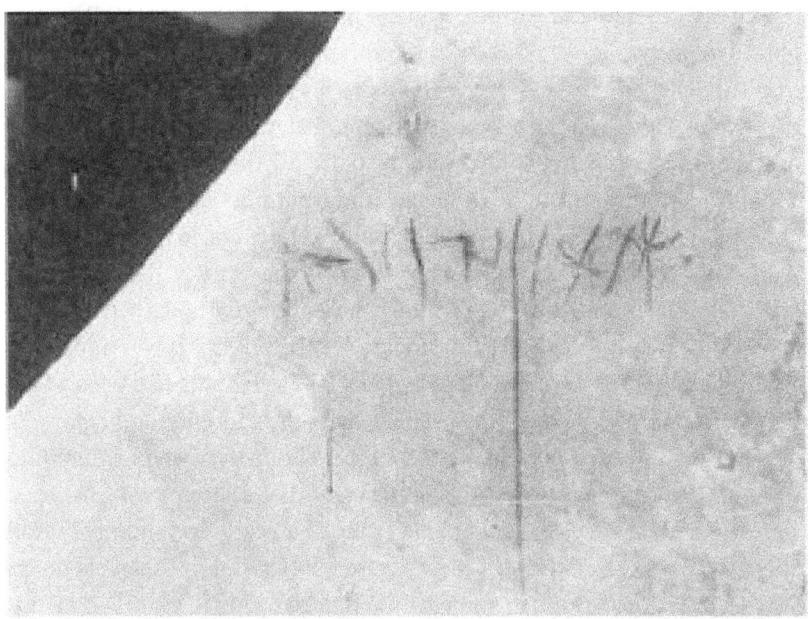

12. Bauckham, pp. 68–69.

Peter probably died in Jerusalem sometime around 52–62 CE when James himself was executed, perhaps earlier. Paul tells us that "when Peter was come to Antioch, I withstood him to the face, because he was to be blamed" (Gal 2:11). This was after the edict of James had been approved. We hear no more of Peter after this occasion, but we can assume he went back to Jerusalem with the men sent by James. This was clearly after the first missionary journey of Barnabas and Paul because the two had a falling out over whether to take John Mark with them the second time (Acts 15:36–37). Apparently, the argument was over more than that, for Paul says "when Peter was come to Antioch, I withstood him to the face, because he was to be blamed. For before that certain came from James, he did eat with the Gentiles: but when they were come, he withdrew and separated himself, fearing them which were of the circumcision. And the other Jews dissembled likewise with him; insomuch that Barnabas also was carried away with their dissimulation" (Gal 2:11–13). The word "dissimulate" means "hypocrite", so Paul was referring to them as hypocrites. From that point forward, Paul began his own gospel of high Christology, while the Jews remained fully within Judaism until the movement began its final schism.

On Paul's third trip to Jerusalem (52–60 CE) Peter is no longer mentioned as being present with James and the elders in the council (Acts 21:18). He had been in Babylon with the large Jewish population in 44–45 in order to evade the authorities. John Mark apparently was sent along with him. Since Paul states that Peter was now the apostle to the circumcised we can well imagine that Peter never left the Jerusalem area after he returned from Babylon and died and was buried on the Mount of Olives.

ANDREW

Andrew bar Jonah was the little known brother of Peter who overshadowed him in the New Testament. We might assume that he was the younger brother since he is always named secondly in the lists of apostles. Mentioned only thirteen times in the entire New Testament, and then mostly in conjunction with his brother, we know very little about him from that source. We learn that he is mentioned with Philip in the Gospel of John where he relays a message to Jesus that the Greeks requested an audience with Jesus (John 12:22), but little beyond that. He is one of the four brothers who surround Jesus most of the time. We learn Andrew had been a follower of John the Baptist in the Gospel of John (1:40). He had "heard John speak" at the very minimum. Peter, apparently, had not been there to see the anointing of Jesus as the messiah, because he [Andrew] "first findeth his own brother Simon, and saith unto him, We have found the Messias, which is, *being interpreted* [that is, into the Greek], the Christ" (John 1:41). If that is so, it is likely then that Andrew was the first disciple called and Peter the second, although the late Gospel of John is the only one to mention Andrew's name first. Tradition states that his missions carried him around the area of the Black Sea, but these traditions are of late date. His death was said to occur between 60 and 62 CE. He might have been executed along with James, the brother of Jesus in 62.

JAMES, SON OF ZEBEDEE (JACOB)

James was one of the two brothers, sons of Zebedee (Zabdi), who might well have been Jesus' great uncle. Their mother was known as Salome, a popular name during the first century. These two sons were known as the "Sons of Thunder" (Boanerges = Benei-Regesh). They might have derived their title from their zeal for Yahweh's word. Yahweh's voice was known as "thunder" (Zech 9:14, for instance). In Zechariah 9:9 the prophecy of the messiah is given: "Rejoice greatly, O daughter of Zion; shout, O daughter of Jerusalem: behold, thy King cometh unto thee; he is just, and having salvation; lowly, and riding upon an ass, and upon the colt the foal of an ass." James and John were disciples of the messiah who comes in the "Name of the LORD", thus it is not too much of a stretch for the title to refer to the zeal of these two for Yahweh's word and kingdom, and as such companions of the messiah. Jesus taught the Kingdom of God, and these two were also sent out to all the cities of Judea with that message.

James was the first apostle to die. In the year 43–44 King Agrippa (41–44 CE) beheaded him on the advice of Jonathan the son of Annas, and Simon Cantheras, son of Simon Boethus, both overlapping high priests during that period of time. These two high priests were especially averse to the family and followers of Jesus and Agrippa sought to please them ("because he saw it pleased the Jews"—Acts 12:3). "Now about that time [meaning during the time of the famine in Judea during the reign of Claudius in 43–44 CE] Herod [Agrippa I] the king stretched forth his hands to vex certain of the church. And he killed James the brother of John with the sword" (Acts 12:1–2).

James probably never left Jerusalem. There is a seventeenth century tradition that he went to Spain, but that is highly unlikely since he was executed in 43–44 CE. Paul had intended to go to Spain (Gaul) first but was prevented by his arrest. In speaking to the Romans, he said: "But now having no more place in these parts, and having a great desire these many years to come unto you; Whensoever I take my journey into Spain, I will come to you . . . When therefore I have performed this, and have sealed to them this fruit, I will come by you into Spain" (Rom 15:24, 28). At this time, Spain had never been approached for conversion.

JOHN, SON OF ZEBEDEE

It is necessary to state here that John, son of Zebedee, was not the author of the Gospel of John. There are traditions that he went to Ephesus; however, this, too, is unlikely. There were two Johns who lived there, John the Evangelist so-called, and John the Presbyter (or Elder), who had been a priest. Christians have also equated him with the "Disciple Whom Jesus Loved", but considering the fact that the high priests referred to him as "unlearned" and "illiterate" (meaning in the Torah), it is not likely he would have been able to enter into the high priest's quarters at the trial of Jesus. Jerome wrote that Polycarp (69–155 CE) was a disciple of John, but this is probably not so since Polycarp was born about the time of the destruction of Jerusalem, and some scholars believe John was killed at the same time as his brother. This is entirely logical. Ignatius, a friend of Polycarp, also claimed to have been a student of John's, but this is also unlikely since he was steeped in the ecclesiastical hierarchy of the Roman church during his bishopric before he died (ca 107 CE). The later Gospel of John is believed to have been written in "Syria", that is, probably Antioch. It was written at a very late date (90–150 CE) during the time between the bishoprics of Ignatius and Cornelius, and that gospel reflects the theology of those "apostolic fathers". There is some suspicion that it was written by one of them or one of the succesors (a discussion follows in the next chapter). Among those who might have written it are Heron (107–127; d. 136), who replaced Ignatius, or Cornelius (127–154).

The church "fathers" were confused as to whether he might have been John the Evangelist, John the Presbyter, or the "Beloved Disciple". It is claimed he died in Ephesus at the age of ninety-four and buried on a mountain outside the town. No archaeological evidence has yet been discovered to determine whether this is true or not. Legends persist about John, but no mention in historical records is made of his ministry outside Jerusalem.

PHILIP

Philip was, apparently, a Hellenistic Jew since it was he who seemed to be the interpreter for the "Greeks" when they requested an audience with Jesus (John 12:20–22). We can, therefore, assume Philip spoke fluent Greek and was highly educated. A native of Bethsaida, Philip was first a disciple of John the Baptist and a friend to Andrew. Further, he was a friend of Nathaniel (Bartholomew) whom he introduced to Jesus. The life of Philip is given in the Acts of Philip (which we now know gives an accurate account of his ministry and his death).

This Philip had twin sisters, Mariamne (probably named after his mother), and Nicanora (See the Acts of Philip). The dialogue between Mariamne (Philip's sister) and Nicanora described them as "twin sisters, daughters of the same mother (c115, AaII/2, 45.15–46.13). Nicanora asks Mariamne to speak to her in Hebrew, her native tongue. Philip's four daughters became healers and prophetesses (Therapeutrides). We are told that the four daughters of Philip were prominent during the first and early second centuries.

> An ancient Greek litany of saints identified them as Hermione [Heb. Malach], Chariline [Heb. Gavriella], Irais [Heb. Keshet], and Eutychiane [Heb. Bruchiah]. All of them had lived to be very old. One of them had married; another 'lived in the Spirit' at Ephesus; and the other two had died unmarried at Hierapolis. All were known as prophetesses, but the oldest sister, Hermione, who was martyred during the reign of Hadrian (A.D. 117–138), was also renowned for her gift of healing. All were evidently important Church leaders. The youngest, Eutychiane, lived to be more than a hundred years old, since Polycrates knew her in the middle of the second century.[13]

In other documents we are plainly told that Hermione was a "doctor"; i.e., a Therapeutride.[14]

The Slavonic Josephus confuses the two Philips (as did also the authors of The Gospel of the Holy Twelve), declaring that "Philip the Tetrarch had

---

13. Ruffin, *The Twelve*, pp. 109–110
14. "Hermione", http://orthodoxwiki.org/Hermione.

four daughters left alive. For thou dost not raise up seed for thy brother, but gratifiest thy fleshly lust and committest adultery, seeing that four children of him are alive."[15]

The fact is that Philip the Tetrarch had married Salome but died childless in 34 CE. Salome was the daughter of Herod Philip Boethus (son of Herod the Great and the Mariamne II, the high priest's daughter). The two Philips, Philip the Tetrarch and Philip the apostle are confused, and it appears Philip the apostle is here believed to be Herod Philip Boethus.

The gnostic community in Egypt adopted Philip, and it was apparently the community there that was responsible for the Therapeutic tendencies in the *Gospel of Philip* in which the voice of the author explains the virginity of Mary as having been anathema to the apostles. Some believe Philip could have been responsible for the earliest gospel of all: the *Gospel of Thomas*. The *Gospel of Thomas* is believed to have been the earliest "sayings" gospel from which the others derived. The heretofore gnostic tendencies of *Thomas* where Mary the Magdalene was "made male" is explained by the fact that the men and women of the community of Therapeutics were considered spiritually equal and shared in common all things. An examination of the "sayings" of the gospel will point to Therapeutic origins.

There are some who believe Thomas might have been a "twin" to Philip. While Philip the Apostle did, in fact, have a sister named Mariamne (apparently named after her mother) who was a "twin" to Nicanora of Hierapolis in Phrygia (Turkey), the wife of the Roman procurator there,[16] it is highly unlikely Thomas was actually his twin.

As a high-ranking figure, Philip would have been privy to the company of government officials and wealthy individuals. This is why we find him in the company of a "eunuch" (a government official, and in particular a treasurer) "of great authority under Candace queen of the Ethiopians, who had the charge of all her treasure" (Acts 8:26–39). It isn't likely this important official would be in conversation with a simple peasant. Aristocrats were rarely in the company of the *am haretz* (common people). It was also Philip to whom the "Hellenized Jews" (called "Greeks") came in order to secure an interview with Jesus (John 12:20). Philip, having lived in a Greek style royal house, himself, would have been most likely to have consorted with these Hellenized Jews. Some scholars try to create two Philips: an

---

15. *Slavonic Josephus*, trans. A. Berendts, 1906, p. 104.
16. ActsPhil.

Becoming Christian

apostle and an "evangelist", but the earliest documents merge the two. In the *Acts of Philip*, we learn that Philip's sister Mariamne (named for her mother it seems) and his constant companion, Bartholomew (Nathaniel Bar–Tolmai or Theodorus, Son of Ptolemy) and some other of their disciples travel to Hierapolis in Asia (Phrygia), where Philip (the apostle) and at least two of his daughters are believed to be entombed. Recently, the tomb of Philip has been discovered in the ancient city of Hierapolis in Denizli, Turkey by Professor Francesco D'Andria. D'Andria said the structure of the tomb and the writings on it proved that it belonged to St. Philip the Apostle. His death occurred sometime around 80 CE.

Nicanora, twin sister to Mariamne, and sister to Philip is the wife of the Roman proconsul there and is healed of her various diseases, including the disease of her eyes. She says to her relatives: "*I am a Hebrew, a daughter of the Hebrews*; speak with me in *the language of my fathers*, because I have heard your preaching, and have been cured of this my disease.[17]

Tomb of Philip the Apostle

BARTHOLMEW (NATHANIEL)

Most interestingly, it was Philip who "findeth Nathanael" (John 2:45); in other words, he went to his home. Bar–Tolmai or Theodorus the son of Ptolemy was likely of noble birth, and it is most likely through Philip's connections that he knew him. Jesus was aware of Nathaniel's royal birth for he

17. Acts, Phil, italics mine.

called him "an Israelite" in whom there is no (political) guile. "An Israelite" was a lay *noble*; i.e., a non–political member of a royal family.[18] For centuries scholars have been baffled by Luke's mention of Nathaniel's family in his gospel. They have wondered why Luke would make mention of such a minor tract of land and royalty as the "Tetrarch of Abilene", considering the minor nature of the tetrarchy, but it was for the honor and recognition of Nathaniel's discipleship that he chose to mention his family:

> Now in the fifteenth year of the reign of Tiberius Caesar, Pontius Pilate being governor [procurator] of Judaea, and Herod [Antipas] being the tetrarch of Galilee, and his [half] brother Philip [Philip, son-in-law of Philip Boethus] of Ituraea and of the region of Trachonitis, and *Lysanias the tetrarch of Abilene*, Annas and Caiaphas being the high priests, the word of God came unto John the son of Zacharias in the wilderness (Luke 3:1–2, italics mine).

Some have accused Luke of having made an error here since the Lysanias of history that most call to mind is Lysanias I, the son of Mennaeus Ptolemy and Alexandra Hasmoneus who was put to death by Mark Antony. That particular Lysanias was King of Chalcis and was never called "tetrarch". Alexandra was the daughter of Judah Aristobulus, the brother of King Alexander Jannaeus and first husband of Queen Salome Alexander (Shlom–Zion/Salampsio). Alexandra had first married Philippion ben Ptolemy, the son of Mennaeus, King of Chalcis, but once Mennaeus cast his eye on Alexandra, he murdered his son and took her for his own wife.

> But Ptolemy, the son of Menneus [Ptolemy], who was the ruler of Chalcis, under Mount Libanus, took his brethren to him, and sent his son Philippion to Askelon to Aristobulus's wife, and desired her to send back with him her son Antigonus, and her daughters; the one of which, whose name was Alexandra, Philippion fell in love with and married her, though afterward his father Ptolemy slew him, and married Alexandra, and continued to take care of her brethren.[19]

Thus Nathaniel was not only related to the Ptolemy families of Egypt but also to the Hasmoneans in Judea. The genealogy of the family vindicates Luke. Ptolemy XIII married 1) Arsinoe II (sister to Cleopatra VII, who was his second wife). They had two children:

18. Freyne, *Galilee*, p. 127.
19. Josephus, *Ant.* 14.7.4.

Becoming Christian

1. Ptolemy bar Ptolemy and
2. Mennaeus bar Ptolemy (also called Mennaeus Ptolemy), King of Chalcis; he married Alexandra, daughter of Aristobulus II and his wife Salome Alexander (Shlom–Zion), who later married his brother King Alexander Janneus. Their child was:
3. Lysanias I, King of Ituraea; his child was:
4. Zenodorus; his child was:
5. Theodoros (Nathaniel in Hebrew) whose great treasure was stolen from him by King Alexander Janneus[20] (and later by Herod and the Caesars); his son was:
6. Lysanias II, Tetrarch of Abila (Abilene), the father of:
7. *Theodoros (Nathaniel "Bartholemew" bar Ptolemy), the disciple of Jesus.*

Josephus gives us a little history of the family and the feud between the Ptolemies and Hasmoneans:

> But when this Ptolemy was pursued by his mother Cleopatra [III], and retired into Egypt, Alexander besieged Gadara, and took it, as also he did Amathus, which was the strongest of all the fortresses that were about Jordan, *and therein were the most precious of all the possessions of Theodorus, the son of Zeno. Whereupon Theodorus marched against him, and took what belonged to himself, as well as the king's baggage, and slew ten thousand of the Jews.*[21]

This first Lysanius had a son named Zenodorus (Zeno/Zenos) who re–leased the land from Cleopatra. From the point of view of the Herodians he was a "robber". Josephus tells us:

> One Zenodorus had hired what was called the house of Lysanias, who, as he was not satisfied with its revenues, became a partner with the robbers that inhabited the Trachonites, and so procured him a larger income; for the inhabitants of those places lived in a mad way, and pillaged the country of the Damascenes, while Zenodorus did not restrain them, but partook of the prey they acquired. Now, as the neighboring people were hereby great sufferers, they complained to Varro, who was then president [of Syria], and entreated him to write to Caesar about this injustice of

---

20. Josephus, *War* 1.4.2–3.
21. Ibid., 1.4.2, italics mine.

The Apostles

Zenodorus. When these matters were laid before Caesar, he wrote back to Varro to destroy the nests of robbers, and to give the land to Herod, that by his care the neighboring countries might be no longer disturbed with these doings of the Trachonites . . . Hereupon Zenodorus was grieved, in the first place, *because his principality was taken away from him, and still more so, because he envied Herod, who had gotten it;* so he went up to Rome to accuse him, but returned back again without success . . . These reproaches they mainly ventured upon by the encouragement of Zenodorus, who took his oath that he would never leave Herod till he had procured that they should be severed from Herod's kingdom, and joined to Caesar's province.[22]

This Zenodorus had a son named Theodorus (or in Hebrew, Nathaniel), whose land and inheritance was confiscated first by King Alexander Janneus and afterward by Herod. The family of Nathaniel was left with a single strip of land called by Josephus and Pliny "the country of Zenos". The descendant of Theodorus (i.e., Lysanias II) became the tetrarch of that very slim strip of land (in the country of Abilene or Abila) which now consisted of the capital city Abila and its surroundings, *running alongside the Tetrarchy of Philip* (at one time said to be situated eighteen Roman miles from Damascus on the way to Heliopolis or Baalbek) and *near Cana* from whence Nathaniel derived in the New Testament. In Ptolemy V 14, 18, (c. 110 CE) Abila is still called *Abila epikaloumene Lusaniou* (Abila called 'of Lysanias'), presumably because Lysanias not only possessed the city at one time, but had originally founded it. There were two Abilas, one near Gadara in the Decapolis, and the other to which Josephus refers as "Abila of Lysanias"[23] which is near Damascas in Coele–Syria.

There was a Cana (Kana) in Coele Syria between the Lebanon and Anti–Lebanon mountain range, the territory in which the tetrarchy of Abilene existed. This was the Cana of Nathaniel (or Theodorus). Even Eusebius and Jerome identify it. The marriages of Cana in southern Lebanon are accompanied by great feasts and, most importantly, Canaean wine. Dr. Youssef El Houraini has worked to prove the identity of the location of the "marriage feast" in the New Testament as the Cana of Coele–Syria. Here the grapevines are grown in fertile red soil and produce the rich red wine of Cana. Dionysus was worshipped in this region of Phoenicia. The first miracle of Jesus, changing the water into the "best" wine would, indeed, be

22. Josephus, *Ant.* 15.10.1–3, italics mine.
23. Ibid., 19.5.1 274–75, italics mine.

reminiscent of this Cana. Both Eusebius and Jerome located "Cana of Galilee" in the land of "Acher" (Asher) near "Tyre". This place is still referred to as "Cana of Galilee". Stone urns similar to the ones used at the wedding feast have been unearthed there by the late "Moussa Amer". There are also stone inscriptions near a cave there that refer to Jesus. In the Onomasticon the word Cana is found: "Cana, till the reaches of Grand Sidon to the tribe of Asher" (Tyre was the larger of the two cities, thus it was referred to as *Grand* Sidon). Eusebius was well informed of the region because he was the Bishop of Caesarea.

The fourth gospel tells us the first miracle of Jesus occurred at the wedding feast in Cana. The raging question is whose wedding was it? When we learn that Mary was there (apparently in some family capacity since it is she who appears to be in charge of the arrangements) and that all the disciples were "called" (invited) to be there with Jesus (John 2:2), we tend to think the bridegroom (who is mentioned only as "the bridegroom") is a friend or relative of the family. Why would the disciples be invited if they were unknown to the bridegroom and bride? It is to be especially noted that the last few verses of John 1 refer to Nathaniel *of Cana*; the next chapter begins with the wedding *at Cana*. Nathaniel was probably the bridegroom! There were no chapter separations in the ancient texts, thus, these two events would be connected.

> Jesus saw Nathanael coming to him, and saith of him, Behold an Israelite [a non-political royal] indeed, in whom is no [political] guile! Nathanael saith unto him, Whence knowest thou me? Jesus answered and said unto him, before that Philip called thee, when thou wast under the fig tree, I saw thee. Nathanael answered and saith unto him, Rabbi, thou art the Son of God; thou art the King of Israel. Jesus answered and said unto him, because I said unto thee, I saw thee under the fig tree, believest thou? Thou shalt see greater things than these. And he saith unto him, verily, verily, I say unto you, hereafter ye shall see heaven open, and the angels of God ascending and descending upon the Son of man. And the third day there was a marriage in Cana of Galilee; and the mother of Jesus was there: and both Jesus was called, and his disciples, to the marriage . . ." (John 1:47–2:2).

In other words, Jesus and his disciples traveled to Cana to attend Nathaniel's wedding. Could he have wed one of Mary's family members? Christian tradition is that the wedding was that of one of Mary's daughters, one of Jesus' sisters. It is entirely possible since Nathaniel would not have met Jesus prior to Jesus "recognizing" him three days earlier. Jesus had just arrived home from Egypt! He would have honored Nathaniel as the bridegroom by "saving the best wine" for the last.

While we are on the subject of the meeting between Jesus and Nathaniel, it might well be useful to examine the mysterious exchange between them. While, presumably, they had never met, Jesus knew exactly who Nathaniel was. He had seen him "under the fig tree". For some reason, that made Nathaniel proclaim that Jesus was Son of God and King of Israel. I suggest that Jesus knew of Nathaniel before he met him. It is possible Nathaniel had also attended the schools of the Therapeutae in Egypt (his Ptolemaic ancestor's ancient home). The tree to which Jesus refers was one the Therapeutae would have used on a regular basis in their healing activities. The sycamore fig tree was sacred in Egypt and was called the Tree of Life. Its healing properties are well known to the ancient world. The Therapeutae would have used it in their ministrations. The fig and its sap were used for natural healing purposes: the sap could be used for a local anesthetic, its fruit also served as an analgesic; by mouth it was taken against ringworm and pruritis ani; it was used as a poultice to open abcesses; the sap was used for burns and skin ailments; it has been used for bone fractures, laxatives, worms, toothache, tongue ailments, paralysis of the joints, displacement of arteries, boils, and inflamations. In Pharonic texts *the Sycamore fig was considered an ideal tree under which to dine and/or a place of rest for travelers*. It grew along the fertile soil of rivers and streams. Pharoahs called them Nehet. A Pharonic poem, translated by the Frenchman Gustaf Maspiro states:

> The young Scycamore that you have planted with your hand has grown and has begun to speak the sweet words like drops of honey. She is slender and her branch beautiful and green as papyrus, and she is laden with food that rival the redness of rubies. The air under her is moist and fresh, so come and spend time in the garden. The gardeners are happy and rejoicing in seeing you and bring you different bread, flowers and fresh fruit. *So come and enjoy this day, sitting under the shade*, and I will keep the secret and I will not mention anything I see.[24]

Jesus was referring figuratively to Nathaniel's Ptolemaic heritage! He knew Nathaniel had descended from one of the Ptolemaic pharoahs (i.e., Mennaeus Ptolemy and his mother Arsinoe, the sister of Cleopatra VII). Nathaniel's response was, likewise, mysterious. He immediately recognized

---

24. http://members.tripod.com/maaber_life/sycamore/tree.htm, italics mine.

Jesus as the Son of God and King of Israel! Because Jesus was able to tell him of his heritage, Nathaniel believed he was the Son of God, the Messiah! Because Jesus mentioned the "fig tree" and that Nathaniel was "under the fig tree", Jesus could have been referring *only* to Nathaniel's royal pharoanic lineage. The second clue we have on his heritage is that Nathaniel was called an "Israelite" and in the first century this meant one who was a *lay nobleman*, one who was not involved in political intrigue. His mother was most likely an Asherite since they were mixed with the inhabitants of Canaan.

The Asherites were known as a rebellious tribe:

> "But the Asherites dwelt among the Canaanites, the inhabitants of the land: for they did not drive them out" (Judges 1:32). "All these were the children of Asher heads of their fathers' house, choice and mighty men of valor, chief of the princes, and of them that were apt to the war and to battle . . ." (Judges 7:40).

Jesus had recognized Nathaniel as "an Israelite in whom is no guile", a non-political *royal* Jew who was righteous. Although Nathaniel was of Cana, he was only partially Asherite as one might expect. He was, also, a Levite, descended from the Hasmonean Alexandra (and thus through the division of Joiarib) and her husband Mennaeus Ptolemy. It seems probable he was the son of the second Lysanius who had married a local woman *from the tribe of Asher* and who had lived in or around Cana. Jewish families living in the region of Coele-Syria accepted Jesus' teachings and healings:

> And he came down with them and stood in the plain, and the company of his disciples, and a great multitude of people out of all Judea and Jerusalem, and from the seacoast of Tyre and Sidon, who came to listen to him, and to be healed of their diseases (Luke 6:17–18).

The distance Jesus traveled to the wedding feast also confirms that this Cana is the Cana of Galilee mentioned in the New Testament. The first day he was on the Jordan River when the son of a Roman legionnaire living in Kefer Nahum (Capernaum) was healed. Kefer Nahum (Capernaum) is on the banks of the "Sea of Galilee" about 90 kilometers from Cana.

An inscription in Greek has been found there with the words "For the salvation of the Lords Imperial and their whole household [Tiberias and his mother Livia], by Nymphaeus, a freedman of *Lysanias the tetrarch*." Another was found in Latin recording the repair of a road "*at the expense of the Abilenians*".[25] All that having been stripped away from his family, however, by the Hasmoneans (who were connected with the Herodians and the Roman Caesars who also stole the land), animosity between the two was bound to build. It is no wonder upon learning that Jesus was from Nazareth that Nathaniel asked, "Can anything good come from Galilee?" He was referring to the Herodians and Hasmoneans who had taken the land in Galilee near Sepphoris. Josephus gives us an account of the event:

> So when Alexander [Hasmoneus] was delivered from the fear he was in *of Ptolemy*, he presently made an expedition against *Coelesyria*. He also took Gadara [in the Decapolis], after a siege of ten months. He took also Areathus, a very strong fortress belonging to the inhabitants above Jordan, *where Theodorus* [Nathaniel in Hebrew], *the son of Zeno, had his chief treasure, and what he esteemed most precious.*[26]

Apparently, Nathaniel (Bar–Ptolemy, or "Bartholomew"), or using his Greek name Theodorus, was named for his ancestor (grandfather?) Theodorus, the son of Zenodoros. Having had his inheritance taken away did nothing to advance his confidence in the Galilean city over whom presided one of the Herodians (Antipas, who rebuilt Sepphoris of which Nazareth became a satellite village). A "son of Ptolemy" (meaning he was a descendant of the Greek–Egyptian monarchy), Nathaniel was probably a sixth generation descendant of Arsinoe, the sister of Cleopatra VII, and her son, Menneus Ptolemy. These Ptolemy families were intermarried with the Hasmonean Royal Dynasty. As mentioned previously, Mennaeus Ptolemy had married Alexandra, the daughter of Aristobulus and Queen Alexandra Salome (Schlom–Zion) (she later married his brother King Alexander Jannaeus). It is this "Alexander" to whom Josephus refers in the passage above. The Ptolemy family, once allied with Herod the Great, was quickly abandoned by Herod when Antony fell from power, another reason for animosity between these families. A branch of Nathaniel's family is also to be found in Cyrenica (Cyrene). Inscriptions for the repair of a Jewish synagogue in 55 CE have been found with the names Lysanias and relative Zenodorus (obviously family names).

> In the second year of the emperor Nero Claudius Caesar Drusus Germanicus, on the 6th of Choarch [December, 55 CE]. It was

25. International Standard Bible Encyclopedia.
26. Josephus, *War* 13.13.3, italics mine.

Becoming Christian

> resolved by the congregation of the Jews in Berenice and its vicinity that (the names of) those who donated to the repairs of the synagogue be inscribed on a stele of Parian marble. Column One ... *Lysanias, son of Lysanias, 25 drachmae; Zenodoros, son of Theophilos, 28 drachmae* ...[27]

Even the heading describing Chapter 10, Book 15, of Josephus' *Antiquities* tells us the family of Nathaniel was clearly at odds with the Herodians:

> *How Herod Sent His Sons To Rome; How Also He Was Accused By Zenodorus And The Gadarens, But Was Cleared Of What They Accused Him Of And Withal Gained To Himself The Good-Will Of Caesar.*

There are church traditions that Bartholomew went to India, Turkey, and Armenia in particular, but there are other traditional journeys as well to unlikely locations. Of all the traditions the most likely is a ministry in Turkey (Heiropolis in Phrygia) or Armenia. We know he accompanied Philip to Heiropolis through the Acts of Philip, and since archaeology has discovered Philip's tomb there, we can assume that Nathaniel was, indeed, with him at the time. There are also legends about Nathaniel's death, but these, too, are traditional and we do not know the date of his demise. We should probably date his death around 80 CE.

JUDAS THOMAS (DIDYMUS, MEANING "TWIN TWIN")

Both Thomas and Thaddeus are named Judas, but Judas is also the Hebrew name for *Aristobulus*, so it would not be unreasonable for two members of the family to carry that name and be referred to as "twins". It is interesting that brothers are mentioned together in the lists of disciples; as examples, James and John of Zebedee and Simon Peter and Andrew are usually named together. In Acts 1:13 we are told that Judas Lebbaeus Thaddeus is the brother of James of Alphaeus. Lebbaeus is more likely the Greek transliteration of *laben*, "white" and, in fact, *leukos* ("Luke") means "white" or "light" (though he is not the author of that gospel). The name Thaddeus by which he was called is also Theudas, or in Hebrew Toda, "thanks". If Thomas is, indeed, a twin of Judas Lebbaeus Thaddeus, then he is also a son of Alphaeus and brother of Simon and Matthew Levi as well. Alphaeus is a name that means "to exchange" and very well could have been a title

27. CJZC 72, italics mine.

for Cleophas, the brother of Joseph. As a tax collector he would have also been a moneychanger since Roman coins were given as "change" to anyone giving more than the amount needed for the half–shekel temple tax. Jews tried to have the correct amount when exchanging their coins because they did not want to receive Roman coins in return.

MATTHEW LEVI

Matthew was a customs agent (collecting port taxes for Antipas) in Capernaum. He was the son of Cleophas and his wife Mary. Matthew could not have used the Alphaeus title (meaning "to exchange") because his father was still alive, but he used instead "Levi", a family name derived from his ancestor (perhaps Matthat ben Levi). If he were a Roman decurio (one of the three city counsellors) like Joseph of Arimathea, that title was inherited, and Cleophas was still alive at the time.

Matthew is credited with having written the first Hebrew gospel entitled the Gospel of the Hebrews. It was written in Jerusalem and was extant in the Library at Caesarea in the fourth century. The Nazaraean community transcribed a copy into Greek, which was lost, for Jerome, who provided quotes from it in his writings. The Ebionites and Nazaraeans had used this gospel exclusively.

Church tradition claims he went to Ethiopia, Parthia, and Egypt. The date of his death is given as 90 CE; however, these claims are based on imagination. Clement of Alexandria (Strom., iv.9) gives the explicit denial of Heracleon that Matthew suffered martyrdom. It is likely that Matthew died alongside James and other Nazaraeans in 62 CE.

JAMES, SON OF ALPHAEUS (CLEOPHAS)

This James was referred to as "James the Less", not because he was little but because he was the second disciple named James (James, the brother of John was the first). He is associated with his mother Mary, Cleophas' (Alphaeus') wife (Mark 15:40; Mark 3:16–19; Mark 16:1; Matt 27:56; John 19:25). Another brother to add to the list of Cleophas' and Mary's children is Joses (a nickname for Joseph). Church tradition places James' death in Egypt. However, once again, this James was probably executed along with James, the brother of Jesus in 62 CE.

THADDEUS, SON OF CLEOPHAS

In Acts 1:13 we are told that Judas Lebbaeus Thaddeus is the brother of James of Alphaeus—Cleophas (James the Less). This makes several of the brothers sons of Cleophas first cousins to Jesus. His name is discussed in detail in the entry for Thomas Didymus above. He is often confused with Thaddeus of Edessa, one of the "Seventy". He is most often referred to as "Jude". He is usually connected with Simon the "Zealot", and both are said to have perished in Syria in 69 CE, although Simon the "Zealot" was also a son of Cleophas and was the second leader of the Jerusalem assembly. Tradition states Thaddeus was born in Paneas (Caesarea Philipi) in Galilee.

SIMON THE KANANAIOS, OR KANANITES (THE "ZEALOT")

The son of Cleophas and Mary (and another brother of other apostles listed above), Simon was zealous for Torah. His title had nothing to do with being a member of the Zealot faction of Pharisees. He, too, was a first cousin to Jesus.

The exodus to Pella is said to have taken place under the leadership of Simon (Simeon) son of Cleophas, also a Zadokite. Hegesippus reported that Simon was chosen bishop directly after the death of James when the *relatives of Jesus* assembled with the surviving apostles and disciples to elect a successor.[28]

We are told by Eusebius, quoting Hegesippus, in at least two places that after the death of James, "Symeon, the son of Cleophas" became the leader of the Jerusalem *ekklesia*:

> (3.11) After the martyrdom of James [62 CE] and the taking of *Jerusalem* which immediately ensued, it is recorded that those apostles and disciples of the Lord who were still surviving met together from all quarters and, together with *the Lord's relatives after the flesh (for the more part of them were still alive)*, took counsel, all in common, as to whom they should judge worthy to be the successor of James; and, what is more, that they all with one consent approved Symeon the son of Clopas, of whom also the book of the Gospels makes mention, as worthy of *the throne of the community* in that place. *He was a cousin—so it is said—of the Saviour; for indeed Hegesippus relates that Clopas was Joseph's brother.*[29]

---

28. Eusebius III. xi. 1.
29. Ibid., III, xi. 1, italics mine.

> (4:22:4a) And after James the Just had suffered martyrdom, as had also the Lord, on the same account, the son of his [Jesus'] uncle, Symeon the son of Clopas, was next appointed bishop, whom, since he was a cousin of the Lord, they all put forward as the second.[30]

If Simon was the son of Cleophas, and Cleophas was Joseph's brother, the *despoysni* derived their lineage from *Joseph*, the paternal genealogy of Jesus, and not from the maternal (Mary's). The evidence is that Simon was, indeed, the first cousin to Jesus. He is also mentioned in Jewish documents as the author of the Gospel of the Hebrews (forerunner of Matthew in Hebrew letters), the Ascents of Jacob (called by Epiphanius the Acts of the Apostles, which in no way is associated with the canonical Acts), and the Book of John (the forerunner of Revelation).

> In a late Jewish source the composition of all three works is ascribed to Simeon ben Calpus, an honorable old man, stated to have been an uncle of Jesus. *The uncle, of course, was Calpus (Cleophas)* ... The man they select is "a certain aged man from among the Elders ... *who frequented the Holy of Holies*." He is called in one text Simeon Cepha, but correctly in another Simeon ben Calpus.[31]

"The substitution of Cephas for Calpus is understandable since Simeon Cephas (Peter) was better known."[32] Since he was known to go into the Holy of Holies, the proper assumption would be, like his cousin James, that he is a priest, and not only an ordinary priest but a high priest. For only a high priest can enter the Holy of Holies and then only one day a year on Yom Kippur (the Day of Atonement). This very fact would preclude that Cleophas, like his brother Joseph and his nephew James, was of the Zadokite priesthood. Their children, likewise, would be Zadokite priests.

> The Nazoraean sect exists in Beroea near Coele Syria, in the Decapolis near the region of *Pella*, and in Bashan in the place called Cocaba, which in Hebrew is called Chochabe. That is where the sect began, *when all the disciples were living in Pella after they moved form Jerusalem.*[33]

---

30. Ibid., IV, xxii. 4.
31. Schonfield, *The Jesus Party*, p. 231, italics mine.
32. Ibid., p. 238, n. 4.
33. Epiphanius, *Panarion* 29.7.7–8, italics mine.

Simon was executed by Trajan's (53–117 CE) governor, Atticus, as a descendant of David in 107 CE; however, it is unlikely he was "120 years" old. As Bauckman suggests, this number was established in the Old Covenant as the limit placed on man's lifetime and Hegesippus merely expressed a theological opinion. He might well have been an elderly man, since he is believed to have been a son of Cleophas and a member of the family, apparently known to Jesus as a young man. He might have been the unnamed disciple walking with Cleophas on the road to Emmaus. If he were twenty years old at the time of Jesus' execution, he would have been 97 or 98 years of age. Although, that is feasible, a Jewish boy becomes a man at the age of 13, so it is entirely possible he was about 89 years of age at the time of his death. "Justus" (Joses, Joseph), perhaps his brother, had succeeded the "throne" or seat at the Jerusalem community of *despoynoi* somewhat earlier. By 135 CE the community at Jerusalem was no longer headed by the "circumcised".

JUDAS ISCARIOT

The most infamous character in the New Testament gospels is Judas Iscariot. We are told that Judas "Iscariot" was a son of "Simon". This is only mentioned and is hardly noticeable in the list of apostles and elsewhere in the Gospel of John (John 6:71; 13:2; 13:26), but it leads us to the only other mention of him being Simon's son in the gospels, and it connects him with the family of Mary, Martha, and Eleazar (Lazarus). He is specifically mentioned as being Simon's son while in the house with Simon "the Leper", where Martha, a widow, was serving, Mary anointed Jesus, and Lazarus "was one of them that sat at table". Martha would not have been serving dinner in a stranger's house, nor would Mary, the student who had chosen the better part and "sat at the feet" of Jesus, wander in off the streets for the anointing. Needless to say, Lazarus was their brother and was also a member of that household. The feast was held in Bethany (Beth Hini) where the residences of the sages and priests were.

John 12:1–11:

> Then Jesus six days before the passover (9 Nisan 31 CE, a Friday) came to *Bethany* [Beth Hini], where *Lazarus* [Eleazar ben Simon] had been dead, whom he raised from the dead. *There they made him a supper* and *Martha* [who was a widow at the time] served: but *Lazarus* [Eleazar] was one of them that sat at the table with him. Then took *Mary* ["the Magdalene" of Bethany, "a woman" in

> the other gospels] a *pound of ointment of spikenard, very costly*, and anointed the feet of Jesus, and wiped his feet with her hair: and the house was filled with the odour of the ointment. Then saith one of his disciples, *Judas Iscariot, Simon's son* [Simon ben Cantheras ben Boethus], which should betray him, Why was not this *ointment sold for three hundred pence* and given to the poor? This he said not that he cared for the poor; but because he was a thief, and *had the bag, and bare what was put therein*. Then said, Jesus, Let her alone: *against the day of my burying* hath she kept this. For the poor always ye have with you; but me ye have not always. *Much people of the Jews therefore knew that he was there*: and they came not for Jesus' sake only, but that they might see *Lazarus* [Eleazar] also, whom he had raised from the dead. *But the chief priests consulted that they might put Lazarus* [Eleazar] *also to death*; because that by reason of him many of the Jews went away and believed on Jesus [italics mine].

Note that since they were in Simon's house it is reasonable to refer to Judas as "Simon's son". On the *surname* "Iscariot" see below.

Matthew 26:6–14:

> Now when Jesus was in *Bethany* [Beth Hini] *in the house of Simon the leper* (the "jar merchant") [remember, in John above, Judas Iscariot is named as "Simon's son"], there came unto him *a woman* [Mary the "Magdalene" of Bethany] *having an alabaster box of very precious ointment*, and poured it on his head, as he sat at meat. But *when his disciples saw it, they had indignation* [not only Judas], saying, to what purpose is this waste? For *this ointment might have been sold for much*, and given to the poor. When Jesus understood it, he said unto *them*, Why trouble ye the woman? For she hath wrought a good work upon me. For ye have the poor always with you; but me ye have not always. For in that *she hath poured this ointment on my body, she did it for my burial*. Verily I say unto you, wheresoever this gospel shall be preached in the whole world, there shall also this, that this woman hath done, be told for a memorial of her. Then one of the twelve called *Judas Iscariot* (the "Man of Kithros", Simon's son) went unto the chief priests . . ." [the family of Kithros or Kathros was known to have held a monopoly in the incense trade] [italics mine].

Mark 14:3–10:

> And being in *Bethany in the house of Simon the leper* [the alabaster jar merchant], as he sat at meat, there came *a woman* [Mary

Becoming Christian

the "Magdalene" of Bethany] *having an alabaster box of ointment of spikenard very precious*; and she brake the box, and poured it on his head. *And there were some that had indignation within themselves* [not only Judas], and said, Why was this waste of the ointment made? For it might have been *sold for more than three hundred pence*, and have been given to the poor. And they murmured against her. And Jesus said, Let her alone; why trouble ye her? *She hath wrought a good work on me.* For ye have the poor with you always, and whensoever ye will ye may do them good: but me ye have not always. She hath done what she could: she is come aforehand *to anoint my body to the burying*. Verily I say unto you, wheresoever this gospel shall be preached throughout the whole world, this also that she hath done shall be spoken of for a memorial of her. And *Judas Iscariot* [the "Man of Kithros", Simon's son], one of the twelve, went unto *the chief priests* [i.e., the Hanan and Kithros families], to betray him unto them [italics mine].

Luke 7:36–50:

And one of the *Pharisees* [Simon ben Cantheras ben Boethus, the "Leper", "jar merchant"] desired him that he would eat with him [remember, Simon ben Cantheras, son of Boethus was a Pharisee per Josephus]. And he went into the *Pharisee's* house, and sat down to meat. And, behold, *a woman in the city* [Mary the "Magdalene" of Bethany], which was a sinner, when she knew that Jesus sat at meat in the Pharisee's house, brought *an alabaster box of ointment*, and stood at his feet behind him weeping, and began to wash his feet with tears, and did wipe them with the hairs of her head, and kissed *his feet*, and *anointed them with the ointment*. Now when the *Pharisee* which had bidden him saw it, he spake within himself, saying, this man, if he were a prophet, would have known who and what manner of woman this is that toucheth him: for she is a sinner. And Jesus answering said unto him, *Simon*, I have somewhat to say unto thee. And he saith, Master, say on. There was a certain creditor which had two debtors: the one owed five hundred pence, and the other fifty. And when they had nothing to pay, he frankly forgave them both. Tell me therefore, which of them will love him most? Simon answered and said, I suppose that he, to whom he forgave most. And he said unto him, thou hast rightly judged. And he turned to *the woman*, and said unto *Simon*, seest thou this woman? I entered into thine house, thou gavest me no water for my feet: but she hath washed my feet with tears, and wiped them with the hairs of her head. Thou gavest me no kiss: but this woman

The Apostles

since the time I came in hath not ceased to kiss my feet. My head with oil thou didst not anoint: but *this woman hath anointed my feet with ointment*. Wherefore I say unto thee, her sins, which are many, are forgiven; for she loved much: but to whom little is forgiven, the same loveth little. And he said unto her, thy sins are forgiven. And they that sat at meat with him began to say within themselves, who is this that forgiveth sins also? And he said to the woman, thy faith hath saved thee; go in peace [italics mine].

If this is the meaning of Judas' patronymic, the "Man of the Kithros" (or "Incense") was also a title of his father and would indicate that the two were involved in both the spice and incense trade and in the finances of the city of Jerusalem through their temple service. The second portion of the name is not a name at all but a description of his occupation. Judas, "son of Simon", as even the New Testament confirms, was a member of the Kithros family. This Judas ben Boethus ("son of Simon") "surnamed Iscariot" was, in fact, most probably employed in providing incense for the temple. While he was probably in some way connected to the financial management of the temple, the patronymic "*kariotes*" might well be, as in the case of his uncle Elioneus, the corrupted Greek for the name *Cithaerus or Catheras,* (or Cantheras). Interestingly, there is one "Kyrthas" [Kirthos, Kerythros or Kithros] whose bones were located in the same tomb cave as those of Shalom–Zion (Salampsio), the daughter of "Simeon the Priest". The name Kyrthas is very similar to Catheras or Cithaerus (Kithros). The tomb site where these ossuaries were located is on the Mount of Offense just below Bethany and *above Alcedama*, or the "Field of Blood", where tradition holds Judas committed suicide. It is logical that his burial site might have been above the place where he committed suicide. His patronymic might well be "Judas, the man of Catheras" (or Cithyros/Kithros/Kithyros/Kytheros).

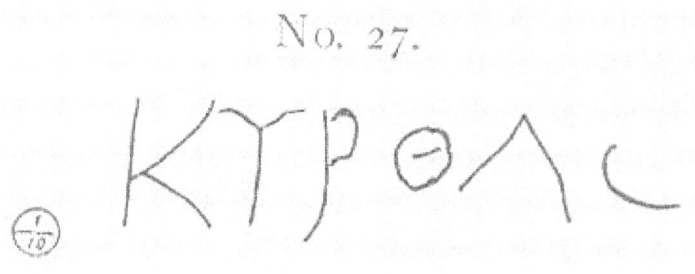

Becoming Christian

Photo Courtesy of Palestinian Exploration Fund

Charles Clermont-Ganneau is puzzled by the name. In his description he says: "A proper name of obscure derivation. Is it Hellenic, or the transcript of some Hebrew name(?)"[34]

It seems likely the origin of the name was Kithros but was corrupted to Caiaphas. Since the grandmother of the "Cantheras" children (Mary, Martha, Eleazar, Judas, Joseph, and Elioneus) is thought to be a sister of Joseph, it is likely the name took on different spellings and pronunciations as time passed.

> Of the four oligarchical families of the high priesthood noted by the Talmud, we know least about the house of Kithros. It is only by means of conjecture that we can assign several high priests to this family. One of them was Elionaeus, the last high priest appointed by Agrippa I, who took the place of Matthias ben Ananus. We read in the Mishnah that this Elionaeus was one of the high priests (the others being Hananel the Egyptian and Ishmael ben Phiabi) who prepared a red heifer. This Elionaeus is called Hakkof in the Mishnah. This suggests a connection between him and the high priest Joseph Caiaphas (known also as *ha kayafay*) of whom it can be conjectured that he too belonged to the house of Kithros.[35]

It is clear that at least four of Simon Cantheras' children were dissidents from their father's religious and political beliefs (Mary, Martha, Eleazar or "Lazarus", and Judas). A short study of Simon the "Leper" should clarify who this family is in relation to the New Testament gospels.

Simon ben Cantheras ben Boethus (served as high priest when James, the brother of John was executed in 43–44 CE) was named for *both* his parents since both families were prominent members of the high priesthood. The name "Cantheras" is found in many variants: Qadros, Qupha, Qyph, Quphai, ha-Qayaf, Qatros, Qatra, Qeypha, Qayapha and Qoph. All are variants of the same name or "house": Caiaphas! Since the younger Simon's mother was a member of the Caiaphas family, and since his own family was also well known—he was the son of Simon Boethus, the high priest—the logical thing for him to do in order to honor both his houses would be to take on the mother's family name as well, not at all unusual

---

34. Claremont-Ganneau, *Archeological*, p. 411.
35. Safrai, *The Jewish People*, Vol. 2, p. 608.

The Apostles

for the first century. He had married Mary, the daughter of Nakdimon ben Gurion (Nicodemus in the New Testament, son of Gurion or Gorion the Great) and his wife, Martha. This Martha was a sister of Joseph ben Gurion.

Simon and Mary the daughter of Nakdimon had several children, all of whom we have heard: 1) Mary the "Magdalene" ("The Great" of Bethany); 2) Martha, who married secondly Joshua (Jesus) ben Gamaliel, son of Simon and grandson of Gamaliel I (he served as high priest 63/64 CE); 3) Eleazar (Lazarus); 4) Judas (ish Kerioth—Kithros—"Man of Incense", "son of Simon"; 5) Joseph; and 6) Elioneus. This goes a long way in explaining why Nicodemus was said to have come to Jesus *by night* in order to pursue being "born from above". It probably didn't have that much to do with *secrecy* but more to do with *convenience* since Jesus was probably staying at the home of Nicodemus' daughter Mary and son-in-law Simon in Bethany. There was certainly no secrecy on behalf of Nicodemus at the time of Jesus' burial. Most likely, the encounter occurred at the house of Simon ben Cantheras ben Boethus and his wife Mary, a daughter of Nicodemus and mistress of the household while Jesus was abiding there.

These first century ossuaries of which we are concerned in Alkedama are inscribed with names like Shalom-Zion (Salampsio, Salome), daughter of Simeon the Priest [#311] Judas (or Judah), son of Eleazar [Lazar] the Scribe, Marias or Mariodos, and Salome, wife of Judah, Nathanel, and Jesus. The tomb site was apparently the resting-place for a family of priests. It is my suggestion that it was the burial tomb for part of the Boethus family who were not entombed in either the Caiaphas crypt or in the catacombs at Dominus Flevit. There is also a Salampsio or Shalom-Zion [#323] in the catacombs at Dominus Flevit where the ossuaries of Simon Peter and Mary, Martha, and Eleazar (Lazarus) are found. The name is quite unique and is found only in the Herodian and Hasmonean families and their allies and kinsmen. Josephus names one Salampsio as a daughter of Herod the Great and his Hasmonean wife, Mariamne (I). The name is apparently derived from Queen Shalom-Zion, her grandmother. Since the Hasmonean and Boethus families each had a daughter named Mariamne, both of whom had married Herod the Great, it is not a great leap to the conclusion that the name was continued in both families.

Judas is surnamed "Iscariot". The Greek word for "surnamed" is *epikaleomai* meaning "entitled" or "called by a title"; it is the equivalent of the Hebrew *kanah*, "to eulogize" or "give a flattering title". Using the English word "surnamed" is at the least misleading, since surnames were not used in the

99

Becoming Christian

first century and developed long centuries afterward. Rather, a person was known and referred to by his occupation or title, or by his father's name. Another example of this is found in Acts 4:36 where Joseph (Barnabas) has been "surnamed" by the apostles. "Barnabas" means "son of consolation" or "son of exhortation", but his name was really Joses (or Joseph), a Levite.

We know Judas took care of the "bag" for the ministry of Jesus. The Talmud and Tosefta (as we have already learned) reveal that the sons of the high priests were treasurers. It was he who went to the high priests (those who managed the money) to ask for a bounty for Jesus. He would have gone to the shekel chamber to meet with three administrative treasurers. They would have distributed the money for a seven-man council of supervisors. These were not the priests. These were men, who along with the supervisors acted in behalf of the high priests. The controller was possibly the *segan* of the Temple. It was probably this man (perhaps Helcias ben Hanan) who would have had the authority to issue the money from the treasury.

It was Judas' sister's (Mary's) behavior, an uncomely behavior in his opinion, that had pushed him over the edge. Even though he was wealthy in his own right, he was also greedy (as was the elder Annas). Greedy, though, he might have been he, apparently, was attempting to force Jesus' hand or trying to protect him. He might have believed that if he betrayed his whereabouts to the guard that Jesus would then "take the kingdom". Perhaps he was young and impetuous and favored the Zealot cause. Or perhaps, *he believed his father, Simon, might have been able to protect Jesus*. The fact is Judas Kithros ("Iscariot") was a Zadokite priest, a son of Simon Cantheras, the son of Boethus, and was permitted to go into the Holy Place in the Temple. Ernest Martin explored this is in his book *The Secrets of Golgotha*.

> Note that after Judas betrayed Christ to the chief priests, they gave him thirty pieces of silver to hand Jesus over to them when they were no crowds around that might prevent his arrest (Luke 22:6). Later, when Judas had realized what he had done (and became remorseful for it), *he took those coins to the Temple and threw them over the floor of the naos* (A Greek word meaning the holy place into which only Aaronic priests could enter) (Matt. 27:5). But note this! The original Greek of a large number of New Testament manuscripts on Matthew 27:5 says that *Judas scattered the coins while in the holy place* (see The Greek New Testament, UBS, p. 108). *This verse shows that Judas was inside a part of the Temple which was reserved only for priests.* It means that Judas was in fact a priest ... but the thirty shekels of silver that Judas obtained (no

doubt from monies deposited in the Temple treasury) were reckoned by the priests to be "blood money" (Matt. 27:6–8). Importantly, we have seen in Matthew 27:5 that Judas the priest scattered the thirty shekels (representing the blood of Christ) while he was *within the very Holy Place where the priests sprinkled the blood of the sin offerings* which we have just mentioned (Lev. 4:1–21). This would have been, in a symbolic sense, an official sprinkling of the blood of Christ by an ordained priest (Judas) within the very place ordained by Moses.[36]

Had Judas been a simple disciple or "fisherman" he would not have been allowed into the Holy Place. Something gave him the authority to be able to enter that restricted area. That "something" was the fact that he was a son of Simon Cantheras, the son of Boethus by whom he would have received his Aaronic blood and thus become a priest like his father. Like "Lazarus" (Eleazar) he was "kin" to the high priest (Caiaphas was his great uncle).

In conclusion, the family of Simon Cantheras (Caiaphas/Kithros) the so-called "Leper" (and high priest) and Mary Nakdimon included:

1. Mary the Magdalene ("The Great")
2. Martha who married both Gorion ben Nakdimon, her uncle, and Joshua ben Gamaliel
3. Eleazar (Lazarus), a priest
4. Judas, a priest
5. Elieonai, a high priest
6. Joseph, a high priest

THE DISCIPLE WHOM JESUS LOVED IN JOHN (NOT ONE OF THE TWELVE)

Eleazar, otherwise known in the Gospel of John as Lazarus, is the most likely candidate for that "Disciple Whom Jesus Loved". He had appeared at the feast at Simon's (his father's) house and again at the "Last Supper", and as heir, leaning on Jesus' breast. To lie in the bosom was a known phrase to indicate heirship. Evan Powell quotes W. H. Brownlee in giving an example: Jacob, while reclining on his deathbed, confers his final blessing on his

---

36. Martin, *Secrets*, pp. 267–268, italics mine.

Becoming Christian

grandson. In other words, this traditional Hebrew procedure of designating an heir and known as "lying in the bosom" is prerequisite for conferring on one the blessings and substance of the testator. It would also include the responsibilities and duties that the decedent would leave behind; i.e., accepting the duty of the firstborn in caring for a widowed mother. Since James, the brother of Jesus, had devoted his life to the Temple, he would not have been able to provide for his mother.

It was this disciple who was able to stand at the foot of the execution tree without fear of death (he'd already experienced it) and did not flee as did the rest of the disciples. It was he who took the care of Mary, the mother of Jesus, and he who likely wrote the first narrative of the gospel attributed to the later redaction of "John" and the book of Revelation. This young man was also probably the "rich young ruler" who had, before his demise, been unable to part with his money (see Clement's *Secret Gospel of Mark* below).

> And they went to Bethany and there was *a woman* [Martha] *whose brother* [Eleazar/Lazarus] *had died.* And coming up to him, she prostrated herself before Jesus and said to him, 'Son of David, have mercy on me.' But the disciples rebuked her. And becoming angry, Jesus went with her to the garden where the tomb was. And immediately a great sound was heard from the tomb, and Jesus, going toward it rolled away the stone from the entrance to the tomb. And going in immediately where the young man was, he stretched out a hand and raised him up, holding his hand. Then, *the man looked at him and loved him* and he began to call him to his side, that he might be with him. And going from the tomb, they went to the house of the young man. *For he was rich . . . And the sister* [Mary] *of the young man* [Eleazar/Lazarus] *whom Jesus loved was there*, as well as his mother [Mary, the daughter of Nicodemus] and Salome [Salampsio bat Boethus, her aunt, the wife of Zebedee].[37]

All the other disciples fled in fear and "hid out" until after the resurrection, including John! It was *this* disciple, Eleazar (Lazarus) who ran with Peter (Simon bar Yonah) to the empty sepulchre. Although he arrived first, he did not enter (due to his indoctrination in priestly purity laws) but let Peter enter first. Only a priest might have had the inclination not to "touch a dead body" or enter a tomb at the time of Passover. There were, however, two priests named Eleazar ben Boethus. The elder was his uncle, a son of Simon ben Boethus the Elder who had served in the temple in 4–3 BCE, shortly after the retirement of his brother.

37. Secret Gospel of Mark, Plate II, II Folios 1 and 2 Recto, italics mine.

This second younger Eleazar [Lazarus], it will be noticed, was able to enter into the temple and trial of Jesus while Peter (who was not a priest) waited outside in the courtyard. Further, he was "known" of the high priest (since his grandmother, Mary, was a sister of Joseph Caiaphas)! The word "known" (*gnostos*), however, does not simply mean acquainted with; it means "well-known", "kin to" or "intimate with".[38] As a priest belonging to the Boethus–Caiaphas family, himself, he would have been allowed into the proceedings. Lazarus and Peter, who were obviously close, were both interred in ossuaries found within feet of each other in the catacombs of the Dominus Flevit Chapel.

The Boethus family had derived from Alexandria in Egypt, a priestly family having descended from the Oniads, the legitimate Zadokite priesthood from the house of Aaron.

MATTHIAS IN ACTS

The appointment of Matthias took place just before Pentecost. Matthias is only mentioned twice by name in the New Testament in the book of Acts as a replacement for Judas Iscariot. "And they gave forth their lots; and the lot fell upon Matthias; and he was numbered with the eleven apostles" (Acts 1:26). There are numerous traditions about his ministry and his death. Nicephorus claimed he had preached in both Judea and in Cochis (modern-day Georgia),[39] but another tradition claims he was stoned and beheaded in Jerusalem. Hippolytus of Rome claimed he died of old age in Jerusalem. His death is generally dated between 52–62 CE. Since there were others who were executed with James, the brother of Jesus, we might well suspect that he was killed at the same time. He has been identified by the church fathers variously as Tolmai, Nathanael, Zacchaeus, and in the Clementine Recognitions as Barnabas.

Matthias was chosen as the "twelfth" apostle from the Seventy disciples who had been appointed by Jesus himself. "Therefore, it is necessary that one of the men who accompanied us the whole time the Lord Jesus came and went among us, beginning from the baptism of John until the day on which he was taken up from us, become with us a witness to his resurrection" (Act 1:21–22). Thus the appointment of the seventy disciples occurred at the very beginning of Jesus' immersion.

38. Thayer, *The New Thayer's*, pp. 119–120.
39. Historia Eccl. 2, 40.

Becoming Christian

The interesting thing about the appointment of Matthias is that he is replacing an original member of the twelve. If there was a need for a twelfth apostle, what about James, the brother of John (43–44 CE)? Who was appointed to replace him? We are not given any information about that at all. Neither do we know how many other apostles were killed or died during the days shortly after the resurrection. Peter himself might well have died between 43–44 and 62 CE, yet we have no replacement that we are aware of for him, either. Matthias himself is believed to have died (at the earliest date) in 52 CE. Again, we have no information on who replaced him. We might assume that it could have been Joseph Barsabbas, known as "Justus" since he is believed to have been the third leader of the Jerusalem community. The definition of an apostle appears to have been one who had been with Jesus from the beginning, meaning from his immersion in the Jordan until the resurrection (Acts 2:21–22). Paul refers to two who might well have been of the Seventy apostles: "Salute Andronicus and Junia, my kinsmen, and my fellow prisoners, *who are of note among the apostles*, who also were in Christ before me" (Rom 16:2, italics mine). This appears to mean they were with Jesus from the beginning.

Matthias, the replacement apostle is said to have been killed in "Ethiopia"; however, that location was Georgia, along the coasts of the Euxine (Black Sea) and not in Africa as most might associate that country. Yet there is another tradition that he had been stoned in Jerusalem (which is probably more accurate), and another that he died of old age in Jerusalem. Georgian Jews date their community there to the sixth century BCE (in other words, during the Assyrian captivity of northern Israel). This would be one location of the captivity of the "lost sheep of the House of Israel" to which Jesus referred. Because Jesus used that phrase in his description of the people he was to preach to, it was generally assumed that he was speaking of that northern captivity, but he was, instead, referring to the Judean kingdom, not these northern Hebrews who were not truly "Jews" at all. The reference to the word "Jew" derived during the Babylonian Captivity of the inhabitants of "Judea", thus they were referred to by the Babylonians as "Jews" or "Judah". The Hebrews of northern Israel were never Jews because they did not belong to Judea; they were, instead, known as "Ephraim" at the time of the Assyrian invasion. The tradition of Matthias being crucified in Colchis then is probably not historical. It would be much more logical for Matthias to have been stoned in Jerusalem during the period of Ananias the High Priest (52–59 CE), a time of conflict between the high priests and the lesser priests and apparently, the apostles and James, beginning in Jerusalem about this time. Ananias is known in the Talmud as a aristocratic glutton, lavishly feeding himself and his household with the sacrifices. They use a play on words as a nickname for him [אקניפ] Pinka, a meat dish. The persecution continued into the reign of Ishmael ben Phiabi II. This was the situation in 61–62 CE when James, the brother of Jesus, was executed by the next priest, Ananus II (son of Annas). It might be that James was defending the poor priests. The conflict went on for quite some time and involved several different high priests.

Just this one example of the mission of Matthias serves as a lesson for the, sometimes, outrageous stories and traditions about the rest of the apostles.

CONCLUSION

Of the above apostles there were teams of brothers: Peter and Andrew, James and John, and the sons of Cleophas and Mary; James the Less, Judas Thomas Didymus, Judas Lebbaeus Thaddeus, Matthew Levi, Joseph (Joses, not mentioned as a disciple), and Simon, five brothers, all cousins to Jesus. Although John Mark was not an apostle either, he was mentioned as a son of Mary and nephew of Barnabas (one of the "seventy") who was her brother, so he also would have been a cousin to Jesus. Her brother, Aristobulus III, mentioned as a brother to Barnabas would have been another cousin as well as Peter's father-in-law. If Lazarus, Martha and Mary were related to Jesus (a circumstance that has been suggested by a number of scholars), then Judas Iscariot was, too, for these are the children of Simon Cantheras Boethus the "Leper" and Mary Nakdimon. This would mean that at least half the disciples were Jesus' cousins. Since Peter was Mary's and Cleophas' brother-in-law, he and his brother Andrew would have been viewed as the family of Jesus as well. Zebedee and Salome are believed to have been Joseph's uncle and aunt, so that, too, would have made the brothers James and John the relatives of Jesus. If Nathaniel had married Jesus' sister, and that appears to have been the case, he would have been his brother-in-law. Philip is the only odd apostle, but if he is Philip Boethus, the son of Herod and Mariamne II, then, he too would have been related through the family of Mary, Barnabas, and Aristobulus III. This would have made the inner circle of apostles and disciples a close-knit family. Since Mary, Jesus' mother, and his brothers followed him to Capernaum as stated earlier, we might assume that this movement was a family affair.

5

Antioch and Transculturation

ANTIOCH ON THE ORONTES, also known as Syrian Antioch, became the new Babylonian capitol near the end of the fourth century BCE. Seleucus Nicator I, one of Alexander's generals, chose the location for its geography. It served as a military and economic location, lying along the Silk Road and the spice trade route. By the Hellenistic and early Roman periods the population has been estimated at 400,000 to 600,000 and Antioch then became the third largest city behind Rome and Alexandria. Rome tried to make it a second "Rome", enhancing its structures and building temples, streets, colonnades, and public baths, but it was really the "New Babylon". What Seleucus Nicator did was to establish the city by transferring the Babylonian priests from the temple of the sun god to Antioch.

> The Babylonian priests became the foremost of Antioch's citizens. Antioch had "a high Greek civilization mixed with various eastern elements and especially with the superstitions of Chaldean [Babylonian] astrology" (Smith's Geography, vol. I, p. 143). It is a simple fact that the Seleucid empire soon became a Babylonian or a Chaldean one in its religious and societal affairs. It was simply a matter of moving the political and religious centers west to Antioch ... In other words, Syria and the Seleucid Empire were saturated with Chaldean and Babylonian teaching. Its religion and philosophies, while using Greek names and Greek cultural words, were nevertheless thoroughly Babylonian. The temperaments of those people who moved to Antioch and Syria were suited to such a religion.[1]

1. Martin, *The People*, pp. 139–140.

Becoming Christian

Those individuals referred to as "Greek" were, in fact, not Greek in ethnicity. They were Babylonians and Mesopotamians who had been steeped in Hellenism. Even the large colony of Hellenistic Jews that had been transported there was, in fact, called "Greek". All these people had been affected by Alexander's Hellenic influence, and although they were ethnically easterners, they had been living in a Hellenistic culture. Thus, not only had they brought the societal norms of the Greeks with them, they also brought the influence of the Babylonian religions, including their calendar.

During the first century the majority of the Jews in Antioch were, in fact, Hellenists. In Acts 11:20 some men of Cyprus and Cyrene (Hellenists themselves) went to Antioch to speak to the "Grecians". The word "Grecians" is the term in the New Testament used for Hellenistic Jews. This was the first instance that we hear of a new "church" in Antioch, and it is comprised of "Grecians" or Hellenistic Jews since they preached "the word to none but unto the Jews only" (Acts 11:19). When James and the community in Jerusalem heard of it, they sent Barnabas (also a Hellenist from Cyprus) to learn about what was occurring there (11:22). Because Saul (Paul) was himself a Hellenized Jew and had experience of speaking to Grecians, Barnabas went to Tarsus (in Turkey) to find him and bring him back to Antioch. Barnabas had been the only disciple to stand with him before the Jerusalem council. He had not had much luck preaching to the Grecians in Damascus. Those who were associated with the Jerusalem community had taken Saul to Caesarea and sent him back to Damascus, after which "the churches [had] rest throughout all Judaea and Galilee and Samaria, and were edified; and walking in the fear of the LORD [Yahweh], and in the comfort of the Holy Ghost [Spirit], were multiplied" (9:31). This means the movement had already been established all over the countries of Judea and Galilee as well as Samaria. It is apparent that the entire movement was in fear of Paul. Once he had been sent back to Tarsus the atmosphere cleared. But this new development far from Jerusalem needed attention, and the person who came to mind was Saul (as he was still referred to—11:25). Barnabas had been unable to cope with the community alone.

This occurred sometime before 42–43 CE at the time of the famine during the reign of Claudius, because at that time "came prophets from Jerusalem unto Antioch" (11:27) prophesying " a great dearth throughout all the world: which came to pass in the days of Claudius Caesar" (28). About this same time King Herod Agrippa I had executed James, the brother of

John (and, perhaps, John as well), later arresting Peter and others during the intermediate days between Passover and Pentecost (Acts 12:1-4). We are not given a reason; however, when we learn that Jonathan ben Ananus (a son of the high priest Annas) was high priest at the time, we might assume that the vendetta between the House of Hanan and the family and disciples of Jesus was the cause. Peter and John had been brought before him and his family a number of years before. "And Annas the high priest, and Caiaphas, and John [Jonathan], and Alexander, and *as many as were of the kindred of the high priest* [Annas here], were gathered together [i.e, as a legal criminal court] at Jerusalem" (Acts 4:6, italics mine).

They had tried, at the time, to have the two disciples executed, and there is little doubt that Jonathan had influenced Agrippa to sanction their capture and execution. They had been unable to do so at the time because of the people. After Peter's escape, he left Jerusalem with John Mark and went to Babylon where a large colony of Jews were still residing and where there was a Nazaraean settlement already established (1 Pet 5:13).

Among the members of the Antiochan assembly were certainly Hellenists: Simeon called Niger, Lucius of Cyrene, and Manaen, who had been brought up with Herod Agrippa II and "Saul" (Acts 13:1). Barnabas was also named among them and was from Cyprus himself. The Cypriot and Cyrenian Jews were also under Hellenistic influence, and that is probably why he had been sent to Antioch as a minister. Joses (Barnabas) had been in the company of the Jerusalem community since the day Peter and John had been arrested and appeared before the criminal court, had seen the miracle they had performed, and was fully indoctrinated in the brotherhood (Acts 4:36-37). Although he had been a wealthy Hellenist Jew, a Levite, from Cyprus he became a disciple and follower of Jesus. He sold his land (presumably in Cyprus where he had been born) and "laid it at the apostles' feet" (37). He became known as the "Son of Consolation" or "Son of Exhortation", but that title has to do with his status as a charitable rich man. He gave "comfort" and "encouragement" to the apostles and the community by providing them with his great wealth.

It was decided that "Saul" and Barnabas, who along with John Mark (called "John" in this portion of Acts) would then depart from Antioch on a missionary journey. They first went to Seleucia and then to Cyprus where Sergius Paulus was then the "deputy" [curator] appointed under Claudius in the year 47 CE. By the time they reached Cyprus, Saul was also referred to as Paul (Acts 13:9). John Mark left them at Pamphylia and returned to Jerusalem, most likely to report of their activities to that point.

After leaving Perga [Pergamon] they went on the Sabbath day to a synagogue in Antioch in Pisidia near the Tarsus Mountains. This was an area Paul probably knew quite well. After Paul preached to the Jews, the Gentiles also wanted to hear their message the following Sabbath. But when they "saw the multitudes, they were filled with envy, and spake against those things which were spoken by Paul, contradicting and blaspheming" (Acts 13:44). These Jews did not want Gentiles to become God-Fearers or Proselytes within their synagogue, so they expelled the evangelists from the land.

Once they arrived in Iconium they again "both together" went into the synagogue of the Jews, and both orthodox Jews and "Greeks" (Hellenized Jews) believed. Those who did not believe stirred up the crowds to stone them, so the pair left there and went on to Lystra and Derbe, where they were hailed as "gods". While in Iconium certain Jews from Antioch and Iconium, "who persuaded the people, and, having stoned Paul, drew him out of the city, supposing he had been dead" (Acts 14:19). Barnabas, apparently, was either not with him or was not stoned. Eventually, they made their way through Pergamon (one of the seven cities of Revelation) and Attalia and returned to Antioch.

Back in Antioch they reported their successes and failures. Word of this must have gotten back to James in Jerusalem because "certain men which came down from Judaea [and] taught the brethren, and said, Except ye be circumcised after the manner of Moses, ye cannot be saved" (15:1). A debate ensued and it was suggested that Barnabas and Paul go to Jerusalem to the apostles and elders about the matter. At this time, Barnabas was uncertain as to whether the Gentiles might be brought into the movement without circumcision (As God-Fearers), and this is probably the cause of the argument between he and Paul later on.

The council took place in about 50 CE, and James decided, and the community of elders and apostles agreed, that the Gentiles could become God-fearers (thus, they did not have to be circumcised), but they could not become Jewish proselytes unless they were circumcised. As proselytes the Gentiles might attend synagogue but did not have the restrictions of kosher diet. Neither might they worship other gods nor commit immoral sexual acts (which went along with idol worship). In other words, they could keep the Noachide commandments but did not have a *full* position

Antioch and Transculturation

in the community. It was decided that Paul was not to preach to the Jews (Hellenistic or otherwise) but only to the Gentiles from this point forward (although he did). This was agreeable to all parties, and he and Barnabas returned to Antioch. For some time afterward the two preached in Antioch, Barnabas presumably preaching to the Jews and Paul to the Gentiles. Silas, who had also gone to Antioch, had remained there, and Paul and he became close, and when it was time to take another journey Paul and Barnabas argued. Presumably, the argument was over whether or not to take John Mark with them; however, under cover it is likely that Paul wanted to preach to Jews in other countries and Barnabas objected. It was at this time that Barnabas took his nephew Mark and went home to Cyprus. Paul, on the other hand, took with him Silas and went "through Cilicia and Syria *confirming the churches*" (15:41, italics mine). This meant that he was returning to the places where he had preached to Jews! He was even forced to circumcise Timothy in order to pacify the Jews because his father was a "Greek" (16:3).

The majority of the congregation in Antioch, in fact, consisted of Hellenist Jews and Gentiles who had become influenced by the eastern mystery religions in their cultural surroundings. They had respected and tolerated other religions around them to the point that they adapted some of their religious practices to their own. Quite early, the Jewish portion of the congregation was overwhelmed by the Gentiles and they began to be derogatorily referred to as "Christians" (Acts 11:26). The Roman church claims Peter had been the first bishop of Antioch, but there is no evidence whatsoever for that conclusion. Peter was only in Antioch once but returned to Jerusalem when confronted by men sent from James for having table fellowship with Gentiles. He was present in Jerusalem at the community council in 50 CE, but we hear nothing further of him. By the year 52 CE Peter was either dead or no longer in Jerusalem.

Paul appears to have been the driving force in Antioch. The next leader of the assembly there is referred to as Evodius who died in 69 CE. Evodius was a pagan who had converted to Christianity, so we can assume he was a Gentile. If he died as early as 69 CE then it is likely (if he served at all) that he was the leader from about 58 or 60 CE until his death. Antioch was a pagan city full of Babylonian Gentiles. Here begins a parting of the ways between the Jesus movement and the universal church (which became known as Christianity).

Becoming Christian

Pagan influences filtered into the Antiochan community after the demise of the apostles and of Paul who were no longer around to curb the tendencies of the Gentile members to return to their old religions. The third leader was Ignatius (ca 50–108 CE), who is referred to as the "bridge" between the early Jesus movement and the Roman church. He was steeped in and influenced by the mystery religions as is evident in his letters. He is acclaimed by later church fathers to have been a student of John the apostle and a friend of Polycarp, who it is said was also a "hearer of John", although this must be taken with a grain of salt. Most likely, John was executed along with his brother James in 42–43 CE in Jerusalem.

It was Ignatius who glorified the "bishops" of the day and it is faith in his alleged words that formed the basis for the following ideas: 1) that Jesus established the Catholic (universal) church; 2) that nothing should be done "without the bishop"; 3) that everything the bishop approves of is approved of God; 4) the virgin birth (even claiming to have had correspondence with Mary); 5) and that his authority derived from John the apostle (probably long dead). Needless to say, there are numerous legends about the earliest "fathers" and the apostles. The letters of Ignatius are the root of the doctrines and dogmas of the church and established what within his lifetime becames the Roman "universal" church. He, too, had been a pagan and was reared in a pagan household but is said to have converted to Christianity at an early age. He carried along with him in his conversion the concepts and ideas of his former religion.

It appears that Ignatius and Polycarp were members of the Johannine Community (as promulgated by Raymond Brown) and that would have been in Antioch. Ignatius is believed to have been the first Christian writer to urge replacement of the Jewish Sabbath (Friday–Saturday) with the church's Lord's Day (Sunday). He also promoted the idea that the bread involved in "Communion" is the literal flesh of Christ who was sacrificed for our sins.

> See that ye all follow the bishop, even as Christ Jesus does the Father, and the presbytery as ye would the apostles. Do ye also reverence the deacons, as those that carry out the appointment of God. Let no man do anything connected with the Church without the bishop. Let that be deemed a proper Eucharist, which is [administered] either by the bishop, or by one to whom he has entrusted it. Wherever the bishop shall appear, there let the multitude also be; by the bishop, or by one to whom he has entrusted it. Wherever

Antioch and Transculturation

the bishop shall appear, there let the multitude also be; even as, wherever Jesus Christ is, there is the Catholic Church.[2]

Theodoret of Cyrrhus claims that Peter himself appointed Ignatius as bishop; however, since we know that Ignatius did not begin to serve in that capacity until the death of Evodius in 69 CE and Peter died long before that (probably about 52 CE), that tradition would be quite impossible.

When Ignatius wrote the Letter to the Smyrnaeans in about the year 107 and used the word *catholic, he used it as if it were a word already in use to describe the church*. This has led many scholars to conclude that the appellation "Catholic Church" with its ecclesiastical connotation may have been in use as early as the last quarter of the first century.

It was during this Antiochan period that the dogma of the Roman church begins to be placed in the New Testament. Arising from Antioch were the infancy gospels and the Protoevangelium of James (also referred to as the Gospel of James) which describes Mary's perpetual virginity, and it was the influence of the Babylonian mystery religions in Antioch that gave rise to those writings. This author claiming to be "James" (long dead) states Jesus was born in a cave like Mithras, the sun god of Babylon and mentions the magi (astrologers), the like of which were also to be found in Antioch as early as 300 CE. This so-called gospel is generally dated about 125 CE, and seems to derive from the fact that Ignatius was supposed to have corresponded with Mary. There are, in the lists of the letters written by Ignatius, in the Latin form "one to the Virgin Mary and one from Mary to Ignatius."[3] He was certainly indoctrinated in the idea that Mary was a virgin when she gave birth to Jesus, a concept found only in the mystery religions, something that would have been repugnant to the early Jewish followers of Jesus.

Returning to the period of time in which the movement first appeared in Antioch, it must be remembered that Judea and Galilee were governed by the Roman Republic under the rule of kings. The world of Jesus was first century Judea, Galilee, and Samaria that were governed by kings and prefects (later procurators), an entirely different social structure than that of Syria. Syria was an area considered a crossroads to the larger empire and socially Hellenistic.

---

2. Ignatius of Antioch, *Epistle to the Smyrneans* 8:2 (c. A.D. 110).
3. 11th ed. Encyclopedia Brittanica, 1911.

Becoming Christian

> Success in Antioch established Christianity socially on a new footing. From here the lines of communication run westwards to the other great cities of the Mediterranean, "Syrus in Tiberim defluxit Orontes" (Juvenal, *Sat.* 3.62), What is heard today on the Orontes, is repeated tomorrow on the Tiber. Thus once the sect is established beyond the homeland of its parent religion, at least within the Roman area, which is as far as our records go, it belongs inevitably, as a social phenomenon, to the Hellenistic republics. Its thinking and behaviour naturally reflect the social institutions of these states. In political terminology it is not now so much a matter of rulers, kings, and nations, as of republics, assemblies, and magistrates.[4]

The communication between Antioch and the larger empire brought together two different types of cultures and two different religions. It was inevitable that the two would eventually merge into a single religion. A battle ensued between the Gentile leaders in Antioch who were opposed by those of the original movement in Judea. The Gentiles began to fall away from the original teachings of the apostles and referred to them as "Judaizers," including Paul himself (Gal 2:1–5; 2:14). He referred to them as "false brethren" (vs. 4). His bitter statements about those who "*seemed to be somewhat*, (whatsoever they were, it maketh no matter to me)" clearly indicates that his gospel is different from that of the apostles. He makes mention (in vs. 9) that "James, Cephas [Peter], and John . . . *seemed to be pillars*." His words imply that he no longer recognizes their authority. He had not, at first, recognized their authority (Gal 1:17). The Galatians had been visited by some of these original apostles because Paul states that "though we, or an angel from heaven, preach any other gospel unto you than that which we have preached unto you, let him be accursed. As we said before, so say I now again, If any man preach any other gospel unto you than that ye have received [from Paul], let him be accursed" (Gal 8–9). There can be little doubt that he is referring to the apostles and community of Jerusalem in that he claims they *seemed* to be those in authority. Thus the conflict still existed. What the Jerusalem community wanted was for Gentiles to be circumcised if they were to become *full members* of the community (proselytes). Otherwise, they might worship in the synagogues but not be members of the larger organization. If they chose to live according to the Noachide commands they could only become God–Fearers (σεβόμενοι), meaning to "live according to Jewish customs". God–Fearers were like

---

4. Judge, *Social Distinctives*, p. 8.

visitors in the synagogue. They might not participate in all the worship services, whereas a proselyte became a "Jew" and was able to conduct himself in any community business or religious rites.

Judaism was attractive to many Gentiles. Many of them became "Jews" called Proselytes and enjoyed all the privileges of an ethnic Jew, but those who simply wanted to visit the synagogue (God–Fearers) were limited in their scope of interaction within the larger community. As God–Fearers they did not have to give up their Hellenistic life styles and were able to continue having "table fellowship" with others who were not of the same religion. Proselytes could not have table fellowship with most God–Fearers because of their associations, the two groups differing in ritual purifications. For example, when Peter converted Cornelius and his household, they became Proselytes and not God–Fearers. Thus, Paul's gospel of faith in an ethereal Christ was suitable for most Gentiles. True Proselytes to the Jesus Movement were Jews in every sense, except ethnicity. They were "believers" in the teachings of Jesus the Messiah, a man who they believed fulfilled the Old Covenant prophecies and was resurrected from the dead by the Almighty God, Yahweh.

Antioch was the first to include Gentiles within the community founded in Jerusalem. Since Antioch was located at the crossroads to the larger empire it served as a parting of the ways. By 53–60 CE it had become a "Gentile church", no longer viewing Jesus as a man at all but as God himself. By the year 69 the rituals and beliefs of the mystery religions had crept into theology and changed the religion forever.

6

Pella and the *Despoysni*

We have not met our forgotten ancestors, but we begin to sense their presence in the dark. We recognize their shadows here and there. They were once as real as we are. We would not be here if not for them. Our natures and theirs are indisolubly linked despite the aeons that may separate us. The key to who we are is waiting in those shadows.

CARL SAGAN

As MENTIONED IN AN earlier chapter the original Nazaraeans from the Jerusalem community split into two groups. This schism probably came at the death of James, the brother of Jesus. It is helpful to give a little background information on the circumstances that led to his death and the destruction of the temple and Jerusalem. Since about 52 CE the high priesthood, beginning with Ananias ben Nebedeus, became more and more corrupt and began sending their servants to steal the tithes from the lesser priests, causing them and their families to starve to death. Ananias son of Nedebaios,[1] called "Ananias ben Nebedeus" in the Book of Acts was the high priest that presided during the trial of Paul at Jerusalem and Caesarea. He officiated as high priest from about 52 to 59 CE. Quadratus, governor of Syria, had accused him of being responsible for acts of violence, and Ananias was sent to Rome for trial but had been acquitted by the emperor

---

1. Josephus, *Ant.* 20.5.2.

Claudius. Being a friend of the Romans, he was murdered by the people at the beginning of the First Jewish–Roman War.

Ananias is known in the Talmud as an aristocratic glutton, lavishly feeding himself and his household with the sacrifices. They use a play on words as a nickname for him [אקניפ] Pinka, a meat dish.

> The Temple Court cried out: 'Lift up your heads O ye gates, and let Johanan the son of Narbai, the disciple of Pinkai, enter and fill his stomach with the Divine Sacrifices. It was said of Johanan b. Narbai that he ate three hundred calves and drank three hundred barrels of wine and ate forty sea'ah of young birds as a dessert for his meal. And it was said: As long as Johanan the son of Narbai lived; nothar was never found in the Temple.[2]

Hananiah spelled backwards gave Yochanan (Johanan). The twenty-fourth psalm of David had the line: "The temple court cried out 'Lift up your heads, O ye gates and let the King of glory enter in.'" The sages used this verse to indicate that Ananias was greedy and a glutton. Pinqai suggested *pinka*, a dish of stewed meat with onions to which the high priest was partial.

Considering the conflict between the priesthood and the lower priests at the time of James' death in 62 CE (and it had been going on since at least 52 CE), there appears to have been a persecution of the priestly community in general by the high priesthood. No doubt some of these priests were probably Nazaraeans: "And the word of God increased; and the number of disciples multiplied in Jerusalem greatly; and *a great company of the priests were obedient to the faith*" (Acts 6:7, italics mine).

Ishmael ben Phiabi II had been appointed to the office by Agrippa II in the year 59 CE, and enjoyed the sympathy of the people because of his ability to purchase their obedience. He was very rich. For instance, his mother made him, for the Day of Atonement, a priestly robe which cost 100 minae. After Yom Kippur, he donated them to the Mikdash.[3]

Josephus gives us a history of the persecution of the lesser priests by the aristocratic high priests.

> About this time king Agrippa (Agrippa II, the tetrarch) gave the high-priesthood to *Ismael*, who was *the son of Fabi* [Ishmael ben Phiabi]. And now arose a sedition between the high-priests and the principal men of the multitude of Jerusalem; each of whom

2. b. Pesah. 57a.
3. b. Yoma 35b.

got them a company of the boldest sort of men, and of those that loved innovations, about them, and became leaders to them; and when they struggled together, they did it by casting reproachful words against one another, and by throwing stones also. And there was nobody to reprove them; but these disorders were done after a licentious manner in the city, as if it had no government over it. *And such was the impudence and boldness that had seized on the high-priest, that they had the hardness to send their servants into the threshing-floors, to take away those tithes that were due to the priests, insomuch that it so fell out that the poorer sort of the priests died for want.* To this degree did the violence of the seditious prevail over all right and justice.[4]

The Boethus priests were also involved in this persecution. "There were sycamore tree-trunks [staves] in Jericho [with which they beat the people], and the men of violence seized them by force, [whereupon] the owners arose and consecrated them to Heaven."[5]

The paragraph continues with the good reason.

Woe is me because of the house of Boethus; woe is me because of their staves! [they beat the lesser priests] Woe is me because of the house of Hanin (Annas), woe is me because of their whisperings! [they were strict in exacting the death penalty using contrived testimony] Woe is me because of the house of Kathros [Kithros/Caiaphas/Cantheras], woe is me because of their pens! [they were scribes and wrote accusations] *Woe is me because of the house of Ishmael the son of Phabi, woe is me because of their fists!* [they beat the people] For they are High Priests and their sons are [Temple] treasurers and their sons-in-law are trustees and their servants beat the people with staves.[6]

This was the situation in 61–62 CE when James, the brother of Jesus, was executed by the next priest to be appointed after Ishmael, Ananus II (son of Annas the high priest). It might be that James was trying to defend the poor priests who, along with their families, were starving to death. The conflict went on for quite some time and involved several different high priests. Ananus II, the second "Annas" served only for a short time (three months) in 62 CE.[7] It was before this Annas that James the Just and

4. Josephus, *Ant.* 20.8.8, italics mine.
5. *b. Pesah.* 57a.
6. *b. Pesah.* 57a, italics mine.
7. Josephus, *Ant.* 20.9.1.

Pella and the Despoysni

other Nazaraeans (perhaps, a few of the apostles) were brought for trial. He illegally called a meeting of the criminal Sanhedrin and was responsible for having them put to death. Josephus tells us he was removed shortly thereafter for having done so.

> Now the report goes, that this elder Ananus [Annas I, the high priest at the trial of Jesus] proved a most fortunate man; for he had five sons [Eleazar, known as "Alexander" in the New Testament, Jonathan, Theophilus, Mathias, and Ananus II], who had all performed the office of a high-priest to God, and he had himself enjoyed that dignity a long time formerly, which had never happened to any other of our high-priests; but this *younger Ananus*, who, as we have told you already, took the high-priesthood, was a bold man in his temper and very insolent; *he was also of the sect of the Sadducees who are very rigid in judging offenders, above all the rest of the Jews*, as we have already observed; when, therefore, Ananus was of this disposition, he thought he had now a proper opportunity [to exercise his authority]. Festus was now dead, and Albinus was but upon the road; so he assembled the sanhedrim of judges, and *brought before them the brother of Jesus, who was called Christ, whose name was James, and some others*, [or, some of his companions]; and when he had formed an accusation against them as breakers of the law, he delivered them to be stoned.[8]

But this was not the only execution that occurred during the three months that Ananus II held the high priesthood. Lawlessness was rife under these high priests, and especially under Ananus II. A daughter of one of the Ananide priests was burned for adultery between the death of Festus (62 CE) and the coming of Albinus (63 CE), during the high priesthood of this second Ananus.

> Eleazar b. Zadok said, as it happened once that a priest's daughter committed adultery, etc. Rabbi Joseph said: *It was a Sadducee Beth din that did this*. Now is this what R. Eleazar b. Zadok said, and did the sages answer him so? Has it not been taught: R. Eleazar b. Zadok said, 'I remember when I was a child, riding on my father's shoulder that a priest's adulteress daughter was brought [to the place of execution] surrounded by faggots and burnt' . . . That was done *because the Beth din at the time was not learned in the law*.[9]

---

8. Josephus, *Ant.* 20.9.1, italics mine.
9. *b. Sanh.* 52b, italics mine.

Becoming Christian

The period just before the outbreak of the Jewish Revolt was filled with lawlessness and avarice. Once James had been executed the community was thrown into mass confusion. At that time a new family leader was elected. "[T]hey all with one consent approved Symeon the son of Clopas, of whom also the book of the Gospels makes mention, as worthy of *the throne of the community* in that place. *He was a cousin—so it is said—of the Saviour; for indeed Hegesippus relates that Clopas was Joseph's brother.*"[10]

Eusebius' claim and his listing of the first overseers of the Jerusalem community "of the circumcision" is an indication that the leadership of the religion *was not through apostolic succession* (as the Christian church indicates) but through the royal dynastic family of Jesus. That family became known as the *despoysni*.

We know that the *desposyni* carried around with them *Joseph's* genealogy as proof of their ancestry.

> A few however of the careful, either remembering the names, or having it in their power in some other way, by means of copies, to have private records of their own, glorified in the idea of preserving the memory of their noble extraction. Of these were the above-mentioned persons, called *desposyni*, on account of their affinity to the family of our Saviour. These coming from Nazara and Cochaba, villages of Judea, to the other parts of the world, explained the aforesaid genealogy from the book of daily records, as faithfully as possible.[11]

The genealogical rolls were kept in Sepphoris where Joseph's family had settled. They had been removed from Jerusalem before the Jewish war. Rabbi Jose ben Halafta whose family had lived in Sepphoris and whose father had been the leader of the Jewish community during the middle of the first century makes mention his remembrance of the fact that the genealogical registers had been kept there. ". . . Rabbi Jose also informs us that old registers were kept in this city [Sepphoris] indicating who were Israelites of pure blood, equal to those whose ancestors were priests, levites, or members of the Sanhedrin (*M. Kidd.* 4:5)."[12] He is buried in Mount Meron in Galilee.

We have already mentioned that the disciples were likely relatives of Jesus and that several sets of brothers were included among them. It would

---

10. Eusebius, HE 3.9, italics mine.
11. Eusebius, quoting Africanus 1.7.
12. Freyne, *Galilee*, p. 127.

Pella and the Despoysni

be logical for these students to be a *collective group* who worked together, some in the fishing trade and/or with the tax system associated with it.

> Fishing was an important part of the Galilean economy in the first century. But it was not the "free enterprise" which modern readers of the New Testament may imagine. Even fishers who may have owned their own boats were *part of a state-regulated, elite-profiting enterprise, and a complex web of economic relationships* . . . Rather, *only political and kinship systems* were explicit social domains; economics and religion were conceptualized, controlled, and *sustained either by the political hierarchy or kin-groups*" (Polanyi, et al. 1957; Dalton 1961; Polanyi 1968; Finley 1985; Malina 1986; Garnsey & Saller 1987:43–63) . . . *This means that relatives normally worked together and that kinship ties were fundamental for "guild" or "trade relations*.[13]

This did not mean they were "poor fishermen". Zabdi (Zebedee), for instance had hired men working for him (Mark 1:20) and, apparently, owned his own boat. In the introduction to *Jesus and His World*, the authors Rousseau and Arav make it clear that the fishermen around the Sea of Galilee were not by any means poverty-stricken as one might glean from the present gospels.

> On the other hand, rural settlements 20 to 150 acres in size from the first century *were not as tiny and humble as is often supposed. Nor did fishers around the Sea of Galilee live in poverty.* The fisherman's house of Bethsaida extends over 400 square meters (4,300 square feet) and, although it contains no Hellenistic architectural elements, it does contain fine pottery, some imported from Asia Minor. In Gamla, only seven miles from Bethsaida, lower class houses stood next to patrician residences and did not differ substantially from them.[14]

Some of our well-to-do citizens in modern society today do not live in homes as large as 4,300 square feet!

Levi (Matthew), the brother of James and John, served as the chief tax collector in the great toll-house in Capernaum, an important position. Hanson claims there were at least two layers of architelonai (tax and toll

---

13. Hanson, "The Galilean Fishing Economy," italics mine.
14. Rouseseau and Rami, *Jesus and His World*, p. 4, italics mine.

administrators). He states: "We see the contracting of taxes to 'the urban elites and rulers' during the Hellenistic period."[15]

The chief tax collectors reported directly to Herod Antipas, who paid tribute to the Caesars from the proceeds. Cleophas (Alphaeus) and his son Matthew Levi were known to have been a family of tax collectors, or basically customs officers. The title "Alphaeus" is the Greek term for the Aramaic *halphaï* meaning "to exchange" from the Hebrew word *chalfon*, moneychanger. The term encompasses tax collection. a tax collector was also a moneychanger.

Tax farmers (Publicani) were used to collect these taxes from the provincials. Rome, in eliminating its own burden for this process, would put the collection of taxes up for auction every few years. The Publicani would bid for the right to collect in particular regions, and pay the state in advance of this collection. These payments were, in effect, loans to the state and Rome was required to pay interest back to the Publicani. As an offset, the Publicani had the individual responsibility of converting properties and goods collected into coinage, alleviating this hardship from the treasury. In the end, the collectors would keep anything in excess of what they bid plus the interest due from the treasury; with the risk being that they might not collect as much as they originally bid.

Caesar Augustus was considered by many to have been the most brilliant tax strategist of the Roman Empire. *During his reign as "First Citizen" the publicani were virtually eliminated as tax collectors for the central government.* During this period cities were given the responsibility for collecting taxes. Matthew and his father, Cleophas, were referred to as publicans (tax collectors) in the New Testament in Capernaum during the reign of Caesar Augustus. They were *not* of the old *publicani but hired by the local government to collect taxes.* The local government would have been that under Herod Antipas (Galilee). The position was hereditary, thus Cleophas' son Matthew Levi is found sitting at a toll station in Capernaum when Jesus calls him as a student.

The Sadducees were Rome's "bankers", while the moneychangers were Rome's tax collectors. Furthermore, the Levitical priests were also the tax collectors of the Jewish community. They would determine how much each person or family owed and would collect that amount for the temple

---

15. Hanson, "The Galilean Fishing Economy".

Pella and the Despoysni

treasury. These taxes were used to fund the temple, its storehouse and the priests themselves.[16]

Jerome, in his translation of the Vulgate, referred to Joseph of Arimathea (a relative of Jesus) as a local Roman Decurion or "nobilis decurio" for Jerusalem, a tax collector and member of a municipal senate who ran local government. This does not mean he was Roman but that he had been appointed as one of the three Jewish councilors over the City of Jerusalem. As a member of the senate, he would have been more influential with Pilate and of a higher rank than prefect. This is probably why he was able to obtain possession of Jesus' body. There are numerous legends that connect Joseph to mines in Cornwall; however, this is highly unlikely. Decurions were appointed for their "local" governments, not for far-away places. It was said that it was easier to become a Senator of Rome than it was to become a decurion in Pompeii. Austustine's father Patrick (Patricius), had "curial" rank—he was a decurion, a town councilor with tax-collecting duties, and not a Christian. Augustine calls him meager in his land holdings (tenuis, T 2.5), but that was the typical stance of his class. Because the position was hereditary, Augustine sold his inheritance in order to become a bishop. (L 126.7). They were bound to their land and their duties, and so were their heirs. This social group on which imperial power rested were members of the upper stratum of urban landowners, who occupied city magistracies and sat on municipal councils. These decurions were considered privileged and "well-born" in contrast to the urban and rural plebeians, the "common people." Joseph's patronymic "Arimathea", was simply two words in Hebrew: *ari*—house or hearth of and *mattathiyah*—Matthat. This indicated he was from the dynasty or "house" of Joseph's grandfather. This accords well with the wealthy Joseph ben Elim (Eli) from the region around Sepphoris since his family was one of the aristocratic landowners in the area (mentioned by Rabbi Jose Halafta, whose father was one of the community leaders, and probably a decurion, at that time).

> Decurions were the *most powerful political figures at the local level*. They were responsible for public contracts, *religious rituals*, entertainment, and ensuring order. Perhaps most importantly to the imperial government, *they also supervised local tax collection*."[17]
> "[T]he *curiales* (from *co* + *viria*, 'gathering of men') were initially

---

16. "Levitical Duties."
17. "Decurion," italics mine.

> the leading members of a *gentes* (clan) . . . Their roles were *both civil and sacred*. Each *gens curiales* had a leader, called a *curio*[18]

In the first century Roman Empire the imperial government did not tax its subjects directly. Rather, a Roman governor would give the province's tax assessments to local city councils, the *decurions*. The decurions were responsible for seeing that it got paid and had to make up any shortfalls from their own pockets. Normally they farmed the actual collecting out to private bidders who then went around the country collecting people's individual assessments. So the hierarchy in the family of Jesus, would have been of three ranks: Joseph, the decurion; Cleophas, the Alphaeus; and Matthew Levy, a tax farmer or collector, a customs agent.

After Simon's death, a Jew named "Justus" was elected leader of the community of Ebionites. Apparently, Joseph (Joses, Justus), a son of Cleophas the Alphaeus and Mary, was named for his uncle Joseph (Barnabas), but we hear his name only in Matthew 27:56 and Matthew 15:40, 47, where he is mistaken for his uncle Barnabas (also Joses). Yet Joseph Barnabus is also said to have been the uncle of Mark: "sister's son to Barnabus", and Mary was his sister, whose child was "Marcus" (Col. 4:10), where Paul uses Mark's proper name.

The family of Joseph and Jesus lived in a satellite community near Sepphoris where Joseph owned land, but it is doubtful the village named "Nazareth" existed by that name at the time of Jesus. "Besides the New Testament, the earliest mention of Nazareth is by Julius Africanus (170–240 C.E.), as cited by Eusebius (Church History 1, 7.6–12). It must have been a very small village at the time, perhaps a satellite hamlet of Sepphoris."[19]

Much of the priesthood (including the Boethus family) had also settled in areas near that city. As a devout and observant man, and a good father, Joseph would have prepared Jesus for a future in the priesthood. He would have taught him the Torah day by day from the time he uttered his first words. He would have also prepared Jesus for a profession (as required of all priests), that of *ho tekton* (not "carpenter" but architect). It must be mentioned here, however, that in Rabbinic terms a "carpenter" was a "builder of Torah". Since we never hear of Jesus working or building a structure of any sort, it is likely this was a metaphor for both his father and himself. This would be logical for a wealthy priestly family.

---

18. "Curiales," italics mine.
19. Rousseau, *Jesus and His World*, p. 214.

Those familiar with the language spoken by Jesus are acquainted with a metaphorical use of 'carpenter' and 'carpenter's son' in ancient Jewish writings. In Talmudic sayings the Aramaic noun denoting carpenter or craftsman (*naggar*) stands for a "scholar" or "learned man" "This is something no carpenter, son of carpenters, can explain." "There is no carpenter, nor a carpenter's son, to explain it". Thus, although no one can be absolutely sure that the sayings cited in the Talmud were current already in first–century AD Galilee, proverbs such as these are likely to be age-old. If so, it is possible that the charming picture of "Jesus the carpenter" may have to be buried and forgotten.[20]

> 1.5 A. "Said R. Joseph bar Abba . . . "people may remove worms from a tree or patch the bark with dung during the Sabbatical Year but people may not remove worms or patch the bark during the intermediate days of a festival . . . *But there is no craftsman let alone a disciple of a craftsman who can unravel this teaching.* B. Said Rabina, "*I am not a craftsman let alone a disciple of a craftsman [kharash or naggar], but I can unravel this teaching.* What is the problem anyhow?[21]

In the Septuagint, the word *tekton* (for carpenter) is rendered for the Hebrew *kharash* (חרש), "craftsman," as in Isaiah 41:7 and Isaiah 44:13. In the Talmud it is sometimes rendered *naggar*. Thus both Jesus and his father were quite literate in Torah.

> Nazareth, a small village in fertile Lower Galilee, could probably not provide enough business for a *tekton*, "builder, carpenter, mason" to support his family . . . and Joseph may have worked in other places. In addition to its indigenous population of farmers, *its favorable location may have made it the secondary residence of absentee owners of fields, orchards, gardens, vineyards, and flocks, people whose primary residences and business interests were in Sepphoris.*[22]

This would accord with what we know of Joseph ben Elim, an apparently wealthy aristocrat "from Sepphoris". Furthermore, it was Joseph's family who had resided and owned land in and around Nazareth and Sepphoris.

---

20. Vermas, *Jesus the Jew*, pp. 21–22.

21. Neusner, *The Talmud of Babylonia*. Tractate *Abodah Zarah*: chapters 3–5—Page 57, italics mine.

22. Rousseau, p. 215, italics mine.

"Mark specifies that Jesus went to preach to his own *patrida*, a Greek word that means '*family from the father's side, clan, native place*'" (Mark 6:1).[23]

Also located nearby was a priestly station and school. This is where Jesus probably studied. It was later inhabited by Rabbi Juda Hanasi, Judah the Prince, president of the Sanhedrin and was the place where the Mishnah was complied around 200 CE.

It is obvious Jesus' training including reading Hebrew, for he stood up to "read" from the Torah just after the Day of Atonement, declaring the jubilee year by reading from the scroll of Isaiah. Most of Jesus' education would have occurred in the school near Sepphoris. He could not have been illiterate. Whatever the name of the village in which Jesus had grown up, these rural areas were inhabited by *extended families* who dwelt in houses surrounding a communal courtyard. It is, therefore, more likely that other relatives (mostly women, children, and the elderly men) were relatives of Joseph rather than of Mary's. They would have shared their lives with Mary during the week while the men worked. This type of living arrangement was known from ancient times. Villages consisted of family groups living within a community of relatives. The villages were known as the *mispahah*.

> Traditional agrarian families are thus inevitably bound to the fabric of a wider social structure, for economic, psychological, social, and often military reasons. For ancient Israel, the suprahousehold social unit was the *mispahah*, for which the descriptive rendering "protective association of families" is appropriate. The *mispahah*—with its sense of being bound by a common heritage, by kinship ties, and by shared subsistence concerns—represented a solidarity of nearby family units that interacted with and sustained one another.[24]

Usually, their homes were built attached to each other in a square with a common courtyard used by all the relatives, where the food was cooked and numerous household chores were shared. Endogamous marriage was encouraged because it kept the land within the family. This was the situation of Jesus' family. At some time early on, Joseph and his family settled in and around Sepphoris. Perhaps he had grown up there. It is well known that descendants of David settled in the area at different times after the Babylonian captivity. Joseph's father, Eli (Elim, Heli in the New Testament) probably had estates there as did the Hanan, Boethus, and Kithros (Caiaphas)

---

23. Ibid., p. 215, italics mine.
24. Meyers, "The Family in Early Israel", p. 37.

families. Many members of the priesthood had homes in Jerusalem and estates and holdings elsewhere, usually their fathers' lands. Perhaps Mattathiyah (Joseph's grandfather) had migrated from Egypt with the Boethus family, settling in Jerusalem but also holding lands around Sepphoris.

Jude or Judas, the "brother of James", and author of the epistle Jude would have also been a priest (as his brothers James, Joseph, and Simon). If he was Judas "the Scribe" he married a woman named Salome, perhaps his cousin. His grandsons, James (Yacov) and Zocher, or Zacharias (which also indicate he was married), are mentioned as having been brought before Domitian and questioned about their royal descent (their names are preserved by Hegesippus; Paris MS 1555A and Bodleian MS Barocc. 142).

> But the same historian [Hegesippus] says, that there were others, *the offspring of one of those considered brothers of the Lord, whose name was Judas,* and that these lived until the same reign after their profession of Christ, and the testimony under Domitian beforementioned.[25]

There is a traditional extant genealogy of Jude that runs like this: Jude, Elchasai, Nashon, Cyleddon (Bishop of Alexandria 150 CE), Narpus, Nascien II, Prefect of Provinciae, Gallienus Quiriacus, Elias, Isaac, Johanan, Gerentonus, Agripanius, Conan "Meriadoc", died 421. The genealogy is probably legendary. We do know that the "church fathers" considered the Elchasites a heretical sect of Ebionites.

There is a good claim that the ministry of the apostles extended to Edessa. There were three Syrian Jews there who had founded an early community of Nazareans in central Mesopotamia in Ctesiphon-Seleucia on the Tigris during the second century by the names of Abris (Eber?—121–137 CE), Abraham (159–171 CE) and Ya'qub (James; ca 190 CE). Bauckham relates that "Abris is said to have been 'of the family and race of Joseph the husband of Mary', while Abraham was 'of the kin of James called a brother of the Lord' and Ya'qub was Abraham's son."[26] There has been a tradition in which Mari, a disciple of Addai (66–87 CE) also known as Thaddeus, one of the "Seventy", believed to have been a disciple of Thomas who had been sent to Edessa), had introduced the new Nazaraean doctrine there at an early date. The cities of Ctesiphon and Seleucia were in Persia, considered at the time to be a part of the Parthian Empire. Although, Fiey[27] claims they

25. Eusebius HE, p. 118, italics mine.
26. Bauckham, pp. 68–69.
27. Fiey, *Jalons pour un histoire de l'Église en Iraq* (Louvain, 1970).

Becoming Christian

were fictitious, the Talmud mentions these Persian groups of Nazaraeans during the early second century, so it is unlikely they could be fictitious in light of the fact that the Jews living in Galilee were aware of them.

> Raba [Jeremiah] said: When they [sc. the persecutors] demand it for their personal pleasure, it is different. For otherwise, how dare we yield to them [sc. the Parsees or fire worshippers] our braizers [or fire bellows]?[28]

The editors note:

> The passage is obscure ... (another reading) bears a strong resemblance to *dominica*: now, *dies dominica* (the Lord's Day) signifies Sunday, and *aedes dominica* signifies church ... In Raba's time there were Christian communities in Persia, observing their Sundays as strictly as the Jews observed the Sabbath, who therefore arranged for the Jews to heat their churches on that day, as they probably did a similar service for the Jews on the Sabbath ... i.e., they do not demand the fire as a religious act, whereby the Jew shall associate himself in idolatrous worship, but merely desires its warmth in their churches.[29]

Raba bar Jeremiah was a second generation Babylonian amora sage, who lived from about 150–230 CE, perhaps earlier. He was well acquainted with the Persian Nazaraean community, which by that time he believed had become idolatrous. Although this is a later period than the founders of the community in Seleucia and Ctesiphon, it proves the new Nazaraeans had been well-established there by that time.

One other individual, a man named Conon, claimed to be a member of Jesus' family. In the Martyrdom of Conon, he states: "I am of the city of Nazareth in Galilee, I am of the *family* (συγγένεια - kinship) of Christ, whose worship I have inherited from my ancestors".[30] He was questioned during the Christian persecution under Decius (250–251 CE). Since there are several of Jesus' brothers who were married (1 Cor 9–5), there are likely to be *several* bloodlines of the *desposyni* in existence even today (not including the rest of the bloodlines of Joseph and Mary). How we can possibly imagine that Jesus has no living relatives alive today is remarkable! When we consider that those of us living today once had ancient ancestors

---

28. *b. Sanh.* 74b.
29. *b. Sanh.* 74b, Note a6.
30. Bauckham, *Jude*, p. 122.

(else we would not be here), we must also consider that there are some descendants of *his* family also alive today. Perhaps they are unidentifiable, but that does not mean they do not exist. In fact, there are numerous Jews with Davidic ancestry today. Only those who can prove their lineage are allowed to use the ancient Davidic crest.

> Although many Jews are not aware of it, such family lines of religious aristocracy exist even today among the Jewish people, and more than a few Jewish families can trace their lineage back to King David.[31]

It is a certainty (although some believe it is legend) that the apostles were married and that they took with them their wives and families when they fled Jerusalem between 62–66 CE. Perhaps it was the death of James the Just that served as the catalyst for their flight. Paul had mentioned that the apostles had wives: "Have we not power to lead about a sister, a wife, as well as other apostles, and as the brethren of the Master, and Cephas?" (1 Cor 9;5). The reason wives were referred to as "sister–wives" is because ancient dynastic leaders (such as Abraham, Pharoah, Solomon, *et cetera*) were known to have married their sisters. The phrase became a Hebrew idiom since a man's wife was to be as close as a sibling. Peter, as we know, from the gospels had a "mother in law" whom Jesus healed in Capernaum; therefore, it is certain he also had a wife and family.

The exodus to Pella is said to have taken place under the leadership of Simon (Simeon) son of Cleophas. Hegesippus reported that Simon was chosen "bishop" (overseer is a better word) directly after the death of James when the *relatives of Jesus* assembled with the surviving apostles and disciples to elect a successor."[32]

> The Nazoraean sect exists in Beroea near Coele Syria, in the *Decapolis near the region of Pella*, and in Bashan in the place called Cocaba, which in Hebrew is called Chochabe. That is where the sect began, *when all the disciples were living in Pella after they moved form Jerusalem*.[33]

In other words, they originally went to the *region* of Pella. There is archaeological evidence that they might have first met in a cave in Rihab in northern Jordan beneath St. Georgeous Church (230 CE), the cave (33–70

---

31. Buxbaum, *The Life*, p. 11.
32. Eusebius III. xi. 1.
33. Epiphanius, *Panarion* 29.7.7–8, italics mine.

Becoming Christian

CE) itself as one of the oldest places of worship in the world. A mosaic in the floor of the church refers to the "70 beloved by God and the divine" and would appear to refer to the seventy apostles appointed by Jesus. Apparently, there was an early settlement of Ebionites there long before the exodus to the Pella region. One of the first places Jesus preached was in the Decapolis of Jordan (Matt 4:25; Mark 5:20; 7:31). He had gone through the "midst of the coasts of Decapolis", meaning the lands of the ten cities. There can be little doubt that his disciples had also been sent to that area throughout the years on their missionary journeys.

> Their sect began after the capture of Jerusalem. For when all those who believed in Christ *settled at that time for the most part in Peraea*, in a city called *Pella* belonging to the *Decapolis* mentioned in the gospel, which is next to Batanaea and the land of Bashan, then they moved there and stayed . . .[34]

> For when the city was about to be captured and sacked by the Romans, all the disciples were warned beforehand by an angel to remove from the city, doomed as it was to utter destruction. *On migrating from it they settled at Pella*, the town already indicated, *across the Jordan*. It is said to belong to the *Decapolis*.[35]

Julius Africanus comments that the relatives of Jesus had spread the gospel everywhere starting from the villages of Nazareth and Cochaba.[36] Pella lies hidden in a valley on the edge of the Transjordan high plateau currently known as Khirbet Fahil. Cochaba, itself, was known to have been the residence for numerous Davidic families after their return from Babylon, and it became the second most important city of the early Nazaraeans.

The community in Jerusalem had earlier met on the Mount of Olives.

> The Mount of Olives is therefore literally opposite to Jerusalem and to the east of it, but also *the holy church of God, and the mount upon which it was founded*, of which the Saviour teaches a city set on a hill cannot be hid, *raised up in place of Jerusalem* that is fallen never to rise again, and thought worthy of the feet of the Lord, is figuratively not only opposite Jerusalem, *but east of it as well*, receiving the rays of the divine light, and became much before Jerusalem, and the Sun of Righteousness himself.[37]

34. Epiphanius, *Panarion* 30:2:7, italics mine.
35. Epiphanius, *On Weights and Measures* 15, italics mine.
36. Eusebius I, vii. 14.
37. Eusebius, *Proof of the Gospel*, VI, 18, itlaics mine.

> And this *Mount of Olives* is said to be over against Jerusalem, *because it was established by God after the fall of Jerusalem*, instead of the old earthly Jerusalem.[38]

After the destruction of Jerusalem the Ebionites went back to Jerusalem until the time of Hadrian who had abolished all Jews from the city in 135.

Thus Justus (Joses) is the third bishop in Eusebius' list. He is the only brother not *actively* mentioned in the New Testament and who only received scant mention in the gospel of Mark (Mark 6:3). However unlikely, it is possible this Joses could have been the brother of Jesus, himself (some call him "Judas" and make him Jesus' brother, but the name Justus is the equivalent to Joses). The dynasty of Joseph and Jesus is referred to as the *desposyni* because of their familial relationship. The members of this family occupied prominent positions in the Nazaraene/Ebionite community (also attested by Hegesippus) in both Jerusalem and in Pella. According to him, the two grandsons of Jude, the brother of Jesus, James (Jacob) and Zocher (Zechariah), were interrogated by the emperor Domitian about their royal descent and determined to be "peasants" (they had lost all their wealth during the fall of Jerusalem). "Afterward they governed their congregations until the time of Trajan."[39] We have already discussed the two groups of the movement in the Talmud, and it was during the time of Hadrian that the study of Torah was banned altogether. Neither could they worship on the Sabbath or keep the feasts. It became illegal for a man to circumcise his son. All this was punishment for the Bar Kochba Revolt.

There must have been an extant community in Jerusalem until the time of Trajan, however. Eusebius gives us a list of their names, *"all of the circumcision"* [italics mine].[40]

1. James the Just (died 62 CE)
2. Simeon, the son of Cleophas (died 107 CE)
3. Justus (Joses or Joseph, brother of Simeon)
4. Zaccheus
5. Tobias
6. Benjamin

---

38. Eusebius, *Proof of the Gospel*, VI, 18, italics mine.
39. Eusebius, III. 20. 6.
40. Eusebius, HE, p. 131.

Becoming Christian

7. John
8. Matthew (Matthias; died 120 CE)
9. Philip (died 124 CE)
10. Seneca
11. Justus (died 107–113 CE)
12. Levi
13. Ephres
14. Joseph
15. Judas (Kyriakus or Quiriacus, meaning "of the king"; died between 134–135 CE).

These were all members of the *desposyni* since Jesus' family was considered a "royal" dynasty. Each would have a claim to leadership in the Jesus movement. The last of these, Judas, lived during the age of Hadrian and the Bar Kochba Revolt (he is *not* to be confused with the third century Hebrew Judas who was *given* the name Kyriakus by Helena, the mother of Constantine).

After leaving Pella, they returned to Jerusalem (72 CE) and built a community synagogue on the Mount of Olives, where Simeon, son of Cleophas, had first officiated.

> *Believers in Christ congregate from all parts of the world, not as of old time because of the glory of Jerusalem, nor that they may worship in the ancient Temple at Jerusalem, but . . . that they may worship at the Mount of Olives opposite to the city . . .*[41]

As a matter of fact, the site of the place of worship was later covered by the ancient Eleona Church and, even later, by the Pater Noster Church. Below the Eleona Church is a cave where the Gentile "bishops" (not the *despoysni*) of the Jerusalem assembly are believed to have been buried.

---

41. Eusebius, *Proof of the Gospel* VI. 18 (288), italics mine.

Pella and the Despoysni

Courtesy of Ecole Biblique, Jerusalem

The region must have been the most important area in pre-Constantine Jerusalem. *Even the bishops of Jerusalem were buried near the cave/tomb on the Mount of Olives* and it was significant enough in the early history of Christianity that Constantine had a church built over this site [the Eleona Church] shortly after A.D. 325. And sometime in the second century, a tomb chamber was carved out of the rock adjacent to the cave itself (with spaces for five bodies). It appears from this that some people felt inspired to be buried near the cave/tomb.[42] (see figure above)

The tomb chamber referred to in the above quotation, however, was the tomb of the Gentile bishops and not the *despoysni* who were probably buried nearby, perhaps in the Dominus Flevit tomb complex.

> At some distance from this church [Church of the Ascension] was the *Eleona (from the Greek for "olive grove")*, a church built by Constantine *over a cave in which Jesus was believed to have prophesied about the destruction of Jerusalem* (Matt. 24:13; Mark 13:1-4). According to the apocryphal Acts of John (94-95) Jesus taught esoteric mysteries there. Eleona was thought to be the exact place

---

42. Martin, *Secrets*, pp. 82-83, italics mine.

Becoming Christian

> of the Ascension and the future place of Jesus' return. *The early bishops of Jerusalem were buried in its vicinity.*[43]

It is perfectly logical that the earliest community of the followers of Jesus adopted this site to found their assembly in respect to the presence of Jesus.

Further up the mountain is the Dominus Flevit Chapel. Near it are the first century catacombs that have recently been uncovered. It is in these catacombs that we find the ossuaries of several of the early members of the Jesus movement including Simon bar Jonah (Peter), Mary "the Magdalene" of Bethany, Martha, and Eleazar (Lazarus).

We are told by Eusebius, quoting Hegesippus, in at least two places that after the death of James, "Symeon, the son of Cleophas" became the leader of the Jerusalem *ekklesia*.

But in 135 CE the earliest members of the Jesus movement left Jerusalem again, leaving behind the "throne" on which James purportedly sat and said to have been exhibited in Jerusalem even to the time of Constantine.

If Simon was the son of Cleophas, and Cleophas was Joseph's brother, the *despoysni* derived their lineage from *Joseph*, the paternal genealogy of Jesus, and not from the maternal (Mary's). The evidence is that Simon was, indeed, the first cousin to Jesus. He is also mentioned in Jewish documents as the author of the Gospel of the Hebrews (forerunner of Matthew in Hebrew letters), the Ascents of Jacob (called by Epiphanius the Acts of the Apostles, which in no way is associated with the canonical Acts), and the Book of John (the forerunner of Revelation).

From the earliest days we are told that the family of Jesus was situated in the "Jewish villages of Nazareth and Kokhaba" as "they traveled around the rest of the land" and that they had "interpreted the genealogy they had from the Book of Days."[44] We can add to those two villages the village of Rumeh (or Rumah), or Tell Rumeh (a few miles north of Nazareth) from whence the ben Gorian family estates are situated (the family of Nicodemus). It is possible that this was the village of Kokhaba, or was certainly near it. Another location for the village of Kokhaba might have been Shumshi (Shemsiyeh), the modern Ain-esh-Shemsiyeh located between Dothan and the Jordan near the southern border of the land of Issachar. This is a village very near Pella in the east of Jordan.

---

43. Rousseau, *Jesus and His World*, p. 211, italics mine.
44. Eusebius, HE 1.7.14.

> Astori relates, 'Beth-Shemesh, of Issachar, is *south of Zippori (Sefuri or Sepphoris)*, and is called *Shumshi;*' but I believe that, more correctly speaking, this Beth-Shemesh, near Sefuri [Sepphoris], belonged to Naphtali (Joshua 19:38), and not to Issachar.[45]

Schonfield believes these villages were the base operations for the original Nazaraeans and resided in Batanea (in the Pella region) and the Hauran (Auranitis).

> They are called Jewish villages presumably because they were in an area where there were many non-Jews and not far distant from the Greek cities of the Decapolis. It was to Pella in the Decapolis that the Christian-Nazoreans had removed from Judea and Jerusalem shortly before the war with the Romans.[46]

This exodus from Jerusalem occurred prior to the Roman siege when Jews were leaving Jerusalem in early 66 CE in advance of the Jewish war. Jesus had told them to watch for the sign of the Son of Man in the heavens, and in or about the year 66 CE such a sign did, indeed, present itself at the Feast of Unleavened Bread (Passover). "Thus *there was a star resembling a sword*, which stood over the city, and a comet that continued a whole year."[47]

This "star" was likely to the *Notzrim* the sign that Jesus had warned them to watch for in order to know when the destruction of Jerusalem was to occur and to flee from Judea to the mountains (Matt 24:16; Mark 13:14). The star was always associated with the Messiah and was taken from Numbers 24:17: "[T]here shall come a Star out of Jacob, and a Sceptre [Sword] shall rise out of Israel." The Pharisees and *Notzrim*, along with the Zealots and Essenes interpreted the star as an omen that the "Last Days" were near. It appears to have been a "sign" to the priests also that a war was imminent.

> [A]t the ninth hour of the night, so great a light shone round the altar and the holy house, that it appeared to be bright day time; which light lasted for half an hour. This light seemed to be a good sign to the unskilful, *but was so interpreted by the sacred scribes, as to portend those events that followed immediately upon it*.[48]

---

45. *History and Geography*, http://www.jewish-history.com/palestine/issachar.html, italics mine.
46. Schonfield, p. 291.
47. Josephus, J.W. 6.5.3, italics mine.
48. Josephus, J.W. 6.5.3, italics mine.

Some of the Ebionites and the new Nazaraeans spread through northern Galilee, Babylon, and along the Mesopotamian border, and associated with the Pharisees in those locations. The Ebionites continued to study Torah, keep the Sabbath, and continued to worship Yahweh. They carried with them the Hebrew gospel and expounded the messiah from it. The "new" Nazaraeans were Hellenists and adapted to Gentile religious beliefs. Their communities were responsible for the writing of the gospels referred to derogatorily by the Pharisees as the *aven gilion* (a play on the word evangelion). The schism that had begun in Jerusalem was finally made complete by the Bar Kochba Revolt. Bar Kosiba had begun to enlist Jewish followers to fight with him, and this process included the Jews of the Jesus movement. Any Jew who would not fight with him would be put to death, and this included numerous Ebionites and Nazaraeans. We might assume that most of the Ebionites would not accept his claim as messiah since they already knew Jesus as their messiah. This meant for them certain execution. Eventually Gentiles overwhelmed the new Nazaraean community and brought with them their former pagan habits. This was the death blow for the Jesus movement in its entirety. A few Ebionite clans survived, along with a few of the *despoysni*, but now they worshiped in secrecy, hated by both Jews and the Gentile church.

The *despoysni* and the community of original Nazaraeans then would have fled across the river east of the Jordan and eventually settled in villages that carried the names of the "Star" (Kochaba) and the Nazar (Observers). The Ebionites (the originals of the Nazaraean sect) were still in that location at the time Eusebius was writing his history.

We are told by Malachi Martin that during the reign of Pope Silvester I (January 314 to December 31, 335) eight of the *desposynoi* had come to Rome (in 318 CE) in order to re-establish the Jewish origins of the Jesus movement and were denied. They were told that the church was now in Rome with the bones of Peter. However, the "bones" of Peter are not likely to be in Rome at all. His ossuary has been discovered on the Mount of Olives (as mentioned earlier).

The Vatican, of course, refutes this, claiming that Peter had removed to Rome in about 41 CE. Since we know that King Agrippa had imprisoned him in 42/43 CE and that Agrippa himself died in 44, the claim is highly unlikely. When one realizes that Peter was in Jerusalem in 51/52 CE when Paul went to Jerusalem, and that Paul met Peter in Antioch shortly thereafter, it is utterly improbable that Peter was martyred and buried in

Pella and the Despoysni

Rome. Considering that the ossuaries of Mary, Martha and Lazarus were also discovered nearby in the same tomb complex makes would seem to contradict it.

Pope Silvester I was represented at the Council of Nicea and was instrumental in holding a council at Rome to condemn Arius' teachings as "heresy". Poor Arius! He is so misunderstood by the "church". Christianity still believes he was a heretic. In defense of Arius (who was secretly murdered in the end for his beliefs by instigation of none other than the church father Athanasius and his principal assistant Macarius[49]—here are his beliefs:

> How could one be a Christian and not believe that Christ was God incarnate? The Arians had an answer. To them, Jesus was a person of such sublime moral accomplishments that God adopted him as His Son, sacrificed him to redeem humanity from sin, raised him from the dead, and granted him divine status. Because of his excellence, he became a model of righteous behavior for us. And because his merit earned the prize of immortality, the same reward was made available to other human beings, provided that they model themselves after him. From the Arian perspective, it was essential that Jesus not be God, since God, being perfect by nature, is inimitable. By contrast, Christ's transcendent virtue, achieved by repeated acts of will, is available (at least potentially) to the rest of us. Even though we may fall short of his impeccable standards, his triumph over egoism shows us how we also may become the Sons and Daughters of God.[50]

Arius simply had a common understanding with the earliest Jewish followers of Jesus and the *desposyni*. They never believed Jesus had supplanted God, or that he was Yahweh, himself! The "gospel" was not the good news about *Jesus*; it was the good news about the *kingdom of Yahweh*! They never stopped being Torah-observant Jews.

Although Martin claims the *despoysni* disappeared "one by one", they still exist today, although they might not know it. Some of the various families can be traced to at least the fifth century. From that point forward they are "mixed" with the nations (i.e., Britain, Ireland, France, etc.). Although they cannot be genealogically traced from that point forward with any sense of accuracy, the clans still exist in obscurity.

---

49. See Richard Rubenstein's *When Jesus Became God*, pp. 135–137.
50. Rubenstein, pp. 7–8.

Becoming Christian

The *despoysni* probably blended with other Jewish clans, but there is some evidence they also blended with the Gentile nations. One such example is the Conan from Nazareth who claimed to have been descended from Jesus' family (mentioned earlier). There is some indication that "Conan" was a family name since one lineage of Jude claims a Conan "Meriadoc", the first King of Brittany (d 421) in its genealogy, and who was cousin by marriage to Magnus Maximus.

Benjamin of Tudela, in 1166, claimed there were still estates held by contemporary royal Davidic heirs in the kingdom of Navarre (portions of France and Spain) who were able to prove their pedigree, some of whom were believed to have been some of the *desposyni*.[51]

> D. Sancho el Mayor, the first king of Navarre, endeavored to attract the Jews to his domains. They settled in the seaport towns of Pamplona, Estella, Olite, Tafalla, Viana, Funes, and Cortes, but principally in Tudela.[52]

This is the last we hear of the *desposyni* in history. Since Benjamin does not give us any clue as to the names of those whom he believed to have been relatives of Jesus, we cannot accurately know more. We can be assured, however, that a part of that family escaped the pograms in Spain during the Middle Ages. The *desposyni* could be anywhere and/or anyone today. As Carl Sandburg so aptly puts it: *"When a society or a civilization perishes, one condition can always be found. They forgot where they came from."*

---

51. *The Travels*, pp. 381–426.
52. "Navarre", J.E., http://www.jewishencyclopedia.com/articles/11390-navarre.

7

From Nazaraean to Christian

LONG BEFORE THE END of the Bar Kochba Revolt (135 CE) the converted Gentile pagans and Hellenist Jews had corrupted the teachings of the original Jerusalem movement in Antioch. We can probably assign an early date sometime after the death of James and around the time Evodius, a pagan convert, became the first "bishop" of Antioch (ca 58–60 CE).[1] Peter was already dead and Paul had been arrested and was on his way to Rome to appeal to Caesar (52–60). We know absolutely nothing about Evodius other than the fact that he was a Gentile who had converted from a pagan religion. However, we can assume that he was known to Paul. He is mentioned in Philippians 4:1–2 as Paul's "crown", meaning he had converted Evodius. While Christian tradition claims this "Evodias" was a woman, the name is male, not female. Further Paul clearly refers to them as his "brethren", not his "sisters". "Therefore, *my brethren* dearly beloved and longed for, my joy and crown, so stand fast in the Lord, my dearly beloved, I beseech Euodias [Evodius], and beseech Syntyche, that they be of the same mind in the Lord." He refers to *him* as a "true yokefellow" and mentions his friend Clement as well (vs. 3), saying only that he help "those women which laboured with me in the gospel". Here, he is referring to the Jewish women with Lydia whom he first converted. Paul goes on to say, "Those things, which ye have both *learned, and received and heard, and seen in me,* do: and the God of peace shall be with you." Evodius appears only in a dubious list created by Hippolytus of Rome of the "Seventy" apostles; however, he is

---

1. Eusebius, Chron. ann. Abr. 2058; H. E. iii. 22.

Becoming Christian

not listed among the other several lists.[2] It is impossible that Evodius could have been one of the Seventy since he was a pagan and since he was not with Jesus from the beginning when he was immersed in the Jordan, nor was he with him when he was executed or after his resurrection. Only Jews would have been appointed as the Seventy apostles. "After these things, the Lord appointed other seventy also, and sent them two and two before his face unto every city and place, whither he himself would come" (Luke 10:1).

Jesus himself planned to enter the cities where these "seventy" apostles were sent to prepare the communities for his arrival. Since Jesus was on his way to Jerusalem at the time, this meant they would be going primarily to Judean cities and villages where Jewish populations resided. In order to be able to speak with these people, they would have to have known Hebrew or Aramaic. Furthermore, these were those who fit the criteria of an "apostle" as described in the book of Acts. It is clear that an apostle was one who had been with Jesus from the beginning, meaning at his immersion in the Jordan, continued with him through his ministry, was there at his execution, and again at his resurrection. They would not have been "Greeks" or pagans. Since Evodius was a Gentile pagan convert living in Antioch he could not have been one of the "Seventy" as Hippolytus claimed.

We can only assume that Evodius still followed the teachings of the Jerusalem community. Peter had not ordained Evodius as bishop as the tradition states because Peter had been dead long before Evodius was ordained. Peter had only been to Antioch once himself while Paul was ministering there, and both he and Paul were long dead beforehand.

Church tradition, which is often stuff of legend and fables, declares that Peter was made Bishop of Antioch in 34 CE for seven years, but the earliest tradition giving that information is found in the *Liber Pontificalis* (Latin for *Book of the Popes*) in the fifteenth century. It was based on an *apocryphal letter* purportedly written between Jerome (347–420) and Pope Damascus I (366–383). Jerome, who translated the Bible into the Latin Vulgate was known as an arrogant womanizer, prone to self-flagellation, who was known to have changed the very words of Jesus! His translation of the book of Jonah, even though he had the best of Hebrew tutors and certainly knew better, caused a riot in Tripoli. The Jews there went to the authoritative Rabbi to discern what the Hebrew word should be. Jerome translated the Hebrew word *kikayon* (gourd) into Latin as *hedera*, which is the equivalent of the English word 'ivy', and "ivy" was a pagan symbol

2. Hippolytus, *On the End of the World*, 49.

for Bacchus (Dionysius in Greek), the "god" of the vine. He simply associated the word with the Roman god of which he was fully aware. The word simply reflected the culture in which he had been reared. A pagan who studied in Rome, Jerome used classical authors (such as Virgil) to describe Christian concepts such as hell that indicated both his classical education and his deep shame of their associated practices, such as pederasty which was found in Rome. He was, at first, skeptical of Christianity but eventually converted. These are the kinds of men who created the traditions, fables, and legends of the first apostles.

It wasn't until Ignatius became Bishop of Antioch in 69 CE that pagan concepts actually entered into the original teachings. Ignatius ascribed to Evodius the invention of the word "Christians" to first refer to the Gentile followers of Paul in Antioch. Eusebius mentions him in his history. "And Evodius having been established the first [bishop] of the Antiochians, Ignatius flourished at this time."[3] At the same time, Simon, the son of Cleopas was the leader of the Jerusalem Ebionites (after 62 CE at the death of James, the brother of Jesus). It has been suggested that Cleophas had become the next leader of the Jerusalem community, but he probably only served as an interim leader until the new leader could be elected, if at all. Cleophas was Joseph's brother and his son Simon, as a cousin and heir, was elected as the next leader. This family was referred to as the *despoysni*, or "family heirs".

By the time the second Gentile pagan, Ignatius, became the bishop of Antioch (69 CE), the mystery religions had permeated the teachings of the Gentile "church" there. Ignatius thought quite highly of himself, giving himself the name "Theophorus" (Θεοφόρος "God-bearer").[4] Beginning with Ignatius there is evidence that the Roman church was now "catholic" or universal. One might even conclude that he was the founder of the orthodox Catholic church. Among other things, he was the first "Christian" to argue that the Jewish Sabbath (Friday–Saturday) be replaced with the "Lord's Day" (Sunday). Ignatius, it is written in the legend–filled Ethiopian Apostolic Constitutions, was ordained by Paul. Although this is not true, the Antiochians, mostly Gentile pagans, would have followed Pauline philosophy. As we know from the book of Acts, these Gentiles would not have studied Torah, did not have to be circumcised, nor did they have to keep the dietary restrictions of the Jews. Paul, long before, would have taught Evodius a doctrine of faith in opposition

---

3. Eusebius, HE III 22.
4. Ignatius, *Epistle to Polycarp* I.1.

Becoming Christian

to the rule of James: "Shew me thy faith without thy works, and I will shew thee my faith by my works" (Jas 2:18).

The Roman church, beginning with Evodius and Ignatius would claim apostolic succession from Peter, which is clearly impossible since Peter was already dead. Likewise, it is also impossible that Paul could have ordained Ignatius since Paul had been dead since the early 60s. Since Ignatius was not ordained bishop until 69 CE it simply could not be anything but legendary. "First in Jerusalem, James . . . And in Antioch, first, Evodius [ordained] by Peter; and after him Ignatius, by Paul . . . And in the Church of Rome, first, Linus [ordained] by Paul . . ."[5]

A spurious letter from an author *claiming to be Ignatius* to the Antiochians gives the creed of the later church. Although, the letter itself is known to be spurious, it defines the views of the church from the latter first century to the early fifth century. Some scholars believe that the writer who composed the Apostolic Constitutions (unknown in the west until the Middle Ages) under the name of Clement was probably also the author of this letter falsely ascribed to Ignatius. Though Ignatius did not write it, it became popular with the church which wanted to oust the "Judaizers". It reflected their views between the second and fifth centuries. The letter states:

> Whosoever, therefore, declares that there is but one God, only so as to take away the divinity of Christ, is a devil, and an enemy of all righteousness. He also that confesseth Christ, yet not as the Son of the Maker of the world, but of some other unknown being, different from Him whom the law and the prophets have proclaimed, this man is an instrument of the devil. And he that rejects the incarnation, and is ashamed of the cross for which I am in bonds, this man is antichrist. Moreover, he who affirms Christ to be a mere man is accursed, according to the [declaration of the] prophet, since he puts not his trust in God, but in man. Wherefore also he is unfruitful, like the wild myrtle–tree.[6]

The Nazaraeans and Ebionites, Jews, believed in the one God, Yahweh, but did not believe Jesus was divine in the sense that he was God himself. They certainly rejected the incarnation and based their beliefs on the Old Covenant Scriptures. The concept that Jesus was the incarnate God had begun to develop within the Gentile community in Antioch. Ignatius himself in his authentic letters leads the way to Nicea as one can discern

5. *Apostolic Constitutions*, preserved by the Monophysite Church of Abyssinia.
6. Ignatius, *Epistle to the Antiochians*, V; *The Early Church Fathers*.

by the structure he establishes for the "church". He was the first to deny the Sabbath, the first to claim the bread of the eucharist was the literal body of Jesus, and the first to empower the bishop only as the representative of God, replacing the Holy Spirit. The bishop was raised to become the overseer of the presbyters and his became the ultimate authority.

"And after the observance of the Sabbath, let every friend of Christ keep the Lord's Day as a festival, the resurrection–day, the queen and chief of all the days [of the week]. Looking forward to this, the prophet declared, 'To the end, for the eighth day.'"[7]

He also established the structure of the church within his "seven letters".

> Let no man do anything of what belongs to the church separately from the bishop. Let that eucharist be looked upon as well established, which is either offered by the bishop, or by him to whom the bishop has given his consent. *Wheresoever the bishop shall appear, there let the peoples [multitude] also be; as where Jesus Christ is, there is the Catholic church. It is not lawful without the bishop, neither to baptize, nor to celebrate the Holy Communion; but whatsoever he shall approve of, that is also pleasing unto God*; that so whatever is done, may be sure and well done.[8]

Other spurious letters (eight of them) were also attributed to Ignatius, including letters written in Latin to and from the apostle John and to the "Virgin Mary"![9]

Another "apostolic father" was Clement of Rome. Traditions vary concerning whether he was a follower of Peter or Paul, whether he was the second, third, or even a fourth Bishop of Rome (96 CE). He was, however, likely a follower of Paul rather than of Peter since Paul mentions him in Philippians 4:3: "And I intreat thee also, true yokefellow, help those women which laboured with me in the gospel, *with Clement also*, and with other my fellowlabourers, whose names are in the book of life." Paul's letter to the Philippians was written near the end of his life, probably from Rome, about 62 CE (a date generally agreed upon by scholars).

Clement became Bishop of Rome in 92 CE and died in 99 CE. He was a Gentile taught, again, by Paul, who he mentions in his epistle.[10] "Take the

---

7. Ignatius, *Epistle to the Magnesians*, IX.
8. Ignatius, *Epistle to the Smyrneans*, III, 1–5, italics mine.
9. *11th ed. Encyclopedia Brittanica*, 1911 ed.
10. *The First Epistle of Clement to the Corinthians*, III 13.

epistle of the blessed Paul the Apostle into your hands; What was it that he wrote to you at his first preaching the Gospel among you?"[11]

In his letter to the Corinthians, I Clement, betrays his pagan beginnings by using an Egyptian analogy. He compares the resurrection to the phoenix and the worship of the sun–god.

> Let us consider that wonderful type of the resurrection which is seen in the Eastern countries; that is to say, in Arabia. There is a certain bird called a Phoenix; of this there is never but one at a time: and that lives five hundred years. And when the time of its dissolution draws near, that it must die, it makes itself a nest of frankincense, and myrrh, and other spices into which when its time is fulfilled it enters and dies. But its flesh putrifying, breeds a certain worm, which being nourished with the juice of the dead bird brings forth feathers; and when it is grown to a perfect state, it takes up the nest in which the bones of its parents lie, and carries it from Arabia into Egypt, to a city called Heiropolis: And flying in open day in the sight of all men, lays it upon the altar of the sun, and so returns from whence it came. The priests then search into the records of the time; and find that it returned precisely at the end of five hundred years.[12]

By the time Clement wrote his epistle he, also, was steeped in the ecclesiastical structure of the Roman church (Chapter XIX). The epistle mentions *episkopoi* (overseers, bishops) or *presbyteroi* (elders, presbyters), as the upper class of ministers, served by the deacons of the church. He was also entrenched in pagan concepts that were to influence and affect Christianity in later years. Clement was mentioned in the Shepherd of Hermes, a second century document by an unknown author.

The third apostolic father was Polycarp (70–155 CE) who Jerome (347–420 CE) two centuries later supposed to have been a disciple of John the apostle. A somewhat more reliable witness is Irenaeus (115–202 CE) who claims Polycarp was the first to suggest the observance of Passover for the eastern churches instead of the western observance of Easter.

> And when the blessed Polycarp was sojourning in Rome in the time of Anicetus, although a slight controversy had arisen among them as to certain other points, they were at once well inclined towards each other [with regard to the matter in hand], not willing that any quarrel should arise between them upon this

11. *The First Epistle of Clement to the Corinthians*, XX 20; see also Footnote 7.
12. 1 Clem XII 1–5.

From Nazaraean to Christian

head. For neither could Anicetus [d. 168] persuade Polycarp to forego the observance [in his own way], *inasmuch as these things had been always [so] observed by John the disciple of our Lord, and by other apostles with whom he had been conversant*; nor, on the other hand, could Polycarp succeed in persuading Anicetus to keep [the observance in his way], for he maintained that he was bound to adhere to the usage of the presbyters who preceded him [italics mine].

This means Polycarp, a circumcised Jew, had observed the customs and teachings of the original movement that included, among other things, keeping the Sabbath, keeping Passover, studying Torah under John, the Jewish apostle, who taught him these things since they are the things that the original movement kept.

Polycarp was the first to bring this controversy to the attention of the Roman church. The churches in Asia Minor and in the east had always celebrated the death and resurrection of Jesus on the 14th of the Jewish month Nisan, the day before the Jewish Passover (15th), regardless of on which day of the week it fell on, as the execution of Jesus had occurred on the Passover. This was the custom they had learned from the apostles. The Latin fathers, therefore, referred to them as Quartodecimans. The western church, steeped in the spring rituals of the gods, chose Ashtar's Day, or "Easter" in which to celebrate the resurrection (always a Sunday). The new pagan Christians did not have to change their methods of worship; they simply adapted their new religion to their old. Polycarp, a heresy fighter, went to Rome to see Pope Anicetus who he believed was in error about the date of Passover.

> For long ago, even from the earliest days, the Passover was celebrated at different times in the church ... In the time of Polycarp and Victor, the east was at odds with the west and they would not accept letters of commendation from each other.[13]

Considering the Jewish nature of his letter to the Philippians and his teachings (kingdom of God, resurrection, Sabbath–keeping, the commandments), as well as the fact that the Jewish apostle John would not have accepted a Gentile but only a Jewish student, Polycarp was probably a Jew.

---

13. Epiphanius. *The Panarion of Epiphanius of Salamis*, Books II and III (Sects 47–80), De Fide. Section VI, Verse 9,7. Translated by Frank Williams. EJ Brill, New York, 1994, p.411.

Becoming Christian

Further, fifteenth-century Rabbi Isaac makes that claim: "Polycarp . . . born late in the reign of Nero, he became a Nazarene."[14]

Unfortunately, Polycarp's teachings were not carried forward, and the western Roman church gained a foothold in the east. Raymond Brown in his book, *The Community of the Beloved Disciple*, details the Gospel of John as having gone through at least three and possibly four redactions, the first being a historical account of an eyewitness who became the "link" between the apostles and that community. He states that there were possibly four groups of the community. The earliest was the community of the historical "disciple whom Jesus loved" and consisted of those whom he refers to as Jewish Christians (Nazaraeans) connected with James and the Jerusalem community, those who held a fairly low christology. They would have rejected a highly sacramental understanding of the eucharist. Sometime during the early second century they were rejected as "heretics" by the second group of Jews (Hellenists). The third group was made up of those who he claims were put out of the synagogue. Thus a higher christology began to emerge and begins the schism between the heterodox Jews and the amalgamated Jews (Hellenic, Samaritan, disciples of John the Batpist, *et cetera*).

> The Johannine movement drew its followers from among 'heterodox' Jews, including those who were followers of JBap [John the Baptist] and then of Jesus, and those who were very close to or identical with the Hellenists of Acts 6. The community that emerged was not a small group polemicizing against a larger church, but a group with distinct origins that had its own peculiar components.[15]

Finally, a high christology developed as is evidenced by the letters of Ignatius. The community became more sacramental and structured and the last redaction of the gospel developed with its gnostic flavor and focus on divinity was completed some twenty years later.

> There may be close similarities between Ignatius and [the Gospel of] John in matters of high christology and the eucharist, but they are very unlike each other in ecclesiology, especially in matters of church structure. We have seen that the Johannine community did not seem to have authoritative church officers (presbyter–bishops) who could control doctrine by the very nature of their office, and so differed in this aspect from the churches attested in Luke–Acts,

14. Hoffman, Chronicles from Cartaphilus: *The Wandering Jew*, p. 636.
15. Brown, *The Community*, p. 177.

the Pastorals, and Matthew. Ignatian church structure has gone even further in the direction of authoritative church offices, and Ignatius insists on the role of a single bishop (who was now over the presbyters) almost to the point of obsession. The established hierarchy now had control over baptism and the eucharist (*Smyrn.* 8:1–2); human authority now became the visible sign of divine authority . . .[16]

It is most probable that one of the successors of Ignatius was a member of that community and the author of the *fourth redaction*, one that used Philo's Hellenistic *logos* assigning a divinity to Jesus that was not a belief of the earliest members of the community. The "beloved disciple" gave them a historical basis to which they might add their own theology, a blend of four distinct periods in which the community developed. It is certain that the present Gospel of John has a high christology and a Gentile touch. It must be remembered that both Evodius and Ignatius were pagan Gentiles before they converted to "Christianity". It follows that those succeeding them would also be Gentiles. No Jewish "bishop" sat in a leadership position afterward in Antioch. Instead, Herodian of Antioch (107–127) and Cornelius (127–154), both Gentiles, followed his bishopric. It was during this period of Gentile domination at Antioch that the Gospel of John was redacted for the fourth time.

From the time of Polycarp onward there would be conflict between eastern and western doctrines.

After the apostolic fathers came those who wrote in Greek and are referred to as the "Greek Fathers".

Tertullian one of the early church "fathers" did *not* teach what Jesus had taught. In direct and *bold opposition* to what Jesus had taught, Tertullian (160–225 CE) declared:

> Away with the one who is always seeking, for he never finds anything; for he is seeking where nothing can be found. Away with the one who is always knocking, for he knocks where there is no one to open; away with the one who is always asking, for he asks of one who does not hear.[17]

As we are aware, Jesus said: "Ask, and it shall be given you; seek, and ye shall find; knock, and it shall be opened unto you: For every one that asketh

---

16. Brown, *The Community*, p. 158.
17. Tertullian, *Prescription*, Chap. 7.

receiveth; and he that seeketh findeth; and to him that knocketh it shall be opened" (Matt 7:7-8).

> To stamp out heresy, Tertullian says, church leaders must not allow people to ask questions, for it is "questions that make people heretics"—above all, questions like these: Whence comes evil? Why is it permitted? And what is the origin of human beings? Tertullian wants to stop such questions and impose upon all believers the same *regula fidei*, "rule of faith," or creed... The true Christian, Tertullian declares, simply determines to "know nothing ... at variance with the truth of faith." But when people "insist on our asking about the issues that concern them," Tertullian says, "we have a moral obligation to refute them ... They say that we must ask questions in order to discuss," Tertullian continues, "but what is there to discuss?" [He says] that believers must dismiss all argument over scriptural interpretation; such controversy only "has the effect of upsetting the stomach or the brain." Besides, Tertullian says, such debate makes the orthodox position look weak.[18]

Irenaeus (ca 115-ca 202 CE), the heresy hunter, was the first Greek church father, one of the chief architects of the Catholic system of doctrine. He was the bishop of Lugdunum in Gaul (Lyons, France). His best known book is *Adversus Haereses* or Against Heresies (c. 180). In it he attacks gnosticism and especially Valentinus (100-160 CE), a leader of a gnostic sect that became known as the Valentinians, and Marcion (85-160 CE), who denied the God of the Old Covenant entirely.

It was upon his reasoning that the present four gospels were placed in the canon. His irrational reasoning is given in his book:

> The Gospels could not possibly be either more or less in number than they are. Since there are four zones of the world in which we live, and four principal winds, while the Church is spread over all the earth, and the pillar and foundation of the Church is the gospel, and the Spirit of life, it fittingly has four pillars, everywhere breathing out incorruption and revivifying men. From this it is clear that the Word, the artificer of all things, being manifested to men gave us the gospel, fourfold in form but held together by one Spirit. As David said, when asking for his coming, 'O sitter upon the cherubim, show yourself '. For the cherubim have four faces, and their faces are images of the activity of the Son of God. For the first living creature, it says, was like a lion, signifying his active and princely and royal character; the second was like an ox,

---

18. Pagels, *The Origin*, pp. 164-165.

showing his sacrificial and priestly order; the third had the face of a man, indicating very clearly his coming in human guise; and the fourth was like a flying eagle, making plain the giving of the Spirit who broods over the Church. Now the Gospels, in which Christ is enthroned, are like these.[19]

His reflections on the "trinity" and the "virgin birth" doctrines, referred to as "The Rule of Faith" became the Catholic "creed" and were, after a long conflict between the eastern and western bishops, adopted at the Council of Nicea. It was he who laid the foundation for the ultimate Christian theology.

> For the Church, though dispersed throughout the whole world, even to the ends of the earth, has received from the apostles and their disciples this faith: in one God, the Father Almighty, who made the heaven and the earth and the seas and all things that are in them; and in one Christ Jesus, the Son of God, who became incarnate for our salvation; and in the Holy Spirit, who proclaimed through the prophets the dispensations and the advents, and the birth from a virgin, and the passion, and the resurrection from the dead, and the incarnate ascension into heaven of the beloved Christ Jesus, our Lord, and his future manifestation from heaven in the glory of the Father to sum up all things and to raise up anew all flesh of the whole huiman race in order that . . . he should execute just judgement towards all; that he may send spiritual wickednesses, and the angels who transgressed and came into a state of rebellion together with the ungodly, and unrighteous, and wicked, and profane among men, into the everlasting fire; but may, as an act of Grace, confer immortality on the righteous and holy, and those who have kept his commandments, and have persevered in his love, some from the beginning, and others from their repentance, and may surround them with everlasting glory.[20]

It was Irenaeus who first labeled the Ebionites as "heretics".

> Those who are called Ebionites agree that the world was made by God; but their opinions with respect to the Lord are similar to those of Cerinthus and Carpocrates. They use the Gospel according to Matthew only, and repudiate the Apostle Paul, maintaining that he was an apostate from the law. As to the prophetical writings, they endeavour to expound them in a somewhat singular

19. Irenaeus, *Against Heresies* 3.11.8.
20. Irenaeus, *Against Heresies* 1.10.1.

Becoming Christian

> manner: they practise circumcision, persevere in the observance of those customs which are enjoined by the law, and are so Judaic in their style of life, that they even adore Jerusalem as if it were the house of God.[21]

> Vain also are the Ebionites who do not receive by faith into their soul the union of God and man, but who remain in the old leaven of the [natural] birth; who do not wish to understand that the Holy Spirit came into Mary and the power of the Most High did overshadow her: therefore also what was generated is holy and the Son of the Most High God the Father of all, who wrought His incarnation and displayed a new [kind of] generation.[22]

The second Greek writer that must be mentioned here briefly is Clement of Alexandria (150–215 CE) (not to be confused with Clement of Rome). Clement was influenced by Hellenistic philosophy to a greater extent than any other Christian thinker of his time. He was a pagan who had converted to Christianity and was highly educated in Greek philosophy and literature. In his writing entitled *Protrepticus* his extensive knowledge of pagan religion and Greek mythologies comes to bear. The Hellenistic divine Logos is the theme of the writing. In 211 CE, Alexander of Jerusalem wrote a letter commending him to the *Church of Antioch*.[23] At the time, the bishop there was Asclepiades of Antioch, another Gentile. I mention this here only because it is evidence that the community at Antioch had become integrated with pagan notions derived from the culture and environment in which they lived.

The progression of theology from the Antiochian Community under Paul to the Council of Nicea was full of change, tumultuous and dangerous. The Gentiles had overtaken the leadership of the assembly, and by 135 CE the original Nazaraeans, referred to as Ebionites, or the "humble", had now become "heretics". The roles were now reversed. No longer was there any interest in Jesus' humanity or teachings. He had become three spirits in one. Paul's teachings overwhelmed the teachings of Jesus and were suitable for the Roman church. Not only had the Ebionites become estranged from their own communities that had now become mostly Gentile, they became estranged from the Jewish communities as well. The result was the dissolution of the Nazaraean belief system they had taught from the beginning.

---

21. Irenaeus, *Against Heresies* 1.26.2.
22. Irenaeus, *Against Heresies* 5.1.3.
23. Eusebius, HE 6.14.8.

From Nazaraean to Christian

The true succession was through the heirs and family of Jesus, not through the apostolic succession and bishops that led to the establishment of the Roman church. Any group or sect not adhering to the doctrines as outlined by the "catholic" church was labeled heretic. By the time of Constantine, any Jew who did not convert to Christianity was put under a death sentence. The Ebionite Jews, the original Nazaraeans, continued to practice their customs throughout the centuries that followed in secrecy.

8

Becoming Christian

THE YEARS BETWEEN 70 and 500 CE were filled with conflict between competing sects of Christianity. Although Ignatius of Antioch had laid the foundation for the structure of the Roman Church and Iraeneus built the house, there was no unified doctrine among the numerous churches throughout the empire. The regional bishops followed their own theologies. None were alike, nor did they conform to the original apostolic teachings. Ironically, the only community that followed the teachings of the Jewish Jesus as Messiah was that of the Ebionites (humble in spirit). The gospels are testaments to the differing religious communities.

The Gospel of Mark was thought to have originated in Alexandria since it is taught that he founded the first church there, although there are some scholars who believe it was written for a Roman audience since that author uses Latinisms. Some of these Latinisms include (Greek/Latin) 4:27 modios/modius (a measure), 5:9,15: legion/legio (legion), 6:37: denarion/denarius (a Roman coin), 15:39, 44–45: kenturion/centurio (centurion). Since none of the gospels were written by the apostles (or Mark himself), and they have been revised by church leaders at a later period, it is likely the Latin editors later chose to use Latin for certain words for their respective audience.

The Greek Gospel of Matthew, again not written by Matthew himself, is a redacted Greek copy of an ancient Hebrew gospel purportedly written by that apostle. The Gospel of the Hebrews was rejected as heretical by the

Latin Church with the closing of the New Testament canon at the end of the 4th century, and was no longer cited as a source in Church literature.[1] There is some disagreement as to whether it was the Gospel of the Hebrews, the Gospel of the Ebionites, or the Gospel of the Nazaraeans, though all three were known to have used it. However, the early church fathers testified that it was translated from Hebrew into Greek quite a bit later by Jerome (also known as Eusebius Sophronius Hieronymus; 347–420 CE). He had stated that a copy of the Hebrew Matthew was in the library at Caesarea Maritima, and that he had received it from the Nazarenes.

> Matthew also called Levi, apostle and aforetimes publican, composed a gospel of Christ at first published in Judea in Hebrew for the sake of those of the circumcision who believed, but *this was afterwards translated into Greek though by what author is uncertain.* The Hebrew itself has been preserved until the present day in the library at Caesarea which Pamphilus so diligently gathered. I have also had the opportunity of having the volume described to me by the Nazarenes of Beroea, a city of Syria, who use it. In this it is to be noted that wherever the Evangelist, whether on his own account or in the person of our Lord the Savior quotes the testimony of the Old Testament he does not follow the authority of the translators of the Septuagint but the Hebrew.[2]

The Gospel of Luke (and Acts) was originally believed to have been written by the physician "Luke" or "Lucas" mentioned as Paul's companion in Philemon 24, Colossians 4:14, and 2 Timothy 4:11. "Lucas" and Titus were the authors of 2 Corinthians. Modern scholarship, however, generally rejects the view that Luke was the original author for a number of reasons. One reason is because in Acts there are numerous contradictions to Paul's own letters. The author, whoever he was, wrote for an ecclesiastical organization thoroughly steeped in Gentile Christianity and was a Greek-speaking, educated, and well-read Gentile himself. It is certain that within the book of Acts the author had relied on the histories of Josephus. This author's purpose was to *transfer authority* from the Jerusalem Ebionites (Jesus teaching assembly) under James to the Hellenized Gentile church. His primary point in writing the book of Acts was to transfer authority from James and the Jerusalem congregation to Paul and his teachings. Some believe the Greek Gospel of Luke was taken from Marcion's own gospel. One

---

1. Metzger, *The Canon*, pp. 236–38, 314–15; pp. 169–70.
2. Jerome, *Lives*, Ch. 3, italics mine.

author goes to great lengths to parallel the two gospels and comes to the conclusion that the author of Luke expanded the gospel of Marcion, which was supposed to have been written much later than Luke.[3] Due to the listing of other gospels from which Luke was believed to have been taken, the gospel was written quite late. Church fathers list a number of these gospels in their literature. Among those listed by Jerome are: "The Gospel According to the Egyptians, and Thomas and Matthias, and Bartholomew, that of the Twelve Apostles, and Basilides, and Appelles, and others which it would be tedious to enumerate."[4] Charles B. Waite states that the Gospel of Basilides was written about 125 and Apelles not until 160 CE. If this is so, then the Gospel of Luke as we know it was not written until after that date. Epiphanius, likewise states that "Among them, I suppose, were Cerinthus, Merinthus, and others."[5] Again, Mr. Waite pointed out that Cerinthus flourished and wrote about 145 CE, and Epiphanius believed that it was written before Luke. Later scholars agreed. "Westcott thinks it circulated mostly about Alexandria and Antioch, when first published."[6] It may have been written near Antioch, which entirely makes sense since he was writing to a Hellenized Gentile audience who had become steeped in ecclesiastical structure and doctrine by that time through the efforts of Ignatius.

The Gospel of John, as mentioned in the last chapter was, perhaps, the first to have been written by an eyewitness but revised over the decades by two other editors in order to give that author's community *apostolic* authority. The last redaction is certain to have been edited in Antioch between 90–125 CE. The original author was the "Beloved Disciple", a witness to the events, but later editors are entirely unknown members of the Antiochan community as Raymond Brown has postulated (see Chapter 7).[7] It is likely the second revisionist added the "signs" and its discourses to the skeletal gospel, which was probably a basic testimony about the execution and resurrection of Jesus. By the time of the third revisionist the Antiochan community was fully steeped in doctrines of divinity, trinity, and virgin birth, and other sacramental devices, dogmas that became the hallmark of the Roman church and thus the "divine" aspect of Jesus was added to the gospel. We know there were revisionists to the original gospel because of the

3. Waite, *History*, pp. 274–286.
4. Ibid., p. 385.
5. Ibid., pp. 385–386.
6. Ibid., p. 386.
7. Brown, *The Community*, pp. 22–24.

differences in Greek style. Other elements indicate alterations, insertions, or re-editings, and finally, there are repetitions in the discourses that appear to be the result of two different traditions of the same event.[8] The prologue, a "hymn" circulating among the Johannine community was probably originally independent and is believed to have been added by the last redactor to the gospel.[9]

At the time of Irenaeus, who solidified the structure of the church, the *nature* of Jesus began to be discussed among the bishops. At the time there were numerous views as to his being. Some believed he was a second god, some believed he shared the essence of Yahweh, and some believed he was only a spirit disguised as a human being. The Jewish community believed he was fully a human being who himself worshiped the Jewish God, Yahweh. The confusion led to several writings and edicts that would lead to the Council of Nicea in 325 CE which creed would solidify the political stance of religion of Constantine.

By 177 CE the Athenian Athenagoras (133-190 CE) wrote *Embassy for the Christians* (also known as *Plea for the Christians*). In that treatise there is contained a description of Jesus as being of the "same substance" of the Father. The word *homoousios* ("same substance") would become the crux of the Council of Nicea. Although the "trinity" was not mentioned as a doctrine at the time, in chapter 24 he states: "We employ language which makes a distinction between God and matter, and the natures of the two. For, as we acknowledge a God, and a Son his Logos, and a Holy Spirit, united in essence."[10]

Between 200-220 CE Tertullian, called the Father of Latin Christianity, a Roman lawyer from Carthage in Africa, had left the "church" and had become a Montanist, the nature of which emphasized prophecy and had very strict rules. It was while he was a Montanist that he wrote *Against Praxeas* exposing his trinitarian formula in which the word "Trinity" (*trinitas*) was first mentioned. Other Latin formulations that first appear in his work are "three Persons, one Substance" as the Latin "tres Personae, una Substantia".[11] He was also the first to use the terms Vetus Testamen-

---

8. Brown, *The Gospel*, pp. xxiv-xxv.

9. Ibid., p. xxxviii.

10. Ante-Nicene Fathers, Vol. II, *Writings of Athenagoras*, "A Plea For the Christians", Ch. XXIV.

11. Justo L. Gonzáles, The Story of Christianity, Volume 1: *The Early Church to the Dawn of the Reformation* (New York: HarperCollins Publishers, 2010), 91-93.

tum ("Old Testament") and Novum Testamentum ("New Testament"). His writings consisted of apologetics against paganism and Judaism, polemics, polity, discipline, and morals. He eventually was shamed and criticized for having joined the Montanists who were proclaimed by other church fathers as heretics and rejoined the church but died a heretic.

Between 303 and 311 CE there was a period of persecution. The emperor Diocletian ordered an empire-wide persecution of the early church in 303.

> By the closing years of the century, the question haunting Christians and old believers alike was whether the ancient communal deities were destined to be supplanted by the One God of the Christians and His Son, Jesus Christ. If the empire had continued to stagger from crisis to crisis, generating increasing discontent with the old order, the question would probably have answered itself fairly quickly. But one man was determined to put an end to both crises and Christianity. Force alone might not be effective against the new religion, he recognized, but a great revival of Roman power and glory would restore the health of society and undermine the Christians' popularity. Once weakened in this way, the worshipers of the executed Nazarene could be reduced to the status of an unimportant sect or else persecuted out of existence.[12]

In 305, Diocletion retired, the only Roman emperor ever to do so, and Galerius continued his policy of persecution for 6 more years. On April 330, 311 CE, Galerius issued the Edict of Toleration, and the persecution ended.

In 313, Constantine and Licinius issued the Edict of Milan legalizing *both* Christian and pagan worship.

> When you see that this has been granted to [Christians] by us, your Worship will know that we have also conceded to other religions the right of open and free observance of their worship for the sake of the peace of our times, that each one may have the free opportunity to worship as he pleases; this regulation is made that we may not seem to detract from any dignity of any religion.[13]

Because of the wording of the Edict of Milan, in 314, immediately after its full legalization, the Christian Church began to attack non-Christians.

---

12. Rubenstein, *When Jesus Became God*, p. 21.

13. "Edict of Milan", Lactantius, On the Deaths of the Persecutors (De Mortibus Persecutorum), ch. 48. opera, ed. o. F. Fritzsche, II, p 288 sq. (Bibl Patr. Ecc. Lat. XI).

Becoming Christian

The Council of Ancyra denounces the worship of Goddess Artemis. By 324 the emperor Constantine declared Christianity the only official religion of the Roman Empire. In Dydima, Minor Asia, he sacks the Oracle of the god Apollo and tortures the pagan priests to death. He also evicted all non-Christian peoples from Mount Athos and destroyed all the local Hellenic temples.

In 314 St. Sylvester I is elected Pope (–335). This was the beginning of the death knell for the Jesus movement. Malachi Martin explains:

> They [heirs of the Jesus movement] therefore asked Silvester to revoke his confirmation of Greek Christian bishops in Jerusalem, in Antioch, in Ephesus, in Alexandria, and to name instead desposynos bishops.

In addition, they asked that the Christian practice of sending cash contributions to the desposynos church in Jerusalem as the mother church of Christianity, which had been suspended since the time of Hadrian, be resumed.

Silvester curtly and decisively dismissed the claims of the Jewish Christians. He told them the mother church was now in Rome, with the bones of the Apostle Peter, and he insisted that they accept Greek bishops to lead them.

It was the last known discussion between the Jewish Christians of the old mother church and the non-Jewish Christians of the new mother church. By his adaptation, Silvester, backed by Constantine, had decided that the message of Jesus was to be couched in Western terms by Western minds on an imperial model.

> *The Jewish Christians had no place in such a church structure. They managed to survive until the first decades of the fifth century. Then, one by one, they disappear.*[14]

Shortly after his victory over Licinius near the ancient city of Byzantium in 324, Constantine founded the "New Rome" on the site Byzantium. The new capital city became known as Constantinople (it is now Istanbul, Turkey). Constantine made Constantinople his imperial headquarters. From day one Rome and Byzantium vied for Christian domination.

As a result of different views in the East and in Rome inner conflict grew to an intolerable situation within the two churches. In 325 Constantine grew weary of the conflict within the church and called the First

---

14. Martin, *The Decline*, pp. 43–44, italics mine.

Becoming Christian

Council of Nicea, the first ecumenical council. Bishops were called from their regions to Nicea in Bithynia to decide the nature of Jesus as the Son of God to the Father. The central argument was between Athanasius, Bishop of Alexandria and Arius, Bishop of Antioch. Athanasius, an Egyptian, held the trinitarian view while Arius held the position that Jesus of Nazareth is of a distinct substance from the Father. Athanasius is considered to be the Father of Orthodoxy and the Father of the Canon. He became involved in disputes with both the Arians and the Byzantine Church. Constantine truly did not care which man prevailed; he simply wanted a solidification of doctrine for a single religion.

It is a fairly well known fact that Athanasius and his crony Macarius were responsible for the death of Arius. Athanasius had been responsible for the excommunication of Arius, but Arius appealed to Constantine and was given approval to rejoin the church. As he was on his way to his communion with Bishop Alexander of Alexandria he was stricken in the street with a violent stomach ache. Alexander claimed that "as God is eternal, so is his Son—when the Father, then the Son—the Son is present in God without birth, ever–begotten, an unbegotten–begotten."

> Arius was speaking (talking 'very wildly', according to Athanasius), when he was stricken by an agonizing stomachache and an urgent need to use the toilet. He went to the lavatory to relieve himself and sat down, but a wave of spasms shook him and the pain became unbearable. When his comrades went to find out what was delaying him, they discovered him sprawled on the floor beside the toilet. There was no need to call a physician to verify that their friend was dead (He had been poisoned!).

Athanasius, retelling the story, cannot keep from gloating. He would never exult in a death, he says, but it was the Lord Himself who answered Alexander's prayers and "condemned the Arian heresy, showing it to be unworthy of communion within the Church."[15] He compared the death of Arius to that of Judas Iscariot "falling headlong he burst asunder in the midst."[16]

About the year 356 CE the Church Council of Laodicea ordered that religious observances were to be conducted on Sunday, not Saturday. Thus, Sunday became the new "Sabbath". The wording reads: "Christians shall not Judaize and be idle on Saturday, but shall work on that day." Ignatius'

---

15. Rubenstein, *When Jesus Became God*, p. 135–136.

16. Athanasius, "In Serapion, concerning the death of Arius," in Schaff and Wace, *Athanasius*, Select Works and Letters, pp. 564–565.

Becoming Christian

attempt to change the worship day from the true Sabbath had finally been accomplished.

In 359 and until 383 CE the Edict of Thessalonica was in effect. It read:

> Flavius Gratianus Augustus, Emperor 18 April/23 May 359–25 August 383 Under Gracian in the west - Edict of Thessalonica
>
> EMPERORS GRATIAN, VALENTINIAN AND THEODOSIUS AUGUSTI. EDICT TO THE PEOPLE OF CONSTANTINOPLE.
>
> It is our desire that all the various nations which are subject to our Clemency and Moderation, should continue to profess that religion which was delivered to the Romans by the divine Apostle Peter, as it has been preserved by faithful tradition, and which is now professed by the Pontiff Damasus and by Peter, Bishop of Alexandria, a man of apostolic holiness. According to the apostolic teaching and the doctrine of the Gospel, let us believe in the one deity of the Father, the Son and the Holy Spirit, in equal majesty and in a holy Trinity. *We authorize the followers of this law to assume the title of Catholic Christians; but as for the others, since, in our judgment they are foolish madmen, we decree that they shall be branded with the ignominious name of heretics, and shall not presume to give to their conventicles the name of churches. They will suffer in the first place the chastisement of the divine condemnation and in the second the punishment of our authority which in accordance with the will of Heaven we shall decide to inflict.*
>
> GIVEN IN THESSALONICA ON THE THIRD DAY FROM THE CALENDS OF MARCH, DURING THE FIFTH CONSULATE OF GRATIAN AUGUSTUS AND FIRST OF THEODOSIUS AUGUSTUS.[17]

In 380, the Roman Christian Emperor Theodosius passed a decree declaring the "holy trinity". It reads:

> We shall believe in the single Deity of the Father, the Son, and the Holy Spirit, under the concept of equal majesty and of the Holy Trinity. We command that those persons who follow this rule *shall embrace the name of Catholic Christians. The rest, however, whom We adjudge demented and insane, shall sustain the infamy of heretical dogmas, their meeting places shall not receive the name of churches, and they shall be smitten first by divine vengeance and secondly by the retribution of Our own initiative,* which We shall assume in accordance with the divine judgment [italics mine].

---

17. Codex Theodosianus, xvi.1.2, italics mine.

Becoming Christian

By the year 394 CE the Council of Carthage upheld doctrines of prayers for the dead and purgatory. These were pagan practices that had been so popular among idolatry that they had finally slithered into the church organization, and in 431 CE the Ecumenical Council of Ephesus denounced the teachings of Nestorius (d. 451), who argued that the messiah had completely separate human and divine natures. At this time, Mary is also declared to be the Mother of God (*theotokos*). Just twenty years later (in 450 CE) the Ecumenical Council of Chalcedon voted that messiah is simultaneously "truly man and truly God."

By 500 CE the Church had instituted a number of non-Scriptural practices: purgatory, lent, the hierarchy of the priesthood, mass (no longer taught Scripture but applied rituals), the veneration of the saints (Cult of the Saints), the adoration of martyrs, candles (a pagan practice), magical powers of relics, images, pictures, and vestments (against God's commandment), holy pilgrimages, and persecution of the heathen and those they deemed "heretics". Beginning in the middle ages a corruption of the papacy came about. Simony, immorality, no literacy, and the practice of electing lay popes with no priestly training began. The "Church" was no longer the product of intent that the Jesus Movement had originated.

The church "fathers" were not the men Christians think them to be. They were not very spiritual. Their goals were both ambitious and political. They were also were ignorant and unscholarly. They resorted to persecution and even murder when it was advantageous to their own self-promotion. Jerome and Origen were the only ones who were known to have been able to read Hebrew. Examples of their errors abound. Justin Martyr quotes from Jeremiah and calls it Isaiah. Clement of Rome compares the resurrection to a phoenix rising from its ashes (an Egyptian idea). Clement of Alexandria quotes as Scripture passages that are not even in the Bible. He quotes them as Paul's, words which are not in Paul's writings at all. In quoting from an opponent he would insert words not in the original, and he even does the same quoting from the Bible, taking them out of context. Tertullian quotes as in Leviticus a passage not in that book. He also misquotes history; and cites as in Isaiah a passage not found in that book but which is found in the book of Revelation. He has been known to quote inaccurately.[18]

Among them, Tertullian was known to have been a heretic until his death, Origen was deposed and excommunicated, and Clement was ostracized by the orthodoxy and not revered for his (often) heretical writings.

18. Keeler, *A Short History*.

Becoming Christian

The church historian Eusebius who often contradicts himself, wavered from the Arians to the Alexandrians during the days before the Nicean Council, and elaborated on the works of Josephus. It is believed that he was responsible for removing the true passage about Jesus from the history and replacing it with one that favored Nicean Christianity. Of course, Eusebius was the biographer of Constantine and would sway with the political wind (as he did in the controversy between Arius and Athanasius). It is difficult to ascertain from them what is truth and what is legend. Scores of "fathers" have different legends about the same matters. Just as there are numerous contradictory legends about the "martyrdoms" of the apostles, there are, likewise, the same problems in their writings about other subjects and people of the New Testament.

Jerome, the translator of the Latin Vulgate from the Hebrew and Greek sums up the arrogance of the church fathers in his letter to Augustine:

> But while they (meaning the so-called Jewish Christians) desire to be both Jews and Christians, they are neither the one nor the other. I therefore beseech you, who think that you are called upon to heal my slight wound, which is no more, so to speak, than a prick or scratch from a needle, to devote your skill in the healing art to this grievous wound, which has been opened by a spear driven home with the impetus of a javelin. For there is surely no proportion between the culpability of him who exhibits the various opinions held by the fathers in a commentary on Scripture, and the guilt of him who reintroduces within the Church a most pestilential heresy. *If, however, there is for us no alternative but to receive the Jews into the Church, along with the usages prescribed by their law; if, in short, it shall be declared lawful for them to continue in the Churches of Christ what they have been accustomed to practice in the synagogues of Satan, I will tell you my opinion of the matter: they will not become Christians, but they will make us Jews.*[19]

Hugh Schonfield quotes Fenton John Anthony Hort:

> A common judgment has been expressed by the late Dr. Hort in his lectures on *Judaistic Christianity*. He describes the Jewish Church as; "a natural product of the circumstances of the Apostolic Age, living on for some generations, and that probably not without times of revival, but becoming more and more evidently a futile anachronism as the main body of the Church grew up

---

19. Jerome, Letter 75, italics mine.

> into a stately tree in the eyes of all men; and at length dying naturally away.[20]

The Gentiles had tried to remove all traces of the Jewish Jesus Movement from the "church" since the days of Ignatius (69 CE) in Antioch. The "fathers" finally succeeded in ousting the remnants of the true followers of Jesus in approximately the fifth century.[21] While at first they went into hiding, they were eventually assimilated into either the church or into Jewish synagogues. Certainly, for a time the members of the Jesus Movement met secretly, but the following decades proved to be its undoing. No longer could they worship the God of their fathers openly. They did not fit within Pharisaic Judaism, nor did they fit into the new mold of Christianity. No longer did the heirs of Jesus recite their genealogies for fear of persecution. Their children forgot where they came from. The demise of the Jesus Movement was complete.

---

20. Schonfield, *The History*, p. 5.
21. Taylor, *Christians and the Holy Places*, p. 18.

Bibliography

Ante-Nicene Fathers, Vol. II, *Writings of Athenagoras*, "A Plea For the Christians", http://www.biblestudytools.com/history/early-church-fathers/ante-nicene/vol-2-second-century/writings-of-athenagoras/a-plea-christians.html.

Apostolic Constitutions, Book VIII, Chapter XLVI, preserved by the Monophysite Church of Abyssinia.

Bauckham, Richard. *Jude and the Relatives of Jesus in the Early Church*, Edinburgh: T&T Clark, 1990.

Baumgarten, Albert L. "Ancient Jewish Sectarianism", Judaism: *A Quarterly Journal of Jewish Life and Thought*, September 22, 1998.

Bauxbaum, Yitzhak. *The Life and Teachings of Hillel*, Northvale, New Jersey, London: Jason Aronson, Inc., 1994.

Ben-David, Yirmiyahu. *The N'tzarim Reconstruction of Matiytyahu*. 2 Vols., Ra'anana, Israel: Schueller House, 1994.

Berendts, A. trans. *Slavonic Josephus*.

Bowker, John. *Jesus and the Pharisees*. New York, N.Y.: Cambridge University Press, 1973.

Brown, Raymond E. *The Community of the Beloved Disciple*, New York: Paulist, 1979.

———. *The Gospel According to John* (i–xii), The Anchor Bible, Garden City, New York: Doubleday Company, Inc., 1966.

Bruce, F. F. *Peter, Stephen, James & John, Studies in Non-Pauline Christianity*. Grand Rapids: William B. Eerdman's, 1979.

Bush, L. Russ, ed. *Classical Readings in Christian Apologetics*. Grand Rapids, Michigan: Academie Books, Zondervan Publishing House, 1983.

Bütz, Jeffrey J. *The Brother of Jesus and the Lost Teachings of Christianity*. Rochester, Vermont: Inner Traditions, 2005.

Chilton, Bruce and Jacob Neusner, eds. *The Brother of Jesus, James the Just and His Mission*, Louisville: Westminster John Knox, 2001.

Claremont-Ganneau. *Archeological Researches in Palestine during the years 1873–1874*, Vol. 1.

Cohen, Shaye J. D. "Women in the Synagogues of Antiquity" *Conservative Judaism* 34 (November-December 1980), pp. 23–29.

Cohick, Lynn H. *Women in the World of the Earliest Christians: Iluminating Ancient Ways of Life*, Grand Rapids, Michigan: Baker Academic, 2009.

Crossan, John. *Jesus, A Revolutionary Biography*, San Francisco: HarperSanFrancisco, 1994.

"Curiales," http://en.wikipedia.org/wiki/Curiales.

Bibliography

"Decurion," http://en.wikipedia.org/wiki/Decurion_%28administrative%29.

Dunn, James D.G. *Did the First Christians Worship Jesus? The New Testament Evidence*, Louisville, Kentucky: Westminster John Knox, 2010.

The Early Church Fathers and Other Works, Wm. B. Eerdmans Pub. Co. in English in Edinburgh, Scotland beginning in 1867.

"Edict of Milan", Lactantius, On the Deaths of the Persecutors (De Mortibus Persecutorum), ch. 48. opera, ed. o. F. Fritzsche, II, p 288 sq. (Bibl Patr. Ecc. Lat. XI).

Encyclopedia Brittanica, 1911, 11th ed.

Epiphanius. *On Weights and Measures*.

———. *Panarion*.

Epstein, Rabbi Dr., BA. *The Babylonian Talmud*. London: Soncino Press, 1936, 1938, 1987.

Eusebius, Pamphilus. *The Ecclesiastical History of Eusebius Pamphilus*. Grand Rapids, Michigan: Baker Book House Company, 1991.

———. *Proof of the Gospel*.

Fiey, J. M. *Jalons pour un histoire de l'Église en Iraq* (Louvain, 1970).

Finegan, Jack. *The Archaeology of the New Testament, The Life of Jesus and the Beginning of the Early Church*, Princeton, New Jersey: Princeton University Press, 1992.

The First Epistle of Clement to the Corinthians.

Flusser, David. *Jewish Sources in Early Christianity*. Tel Aviv: MOD Books, 1989.

Fredricksen, Paula. *From Jesus to Christ, The Origins of New Testament Images of Christ*. New Haven and London: Yale University Press, 2000.

Freyne, Sean. *Galilee from Alexander the Great to Hadrian 323 B.C.E. to 153 C.E.: A Study of Second Temple Judaism*, Wilmington, Delaware and Notre Dame, Indiana: Michael Glazier, Inc. and University of Notre Dame Press, 1980.

Gonzáles, Justo L. *The Story of Christianity, Volume 1: The Early Church to the Dawn of the Reformation*, New York: HarperCollins, 2010)

Hanson, K. C. "The Galilean Fishing Economy and the Jesus Tradition", BTB; http://www.Kchanson.com/Aricles/fishing.html.

Herford, R. Travers. *The Pharisees*, Boston: Beacon, 1952.

"Hermione", *http://orthodoxwiki.org/Hermione*.

Hillar, Marian. "The Logos and Its Function in the Writings of Philo of Alexandria: Greek Interpretation of the Hebrew Myth and Foundations of Christianity", *A Journal from The Radical Reformation. A Testimony to Biblical Unitarianism*, Vol. 7, No. 3 Spring 1998, Part I pp. 22–37; Vol. 7, No. 4 Summer 1998, Part II pp. 36–53.

Hippolytus. *On the End of the World*.

History and Geography of Palestine; Jewish-American History Documentation Foundation, Inc., http://www.jewish-history.com/palestine/issachar.html.

History of Jerusalem. http://www.shalomjerusalem.com/jerusalem/jerusalem3.htm.

Hoffman, David. Chronicles from Cartaphilus: *The Wandering Jew*. Published by T. Bosworth, 1853. Original from the University of Michigan. Digitized Sep 7, 2007.

Ignatius of Antioch. *Epistle to the Antiochians*.

———. *Epistle to the Magnesians*.

———. *Epistle to Polycarp*.

———. *Epistle to the Smyrneans*.

International Standard Bible Encyclopedia.

Irenaeus. *Against Heresies*.

Jeremias, Joachim. *New Testament Theology*, London: SCM, 2012.

Bibliography

———. *The Eucharistic Words of Jesus*, London: SCM, 2011.
Jerome. *Lives of Illustrious Men*.
Judge, E. A. *Social Distinctives of the Christians in the First Century*, Peabody, Massachusetts: Hendrickson, 2008.
Kuehl, Nancy L. *A Book of Evidence: The Trials and Execution of Jesus*, Eugene, Oregon: Wipf & Stock, 2013.
"Levitical Duties." eHow.com, http://www.ehow.com/list_6530925_levitical-duties.html#ixzz2N6Pc6y. 5B.
Ludemann, Gerd. *The Acts of the Apostles: What Really Happened in the Earliest Days of the Church*, Amherst, New York: Prometheus Books, 2005.
Mack, Burton L. *Who Wrote the New Testament? The Making of the Christian Myth*. San Francisco: HarperSanFrancisco, 1995.
Martin, Ernest. *The People That History Forgot*, Portland, Oregon: ASK, 1993.
———. *Restoring the Original Bible*, Portland, Oregon: ASK, 1991.
———. *Secrets of Golgotha*, Alhambra, California: ASK Publications, 1988.
Martin, Malachi. *The Decline and Fall of the Roman Church*, New York: G. P. Putnam's Sons, 1981.
Metzger, Bruce M. (1997) [1987]. *The Canon of the New Testament: Its Origin, Development, and Significance*, Oxford University Press.
Moore, George Foot. *Judaism in the First Centuries of the Christian Era*, Vol. I, New York: Schocken, 1971.
"Navarre", J.E., http://www.jewishencyclopedia.com/articles/11390-navarre.
Neusner, Jacob. *Judaism in the Beginning of Christianity*, Philadelphia: Fortress, 1984.
———. *Judaism When Christianity Began*, Louisville, Kentucky: Westminister John Knox, 2002.
———. *A Rabbi Talks With Jesus*, Montreal & Kingston, London, Ithaca: McGill-Queen's University Press, 2000.
———. *Rabbinic Literature & the New Testament*, Valley Forge, Pennsylvania: Trinity Press International, 1994.
———. *The Talmud of Babylonia*. Tractate *Abodah Zarah*, Florida: University of South Florida, 1991.
Nolan, Albert. *Jesus Before Christianity*, Maryknoll, New York: Orbis Books, 1978.
Origen and Jerome; Comment. in Matt. vol. xvi. cap. xvii. (Lommatzscli, iv. 52) In loc. & ad Eustoch, fol. 59. 3. Tom. 1.((r) Misn. Menachot, c. 11. sect. 2. B. Menachot fol. 63. 1. & 78. 2. Maimon. Hilch. Pesul. Hamukdash, c. 12. sect. 16. Gloss. in Pesach. fol. 63. 2.((s) T. Bab. Pesach. fol. 53. 1. & Erubin, fol. 28. 2.((t) Zechariah 14 4. Targum in Ezek. xi. 23. & Bartenora in Misn. Mid. dot. c. 1. sect. 3.
Oshri, Aviram," Where was Jesus Born?," *Archaeology Magazine*, Volume 58 Number 6, 2005-NOV/DEC.
Pagels, Elaine. *The Origin of Satan*, New York: Random House, 1995.
Painter, John. *Just James, The Brother of Jesus in History and Tradition*, Columbia: University of South Carolina Press, 1997.
Panayotov, D., A. and H. Bloedhorn (eds.). *Inscriptiones Judaicae Orientis*, vol. 1: Eastern Europe, Tübingen 2004; English translation in Noy, Panayotov & Bloedhorn 2004, 252.
Perdue, Leo G.; Joseph Blenkinsopp; John J. Collins, Carol Meyers. "The Family in Early Israel" in *Families in Ancient Israel*, Louisville, Kentucky: Westminster John Knox, 1997.

Bibliography

Pomykala, Kenneth E. *The Davidic Dynasty Tradition in Early Judaism, Its History and Significance for Messianism*, Atlanta, Georgia: Scholars, 1995.

Rasmussen, Carl G. *NIV Atlas of the Bible*. Grand Rapids, Michigan: Regency Reference Library, Zondervan Publishing House, 1989.

Ritmeyer Archaeology Design, http://store.ritmeyer.com/node/555.

Rouseseau and Rami Arav. *Jesus and His World*, Minneapolis, MN: Augsburg Fortress, 1930.

Rubenstein, Richard. *When Jesus Became God, The Struggle to Define Christianity during the Last Days of Rome*, San Diego, New York, London: Harcourt, Inc., 1999.

Ruffin, C. Bernard. *The Twelve, The Lives of the Apostles After Calvary*. Huntington, Indiana: Our Sunday Visitor, Inc., 1984.

Safrai, Shmuel. *The Jewish People of the First Century*, Vol. 2

———, "The Place of Women in First Century Synagogues", *Jerusalem Perspective*, September 1, 1992.

———. "Were Women Segregated in the Ancient Synagogue?", *Jerusalem Perspective*, July-Sept. 1997, 34.

Saldarini, Anthony J. *Pharisees, Scribes and Sadducees in Palestinian Society*, Grand Rapids, Michigan: William B. Eerdmans, 2001.

Schonfield, Hugh. *The Jesus Party*, New York: Macmillan, 1974.

———. *The Original New Testament*, San Francisco: Harper & Row, Publishers, 1985.

———. *Those Incredible Christians*, Longmead, Shaftesbury, Dorset: Element Books, Ltd., 1985.

Schonfield, Hugh and Bruce R. Booker. *The History of Jewish Christianity From the First to the Twentieth Century*, (Amazon.com): CreateSpace Independent Publishing Platform, May 2009.

Secret Gospel of Mark, Plate II, II Folios 1 and 2 Recto.

Sifrei on Numbers.

Shanks and Witherington. *The Brother of Jesus, The Dramatic Story & Meaning of the First Archaeological Link to Jesus & His Family*, New York: HarperCollins, 2003.

Tanakh, The Holy Scriptures, JPS translation. Philadelphia: The Jewish Publication Society, 5748–1988.

Tertullian. *Prescription*.

Thayer, Joseph Henry, D. D. *The New Thayer's Greek-English Lexicon of the New Testament*. Peabody, Massachusetts: Hendrickson Publishers, 1981.

"Therapeutae", JE, http://www.jewishencyclopedia.com/articles/14366-therapeutae.

The Travels of Benjamin Tudela.

Vermas, Geza. *Jesus the Jew: A Historian's Reading of the Gospels*, London: Fontana/Collins, 1976.

Waite, Charles B. *History of the Christian Religion to the Year Two Hundred*, Chicago: C. V. Waite & Co., 1900.

Whiston, William, trans. *The Works of Flavius Josephus*. 4 Vols., Grand Rapids, Michigan: Baker Book House, 1974.

———. *Primitive Christianity. The constitutions or decrees of the Holy Apostles; being the commandments or ordinances given to them by the Lord Jesus Christ, for the establishment and government of His kingdom on the earth*, London: Simpkin, Marshall, 1851.

Bibliography

White, L. Michael. *From Jesus to Christianity: How Four Generations of Visionaries & Storytellers Created the New Testament and Christian Faith*. New York: HarperSanFrancisco, 2004.
Wilkinson, J. *The Jerusalem Jesus Knew*, Edinburgh: Nelson, 1978.
Williams, Frank, trans. Epiphanius. *The Panarion of Epiphanius of Salamis*, Books II and III (Sects 47–80), De Fide. Section VI, Verse 9,7, EJ Brill, New York, 1994.
Wilson, Colonel R. E., ed. *Picturesque Palestine, Sinai and Egypt*. Palestine Exploration Society, New York: D. Appleton and Company, 1881.
Wylen, Stephen M. *The Jews in the Time of Jesus, An Introduction*. New York/Mahwah, N. J.: Paulist Press, 1996.
Zeitlin, Irving M. *Jesus and the Judaism of His Time*. Cambridge: Polity, 1994.

www.ingramcontent.com/pod-product-compliance
Lightning Source LLC
Chambersburg PA
CBHW050804160426
43192CB00010B/1637